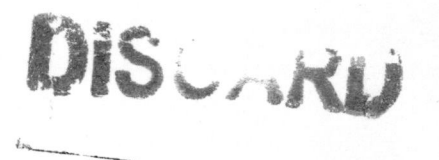

Also by Mark McGuire
and Michael Sean Gormley

Moments in the Sun: Baseball's Briefly Famous
(McFarland, 1999)

The 100 Greatest Baseball Players of the 20th Century Ranked

by MARK MCGUIRE
and MICHAEL SEAN GORMLEY

McFarland & Company, Inc., Publishers
Jefferson, North Carolina, and London

Library of Congress Cataloguing-in-Publication Data

McGuire, Mark, 1963–
    The 100 greatest baseball players of the 20th century ranked / by
Mark McGuire and Michael Sean Gormley.
        p.   cm.
    Includes index.
    ISBN 0-7864-0914-2 (softcover : 50# alkaline paper) ∞
    1. Baseball players—Ranking of—United States.   2. Baseball
players—United States—Statistics.   I. Title: One hundred greatest
baseball players of the twentieth century ranked.   II. Gormley,
Michael Sean, 1960–   III. Title.
    GV865.A1M375   2000
    796.357'0973—dc21   00-20230

British Library cataloguing data are available

Manufactured in the United States of America

*McFarland & Company, Inc., Publishers
    Box 611, Jefferson, North Carolina 28640
    www.mcfarlandpub.com*

To Bill, the best friend, hero
and fungo hitter a little brother could have—Mark

To my big brother, Matt, whom I never beat in anything
but who taught me everything about trying.
And to Denise, Ethan and Shaina,
to whom I dedicate every day—Mike

Acknowledgments

Our deep appreciation and thanks go to Scot Mondore, Jeff Idelson and the other dedicated staffers at the National Baseball Hall of Fame and Museum in Cooperstown, NY. Their knowledge of the game is matched only by their commitment to its fans. A special note of thanks is extended to the photo department's W. C. "Bill" Burdick, who went above and beyond despite the magnitude of our request—and the post-season games on TV.

A note of thanks, too, goes to Matthew F. Gormley and Don Crotty, witnesses to one of baseball's greatest eras. Their insight provided the view of learned fans who were there.

Sam Donnellon, the *Philadelphia Daily News* columnist who is a rising star on the national scene, shared insight on the McGwire-Sosa saga. And James Goolsby, a staff photographer for the *Times Union* in Albany, NY, provided the McGwire photographs.

To former coworkers Phil Brown, Harvy Lipman and Bill Eager, our thanks for being a sounding board in the formidable task of ranking the 100 best.

Illustrations

Contents

1

Introduction

At last, a definitive and authoritative compilation of the top 100 baseball players of the twentieth century, one that will end all such arguments.

Yeah, right. Sure.

We are not kidding ourselves. There could never, should never, be such a list to end all lists. The donnybrook that surrounds where the legends stack up against each other is the kind of Socratic argument that keeps the game, Web sites and probably more than a few sports bars alive.

The truth is that once you get past the No. 1 player of all time—ooh, the suspense *must* be just killing you — every slot on the following pages is up for vigorous emotional, statistical and, for those out of control, physical debate. In fact, you could probably even argue with some merit for a different top player, although we ain't buying it.

Frankly, after you get past the first, say, 70 players, just about any of the ranked players' inclusion in the Top 100 is an arguable proposition. Tell you what: we could make up a team of Hall of Famers and current greats who are not in this book that would certainly challenge and probably maul any of the greatest teams ever assembled.

It gets even more complicated when you try to rank position players versus pitchers. Who is a better ballplayer, Warren Spahn or Roberto Clemente? Yogi Berra or Tom Seaver? Walter Johnson or Stan Musial? You get the idea.

One of the trickiest elements was active players. Thirteen players active at the end of the 1999 season are on this list, including two players in the Top 25. This should serve as a strong indication that time may soon allow us the perspective to view baseball today as one of the sport's golden ages. Some of these players will move up on the all-time (if not all-twentieth-century) Top 100 list; others will drop down — or even out. As the sage Satchel Paige once noted, "Don't look back. Something might be gaining on you."

And just look at some of the players not on the twentieth-century list who very well could someday knock out some of their ancestors and edge into the Top 100: Alex Rodriguez, Derek Jeter, Juan Gonzalez, Nomar Garciaparra, Pedro Martinez, Craig Biggio, Jeff Bagwell and Sammy Sosa are just a few. There are certainly others who may be just embarking on all-time careers.

Thirty-one of 100 players here played the majority of their career prior to World War II. The most represented team (based on longevity or greatest productivity) is, of course ... *not* the New York Yankees (despite holding three of the top six spots). It would in fact be the Philadelphia/ Kansas City/Oakland Athletics, followed by the New York/San Francisco Giants, Yankees and then the St. Louis Cardinals. As expected, outfielders dominate the Top 100 (32), followed by pitchers (24), first basemen (13), second basemen (9), catchers (8), shortstops and third basemen (6 each). There is also one utility player and a designated hitter.

With the close of the century, lists like this are plentiful. (Author McGuire, as a television critic, recently compiled a list of the Top 100 television characters of all time. Trust us, it did not settle the debate.) One of the most notable such baseball compendiums was compiled by a vote of members of the Society for American Baseball Research (the authors are SABR members but did not participate). In that compilation Negro Leaguers were not considered because of the scarcity or susceptibility of records associated with those players but were listed separately.

Well, they're in here. While many Negro Leaguers played the majority of their games as "exhibitions," there can be no denying the talents of Josh Gibson, Paige and many others (in addition to Negro Leaguers, one Japan League legend is included. Oh, you knew that?). While we can argue about how many wins Paige had, or exactly how many home runs Gibson hit, or the level of talent they played against, the consensus is that they are immortals.

So what criteria did we use? Obviously statistics come into play. But we also tried to judge the players on where they stood in the eras that they played, which mitigates somewhat the disparities in the numbers.

All the tools of a player were considered; when it comes to fielding, oral legend has to be a factor. Ozzie Smith is a great example; other shortstops may have better fielding percentages, but only Rey Ordonez is even close in terms of playing the position. This leaves a lot of room for subjectivity.

The research ranged from statistical and historical resources to books, newspapers, Web sites (warning: for those wishing to have any semblance of a life, limit yourself to four hours a day on *www.totalbaseball.com*), the nightly highlights on *SportsCenter* and the indelible plays and images etched in our memory. But this is not science. It may not be art, either. But it is fun.

This is a fan's study. It is dogged study to be sure, but it's one that could probably be done by many a baseball nut who has a library card and an honor system policy for sick days.

Yet we hope this surprises the most learned fans by its subjects, their achievements, even the points of reference from Shakespeare to Mel Brooks's *Blazing Saddles*. We also hope it serves as a primer for new fans and kids who, more than Mark McGwire and Sammy Sosa, are the key to baseball in the twenty-first century. Baseball, perhaps more than any sport outside of rodeo, requires earnest attention to its past if it is to have as rich a future.

So here is our one shot at this. We tried not to blow it, but many of you will think we did. In fact, if you agree with us from numbers 1 to 100, in the order we have, you may want to question your standing as a baseball fan.

For this is just a stab at resolving the unresolvable, concluding the eternal. Our grandfathers' grandfathers were likely debating who were the best players of the nineteenth century, and our kids' great-grandkids may be doing the same for the twenty-first century 100 years hence. We hope so.

Then somebody else will write a book just like this. And your descendants can get just as mad, this time at them.

Have fun fuming.

Mark McGuire
Michael Sean Gormley

The Players

No. 1

BABE RUTH

Humanity has been befuddled by the mysteries of the universe dating back to the days when we were dragging our knuckles. Despite exponential advances over the millennia in science and technology, philoso-

Full Name: George Herman "The Sultan of Swat" Ruth

Position: OF, P, 1B   Debut: July 1914, Boston Red Sox

Born: 2/6/1895, Baltimore, Maryland   Bats: Left

Height: 6'2"; Weight: 215   Throws: Left

BATTING SUMMARY STATISTICS

Year	Team	AVG	G	AB	R	H	HR	RBI	BB	SO	SB
1914	Boston-AL	.200	5	10	1	2	0	2	0	4	0
1915	Boston-AL	.315	42	92	16	29	4	21	9	23	0
1916	Boston-AL	.272	67	136	18	37	3	15	10	23	0
1917	Boston-AL	.325	52	123	14	40	2	12	12	18	0
1918	Boston-AL	.300	95	317	50	95	11	66	57	58	6
1919	Boston-AL	.322	130	432	103	139	29	114	101	58	7
1920	New York-AL	.376	142	458	158	172	54	137	148	80	14
1921	New York-AL	.378	152	540	177	204	59	171	144	81	17
1922	New York-AL	.315	110	406	94	128	35	99	84	80	2
1923	New York-AL	.393	152	522	151	205	41	131	170	93	17
1924	New York-AL	.378	153	529	143	200	46	121	142	81	9
1925	New York-AL	.290	98	359	61	104	25	66	59	68	2
1926	New York-AL	.372	152	495	139	184	47	146	144	76	11
1927	New York-AL	.356	151	540	158	192	60	164	138	89	7
1928	New York-AL	.323	154	536	163	173	54	142	135	87	4
1929	New York-AL	.345	135	499	121	172	46	154	72	60	5
1930	New York-AL	.359	145	518	150	186	49	153	136	61	10
1931	New York-AL	.373	145	534	149	199	46	163	128	51	5
1932	New York-AL	.341	133	457	120	156	41	137	130	62	2
1933	New York-AL	.301	137	459	97	138	34	103	114	90	4
1934	New York-AL	.288	125	365	78	105	22	84	103	63	1
1935	Boston-NL	.181	28	72	13	13	6	12	20	24	0
Career Totals:		.342	2503	8399	2174	2873	714	2213	2056	1330	123

PITCHING SUMMARY STATISTICS

Year	Team	W	L	PCT	ERA	G	SV	IP	BB	SO
1914	Boston-AL	2	1	.667	3.91	4	0	23.0	7	3
1915	Boston-AL	18	8	.692	2.44	32	0	217.2	85	112
1916	Boston-AL	23	12	.657	1.75	44	1	323.2	118	170
1917	Boston-AL	24	13	.649	2.01	41	2	326.1	108	128
1918	Boston-AL	13	7	.650	2.22	20	0	166.1	49	40
1919	Boston-AL	9	5	.643	2.97	17	1	133.1	58	30
1920	New York-AL	1	0	1.000	4.50	1	0	4.0	2	0
1921	New York-AL	2	0	1.000	9.00	2	0	9.0	9	2
1930	New York-AL	1	0	1.000	3.00	1	0	9.0	2	3
1933	New York-AL	1	0	1.000	5.00	1	0	9.0	3	0
Career Totals:		94	46	.671	2.28	163	4	1221.1	441	488

phy and theology and the host of other disciplines, the human mind is still confounded by the most basic of all questions: Why in the name of Cecil B. DeMille hasn't anyone been able to make a decent Babe Ruth movie?

C'mon. What element of a great drama is missing? He was the face on the Roarin' Twenties, a time of Fords with running boards, speakeasies and the Babe. He was a big, goofy kid who loved kids, food, beer and the nightlife. When the Depression hit in 1929 and the good times skidded to a halt, the Babe still rolled on and off the field, while making the ungodly sum of $80,000 a year, more than President Hoover. "I had a better year," Ruth noted. And he did.

Here was a man who was an icon of his nation and his time, so much so that even eight years after he retired from the game, during World War II, Japanese soldiers concluded the worst epithet they could hurl at American GIs was: "To hell with Babe Ruth."

George Herman Ruth spent a portion of his childhood in a Baltimore home for disadvantaged youths, only to emerge as one of the greatest pitchers of his era—and of any era in the postseason. Then he moved

Opposite: **This image bears little resemblance to the chubby, spindly legged star who is ingrained in America's collective memory. But a look at a 20-something Babe Ruth reveals much about the athlete beneath the hype: perfect follow-through, intensity, a body agile enough to twist for that extra torque, whether for throwing strikes or knocking them out of the park. Around the time of this photo—1916—Ruth won 23 games for the Boston Red Sox with an ERA of 1.75. Almost unforgettable numbers for a 23-year-old. But fans hadn't seen anything yet.**

full-time to the outfield and became synonymous with greatness, a pigeon-toed Greek god with a bulging girth and mincing steps. He drank harder, ate more and hit balls farther with a bigger bat than anyone. His name lives on, not only as a myth but as an adjective: *Ruthian.*

The Sultan of Swat. The Bambino. His teammates called him Jidge, his opponents The Big Monk or Monkey; some, like notorious racist Ty Cobb, believed (without verification) that Ruth was part black. But for the masses he was The Babe, or simply Babe. Given to him in his youth, it is the most perfect nickname ever given.

For a moment, just consider Ruth as a pitcher. He sported a 94-46 career pitching record with a 2.28 ERA. In 1916 he went 23-12, leading the American League for the Red Sox in ERA (1.75), games started (41) and shutouts (9). The next year he led the league in complete games. His postseason record: 3-0, 0.87 ERA. And remember, the Red Sox haven't won a series since he was sold down the coast to the New York Yankees.

You know the legend. As a hitter Ruth led the American League in slugging average and home run percentage 13 times, home runs 12 times (including six in a row), walks 11 times, runs 8 times, RBI 6 times and strikeouts (by a hitter) 6 times. Despite a .342 lifetime average, Ruth led the league in hitting only once (.378 in 1924).

But his most startling statistic may be number of MVP awards: one.

What could be more unbelievable? Well, how about what Hollywood has given us?

William Bendix. That's right, William @#$@*& Bendix and *The Babe Ruth Story*, possibly the worst sports movie ever made.

The "Called Shot," that subtle gesture Ruth made (or didn't make), in the third game of the 1932 World Series in Chicago? Bendix made it look like an overt and repeated *Sieg Heil* being made by a deranged storm trooper. The only thing sillier was watching Bendix try to swing a bat. It was actually painful.

The Babe, with John Goodman? Now Goodman is a very good actor and was able to capture Ruth's off-the-field excesses reasonably well. But when he put on the pinstripes, well, it was just an embarrassment. There have been other minimal stabs at theatrical versions (the voluminous documentaries on Ruth are largely exempt from this rant), but none managed to stand out. (One realistic portrayal of the Babe was in *Pride of the Yankees*. Ruth played himself.) No wonder he didn't have much fondness for stage folk.

"I don't give a damn about any actors," the Babe told Harry Frazee, the Boston Red Sox owner who winced when Babe asked for more money than one of the great actors of the day. "What good will John Barrymore do you with the bases loaded and two down in a tight game?"

Maybe the problem is there is so much to Babe, so much grandness and excess in all his pursuits, that on the big screen it just looks ridiculously askew, blown out of proportion. Maybe it's just that doing a film about a man who was all appetite leaves actors and directors unable to resist dipping down into mere caricature. Even though Ruth was the subject of maybe the greatest biography ever written, Robert W. Creamer's 1974 *Babe: The Legend Comes to Life,* Hollywood, which has spawned scores and scores of World War II movies, biblical pics and sweeping historical sagas, has simply never been able to tackle the Babe.

Maybe he was just too big.

No. 2

WILLIE MAYS

You can feel it in the windswept sails from Winslow Homer's brush, you can hear it in the lilt from James Galway's flute, and you can be moved by it, too, in the stride, the swing, the throw of Willie Mays.

Here's the place to type the word for whatever "it" is. But we don't know what "it" is. We don't know what that thing is that captures, let alone explains, why Homer, Galway and Mays lift us.

But they do. And, for a phenomenal 22 years bridging the post–World War II boom to Watergate, Willie Mays moved many of us most of all.

For years he carried the burden of being the most likely to surpass Babe Ruth's career home run record (he never made it). Along the way he led the National League in stolen bases and collected a dozen Gold Gloves, part of it roaming a center field the size of Kansas.

Less than 20 years after Jackie Robinson broke the color barrier, Willie Mays was the captain of the San Francisco Giants, the highest paid

Full Name: Willie Howard "Say Hey" Mays

Position: OF, 1B   Debut: May 1951, New York Giants

Born: 5/6/1931, Westfield, Alabama   Bats: Right

Height: 5'11"; Weight: 180   Throws: Right

BATTING SUMMARY STATISTICS

Year	Team	AVG	G	AB	R	H	HR	RBI	BB	SO	SB
1951	New York-NL	.274	121	464	59	127	20	68	57	60	7
1952	New York-NL	.236	34	127	17	30	4	23	16	17	4
1954	New York-NL	.345	151	565	119	195	41	110	66	57	8
1955	New York-NL	.319	152	580	123	185	51	127	79	60	24
1956	New York-NL	.296	152	578	101	171	36	84	68	65	40
1957	New York-NL	.333	152	585	112	195	35	97	76	62	38
1958	San Francisco-NL	.347	152	600	121	208	29	96	78	56	31
1959	San Francisco-NL	.313	151	575	125	180	34	104	65	58	27
1960	San Francisco-NL	.319	153	595	107	190	29	103	61	70	25
1961	San Francisco-NL	.308	154	572	129	176	40	123	81	77	18
1962	San Francisco-NL	.304	162	621	130	189	49	141	78	85	18
1963	San Francisco-NL	.314	157	596	115	187	38	103	66	83	8
1964	San Francisco-NL	.296	157	578	121	171	47	111	82	72	19
1965	San Francisco-NL	.317	157	558	118	177	52	112	76	71	9
1966	San Francisco-NL	.288	152	552	99	159	37	103	70	81	5
1967	San Francisco-NL	.263	141	486	83	128	22	70	51	92	6
1968	San Francisco-NL	.289	148	498	84	144	23	79	67	81	12
1969	San Francisco-NL	.283	117	403	64	114	13	58	49	71	6
1970	San Francisco-NL	.291	139	478	94	139	28	83	79	90	5
1971	San Francisco-NL	.271	136	417	82	113	18	61	112	123	23
1972	San Francisco-NL	.184	19	49	8	9	0	3	17	5	3
1972	New York-NL	.267	69	195	27	52	8	19	43	43	1
1972	NL Totals	.250	88	244	35	61	8	22	60	48	4
1973	New York-NL	.211	66	209	24	44	6	25	27	47	1
Career Totals:		.302	2992	10881	2062	3283	660	1903	1464	1526	338

baseball player in either league, on his way to a second Most Valuable Player award and was recognized by all as the man who led the New York Giants to a world championship in 1954.

Opposite: **Babe Ruth inspired ballads. Ty Cobb inspired curses. But Willie Mays turned hitting, fielding, throwing, running and sliding into a lyric. Some stars make the game look easy. Mays made it look impossible—at least at his level. Few have matched his statistics in any category. No one has matched them all.**

And he did it all with joy. It's not that he made baseball look easy. He made it look fun. And he let us share in it.

Manager Leo Durocher once said that if Mays could cook, too, he'd marry him.

But numbers, as spectacular and unequaled as they are, don't add up to Willie Mays.

You had to see him, or maybe just know someone who did.

It's September 29, 1954, in New York's Polo Grounds. Score is tied, 2–2, in the eighth inning of the first game of the World Series. Two men on, no outs. The Cleveland Indians had won 111 games that year and were picked to enjoy the off-season early with gaudy rings and bonus checks.

Vic Wertz, already three-for-three that day, pounced on the first pitch like an ugly rumor about your mother.

In center field Mays put his back to the ball and sprinted. At 450 feet he looked over his shoulder, saw the ball, caught it like a Johnny Unitas pass 10 feet from the wall, pivoted, whipped his strong right arm and threw a strike at second base.

No one scored. And no one forgot.

Willie Mays. He's still with us as the century he so influenced slams closed. But deep down we know we'll never again see the game embodied so well, so completely, in one man.

Shakespeare's Romeo saw it in Juliet: "Beauty too rich for use for Earth ... Did my heart love till now? Foreswear it, sight! For I never saw true beauty till this night."

No. 3

Henry Aaron

Henry Aaron deserved more. Deserves more.

Sure, when we talk about the greatest players ever, his name gets mentioned. Eventually. Usually it's preceded by an *and*, as in, "Well, in talking about the best, you are talking Ruth, Gehrig, Mays, DiMaggio, Williams ... oh, *and* Hank Aaron."

Full Name: Henry Louis "Hammerin' Hank" Aaron

Position: OF, 1B, DH

Born: 2/5/1934, Mobile, Alabama

Height: 6'; Weight: 180

Debut: April 1954, Milwaukee Braves

Bats: Right

Throws: Right

BATTING SUMMARY STATISTICS

Year	Team	AVG	G	AB	R	H	HR	RBI	BB	SO	SB
1954	Milwaukee-NL	.280	122	468	58	131	13	69	28	39	2
1955	Milwaukee-NL	.314	153	602	105	189	27	106	49	61	3
1956	Milwaukee-NL	.328	153	609	106	200	26	92	37	54	2
1957	Milwaukee-NL	.322	151	615	118	198	44	132	57	58	1
1958	Milwaukee-NL	.326	153	601	109	196	30	95	59	49	4
1959	Milwaukee-NL	.355	154	629	116	223	39	123	51	54	8
1960	Milwaukee-NL	.292	153	590	102	172	40	126	60	63	16
1961	Milwaukee-NL	.327	155	603	115	197	34	120	56	64	21
1962	Milwaukee-NL	.323	156	592	127	191	45	128	66	73	15
1963	Milwaukee-NL	.319	161	631	121	201	44	130	78	94	31
1964	Milwaukee-NL	.328	145	570	103	187	24	95	62	46	22
1965	Milwaukee-NL	.318	150	570	109	181	32	89	60	81	24
1966	Atlanta-NL	.279	158	603	117	168	44	127	76	96	21
1967	Atlanta-NL	.307	155	600	113	184	39	109	63	97	17
1968	Atlanta-NL	.287	160	606	84	174	29	86	64	62	28
1969	Atlanta-NL	.300	147	547	100	164	44	97	87	47	9
1970	Atlanta-NL	.298	150	516	103	154	38	118	74	63	9
1971	Atlanta-NL	.327	139	495	95	162	47	118	71	58	1
1972	Atlanta-NL	.265	129	449	75	119	34	77	92	55	4
1973	Atlanta-NL	.301	120	392	84	118	40	96	68	51	1
1974	Atlanta-NL	.268	112	340	47	91	20	69	39	29	1
1975	Milwaukee-AL	.234	137	465	45	109	12	60	70	51	0
1976	Milwaukee-AL	.229	85	271	22	62	10	35	35	38	0
Career Totals:		.305	3298	12364	2174	3771	755	2297	1402	1383	240

Aaron usually doesn't get listed first, second or even third, unless the rankings are alphabetical. Or by career achievement. Consider:

No. 1 all-time in career home runs: 755.

No. 1 all-time in RBI: 2,297.

No. 2 all-time in at bats: 12,364.

No. 2 all-time in runs: 2,174.

No. 3 in hits (3,771) and games (3,298).

Aaron is also ninth all-time in doubles, and in the Top 10 in career World Series average. He and Tommy Aaron are also No. 1 in career home runs by brothers. Tommy hit 13.

It was the wrists, wrists that could snap to uncoil on an outside fastball, and amazing consistency and durability that made Aaron what he was in his 23-year career. "Bad Henry"—later "Hammerin' Hank"—hit 20 or more home runs 20 straight seasons, and 30 or more homers 15 out of 17 seasons. He led the league at least one season in every major hitting statistic except at bats (ironic, considering his career standing), triples, walks and stolen bases.

Those seasons of hitting .320 with 35 home runs and 120 RBI started to add up. As Aaron rolled into the 1970s, Babe's 714 came into sight. As the record came into reach, the racists and other nutbags came out. The letters, the catcalls from the stands, racial epithets and questions of his manhood mushroomed, reminders that the early 1970s were not that far removed from the 1950s. The march was steady but maddeningly slow, especially with Aaron locked on number 713 at the end of the 1973 season. A whole off-season to deal with it.

The parallels to the hell Roger Maris went through in his pursuit of Ruth's 61 homers in a season were evident. But with Aaron, because of race, this was uglier. "Babe Ruth," Aaron said, "never had to contend with anything like that when he was establishing his record."

Actually, Ruth did. The one way to rile The Babe was to call him the N-word, since some opponents—most notably racist Ty Cobb—thought Ruth was part black. It just makes the racists "defending" Ruth four decades later look that much more ridiculous.

On April 8, 1974, at 9:07 P.M. EST, before a national television audience, Aaron took veteran Los Angeles Dodger Al Downing deep to left for number 715. Afterward Aaron called the campaign toward the record "a nightmare." And when talking about sad things in sports, that has to rank pretty high up there.

Just like Hank Aaron.

Opposite: Henry Aaron pursued the biggest record in baseball, took us along for the joy ride, and rarely let on that it was such a nightmare for him. Death threats, insults and more arrived in the mail as Aaron whittled down Babe Ruth's career home run record. But Aaron gave baseball so much more. Only a handful of players have ever matched his production for hits, doubles, runs and RBI. How good was he? At age 39 the outfielder hit .301, with 40 homers and 96 RBI.

No. 4

Ty Cobb

Ty Cobb was a punk, a surly, mean-spirited cuss who believed that baseball of his day was "as gentlemanly as a kick in the crotch." He was disliked by many teammates, hated by more opponents, many of whom he spiked with his trademark slides.

How mean? He once jumped into the stands in New York to beat up a heckler ... who had no fingers on his hands.

"I don't care if he has no legs," Cobb shouted at a bystander during the assault.

So what we are saying is that Cobb was a jerk, probably deriving more of a smug sense of superiority rather than joy from the game. He was not the first guy you would want to hang out with in a bar, unless a brawl was brewing and he was on your side.

"Cobb is a pr@#!," Babe Ruth once said. But then he added what everyone had to concede: "But he sure can hit. God Almighty, that man can hit."

How good was Ty Cobb? When the first class of inductees to the Hall of Fame was installed in 1936, it was Cobb, not Ruth, who was the highest vote getter.

Twelve batting titles. Three seasons over .400. A Triple Crown. A total of 4,189 hits and 892 steals in a 24-year career, all but two with the Detroit Tigers (he finished up with the Philadelphia Athletics). Three pennants from 1907–9.

The Georgia Peach also hit .366. Only a handful of players have reached that lofty mark in a season.

That was Cobb's average for a career.

Opposite: Ty Cobb's personal flaws were as monstrous as his statistics. Four decades after his death, the stuff that made opponents, fans, even teammates hate the guy in the first third of the century threaten to overtake his on-field accomplishments in the last third. And that seemed impossible. Yet the baseball love story *Field of Dreams* noted Cobb simply as someone no ghost wanted to play with. Regardless of his crevasses in character, Cobb left some amazing numbers that leave at least his on-field persona intact. He hit over .400 three seasons—over .370 a dozen years—for a career batting average of .366. The average dropped a bit at the end. His last season, at age 41, he only hit .323.

Full Name: Tyrus Raymond "The Georgia Peach" Cobb

Position: OF, P/M

Born: 12/18/1886, Narrows, Georgia

Height: 6'1"; Weight: 175

Debut: August 1905, Detroit Tigers

Bats: Left

Throws: Right

BATTING SUMMARY STATISTICS

Year	Team	AVG	G	AB	R	H	HR	RBI	BB	SO	SB
1905	Detroit-AL	.240	41	150	19	36	1	15	10	-	2
1906	Detroit-AL	.316	98	358	45	113	1	34	19	-	23
1907	Detroit-AL	.350	150	605	97	212	5	119	24	-	49
1908	Detroit-AL	.324	150	581	88	188	4	108	34	-	39
1909	Detroit-AL	.377	156	573	116	216	9	107	48	-	76
1910	Detroit-AL	.383	140	506	106	194	8	91	64	-	65
1911	Detroit-AL	.420	146	591	147	248	8	127	44	-	83
1912	Detroit-AL	.409	140	553	120	226	7	83	43	-	61
1913	Detroit-AL	.390	122	428	70	167	4	67	58	31	51
1914	Detroit-AL	.368	98	345	69	127	2	57	57	22	35
1915	Detroit-AL	.369	156	563	144	208	3	99	118	43	96
1916	Detroit-AL	.371	145	542	113	201	5	68	78	39	68
1917	Detroit-AL	.383	152	588	107	225	6	102	61	34	55
1918	Detroit-AL	.382	111	421	83	161	3	64	41	21	34
1919	Detroit-AL	.384	124	497	92	191	1	70	38	22	28
1920	Detroit-AL	.334	112	428	86	143	2	63	58	28	15
1921	Detroit-AL	.389	128	507	124	197	12	101	56	19	22
1922	Detroit-AL	.401	137	526	99	211	4	99	55	24	9
1923	Detroit-AL	.340	145	556	103	189	6	88	66	14	9
1924	Detroit-AL	.338	155	625	115	211	4	78	85	18	23
1925	Detroit-AL	.378	121	415	97	157	12	102	65	12	13
1926	Detroit-AL	.339	79	233	48	79	4	62	26	2	9
1927	Philadelphia-AL	.357	134	490	104	175	5	93	67	12	22
1928	Philadelphia-AL	.323	95	353	54	114	1	40	34	16	5
Career Totals:		.366	3035	11434	2246	4189	117	1937	1249	357	892

If there was anything more fearsome than the left-hander with the cross-handed grip at the plate, it was Cobb on the base paths. Cobb argued in later years he never intentionally tried to hurt anybody, but if a middle fielder had the temerity to try to tag him out on a steal, well, then he was fair game.

There is a sad quote attributed to Cobb; it may be apocryphal (like so many baseball quotations are), but basically it has Cobb stating if he had the chance he would have done some things differently—and probably would have had more friends. Even the ghosts in *Field of Dreams* didn't want to be around him.

Maybe he would have had more friends, but probably not more admirers, albeit grudging ones.

What a cuss.

But, God Almighty, that man could hit.

No. 5

LOU GEHRIG

There's a rare photograph floating among collectors of baseball memorabilia. It fetches thousands of dollars and was once among the most coveted of master collector Barry Halper's stash. Its rarity speaks volumes of its subject.

The black-and-white glossy shows Lou Gehrig, jawing hard in an argument with an umpire. You see, Gehrig was not one to complain.

Not that he didn't have reason. The man followed Babe Ruth, not just in the batting order but in life. Check virtually any major league hitting record. You'll find Gehrig, almost always a line or two below Babe Ruth.

It mattered little that on the list of players with seasons of 150 or more RBI, Gehrig is listed seven times. Ruth also hit 150 or more RBI in a season several times, five times in fact. But on this list, he was no better than No. 5.

Yet not many people talk about that. Neither do they talk much about Gehrig in recent decades, not until Cal Ripken, Jr., broke his streak of consecutive games played. A revival of appreciation for Gehrig was heartwarming, if short lived in today's game, in which the current star is more bankable than the '27 Yankees.

Baseball again found someone else to root for, and Gehrig drifted back into the shadows.

Full Name: Henry Louis "The Iron Horse" Gehrig

Position: First Base   Debut: June 1923, New York Yankees

Born: 6/19/1903, New York, New York   Bats: Left

Height: 6'; Weight: 200   Throws: Left

BATTING SUMMARY STATISTICS

Year	Team	AVG	G	AB	R	H	HR	RBI	BB	SO	SB
1923	New York-AL	.423	13	26	6	11	1	9	2	5	0
1924	New York-AL	.500	10	12	2	6	0	5	1	3	0
1925	New York-AL	.295	126	437	73	129	20	68	46	49	6
1926	New York-AL	.313	155	572	135	179	16	112	105	73	6
1927	New York-AL	.373	155	584	149	218	47	175	109	84	10
1928	New York-AL	.374	154	562	139	210	27	142	95	69	4
1929	New York-AL	.300	154	553	127	166	35	126	122	68	4
1930	New York-AL	.379	154	581	143	220	41	174	101	63	12
1931	New York-AL	.341	155	619	163	211	46	184	117	56	17
1932	New York-AL	.349	156	596	138	208	34	151	108	38	4
1933	New York-AL	.334	152	593	138	198	32	139	92	42	9
1934	New York-AL	.363	154	579	128	210	49	165	109	31	9
1935	New York-AL	.329	149	535	125	176	30	119	132	38	8
1936	New York-AL	.354	155	579	167	205	49	152	130	46	3
1937	New York-AL	.351	157	569	138	200	37	159	127	49	4
1938	New York-AL	.295	157	576	115	170	29	114	107	75	6
1939	New York-AL	.143	8	28	2	4	0	1	5	1	0
Career Totals:		.340	2164	8001	1888	2721	493	1995	1508	790	102

The Iron Horse, however, was never interested in headlines. He kept his consecutive game streak alive, through sprains and strains and illness and homesickness. This streak, Gehrig said, was something he could control, something all his, something a part of him.

It began on May 31, 1925. A 21-year-old Gehrig pinch-hit for Pee Wee Wanninger against Washington. Gehrig failed to get on base. The next day Wally Pipp was hit in the head during batting practice, and one of the most valuable lineup cards in history carried the line: First Base,

Opposite: **Lou Gehrig simply standing in the batter's box is art. In his prime, Gehrig was overshadowed by Ruth, the only one then or now who could. In seven World Series Gehrig batted an amazing .361 with a slugging average of .731, all this despite sliding in less than three years from a .351 average to .143 because of the disease that took his name. By his thirty-sixth birthday, the game he loved so much was over for him.**

Lou Gehrig. That name would appear on the next 2,128 cards over 14 years.

In between he played well enough to be baseball's greatest star in just about any era. His career batting average was .340; he finished third in slugging average and third in career RBI.

Although captain of arguably the best teams in sports history, Gehrig wasn't anyone's "best" in his own era. He wasn't even the best on his team. And if the fan adulation didn't make that clear, Gehrig's salary, at one-third of Ruth's, did. Every year Gehrig hit nearly as many homers as the Babe. But hitting the second-most homers on your team isn't the kind of thought kids drift off to sleep dreaming about.

But Gehrig didn't complain.

"I'm not a headline guy," he'd say.

Second billing, however, couldn't last forever. By 1935 Ruth was gone from the Yankees. He had waddled to the Boston Braves, baseball's worst team, chasing a dream to manage.

Back in New York Gehrig was at his peak. In 1936 he hit 49 homers to go along with 152 RBI and a .354 average, was the league's Most Valuable Player and kept his streak alive.

But there was this rookie. His name was Joe DiMaggio, and he hit 29 homers and scored 125 runs. DiMaggio was being called the next Yankee star, the next Ruth. But Gehrig didn't complain.

The Yankee captain quietly led the Bronx Bombers to World Series championships in 1936, 1937 and 1938.

Then in 1939 something happened to the Iron Horse, the man cast in 6-feet, 200 pounds of muscle. The rippling back began to weaken. The tireless became fatigued.

In the spring of 1939 opponents began to treat him as an easy out. Worse, teammates treated him as an invalid. On May 2, 1939, Gehrig walked the lineup card to the umpire, slowly. It included: First Base, Babe Dahlgren. Weeks later the horror was diagnosed: amyotrophic lateral sclerosis. In the end it would take away Gehrig's strength, his life, and his name.

But Gehrig didn't complain. He wrote his wife from the hospital bed: "Who can tell that it might lead right on to greater things."

For baseball, and for fans born generations after Gehrig's death, it did.

More than 62,000 fans packed the stadium on July 4, 1939, for Lou Gehrig Appreciation Day. Unable to straighten his spine, wavering to the point that teammates feared he'd fall, Gehrig spoke with the strength of character, of will, that was his trademark.

"Fans," he echoed through the public address system, "for the past two weeks you have been reading about a bad break I got. Yet today I consider myself the luckiest man on the face of the earth."

Babe Ruth was the first to hug him. As fans and players enveloped Gehrig with tears in their eyes, Ruth faded into Gehrig's shadow.

No. 6

JOE DIMAGGIO

Why did we care so about Joe DiMaggio? Why do we still, even after his passing in 1999? Sure, he was the most graceful player to play the game, with a sound swing and an ability to play the cavernous center field of Yankee Stadium with an assurance and instincts that made it look easy. Of course, there is 56, the magic number in a game of statistics.

But no, that's not it. It was the distance, the regal aloofness absent of contemporary surliness, that draws us still to the Yankee Clipper. Our interest remains piqued because we wanted to know more, and he wouldn't let us.

Would it be different if we had thousands of tapes of *Sports Center* to look back on, with DiMaggio in the clubhouse waxing on about another late-inning home run, or catch in the Stadium's left center Death Valley? What if he were among the many of the game's alums who justifiably continue to accept, no, crave, the limelight, and did the interview circuits from Fox to *Sports Illustrated* to *People* and back? What if he needed to step out in front of the masses to have his ego massaged, instead of accept adulation from the shows. He would have had so much to talk about, from Joe McCarthy to Casey Stengel to Norma Jean—Marilyn Monroe—the starlet he once called "a plain kid (who) would give up the business if I asked her." And as for the game, well, who wouldn't want to cling to everything that came from the mouth of the man who, in one vanity, insisted on being introduced as "Baseball's Greatest Living Player," a title bestowed on him three decades ago.

Full Name: Joseph Paul "Joltin' Joe" DiMaggio

Position: Outfield   Debut: May 1936, New York Yankees
Born: 11/25/1914, Martinez, California Bats: Right
Height: 6'2"; Weight: 193   Throws: Right

BATTING SUMMARY STATISTICS

Year	Team	AVG	G	AB	R	H	HR	RBI	BB	SO	SB
1936	New York-AL	.323	138	637	132	206	29	125	24	39	4
1937	New York-AL	.346	151	621	151	215	46	167	64	37	3
1938	New York-AL	.324	145	599	129	194	32	140	59	21	6
1939	New York-AL	.381	120	462	108	176	30	126	52	20	3
1940	New York-AL	.352	132	508	93	179	31	133	61	30	1
1941	New York-AL	.357	139	541	122	193	30	125	76	13	4
1942	New York-AL	.305	154	610	123	186	21	114	68	36	4
1946	New York-AL	.290	132	503	81	146	25	95	59	24	1
1947	New York-AL	.315	141	534	97	168	20	97	64	32	3
1948	New York-AL	.320	153	594	110	190	39	155	67	30	1
1949	New York-AL	.346	76	272	58	94	14	67	55	18	0
1950	New York-AL	.301	139	525	114	158	32	122	80	33	0
1951	New York-AL	.263	116	415	72	109	12	71	61	36	0
Career Totals:		.325	1736	6821	1390	2214	361	1537	790	369	30

But the man who as a young player coming up didn't know what a quote was—"I thought it was some kind of soft drink"—decided what he gave to the fans would for the most part be limited to what they saw on the field, in fading memory or grainy film. He did do television commercials for Mr. Coffee in the 1970s and appeared on some game shows in the 1950s, but that was mostly it, except for a rare interview here or there. Then he faded into the background, a silent sentinel who would doff his cap at Old Timers' Day games, sit earnestly in the stands and serve as the bridge between Gehrig and Mantle.

Hemingway wrote about DiMaggio the year after he retired, how the old man of his *The Old Man and the Sea* said he would have liked to have taken Joltin' Joe fishing: "They say his father was a fisherman. Maybe he was as poor as we are and would understand." Of course, Simon and Garfunkel asked where Joe DiMaggio had gone. DiMaggio didn't get it. He felt he hadn't gone anywhere. The rest of us understood. Then there is the name: Joe DiMaggio. It is perfect for the man and a ballplayer, musical itself as it rolls off the tongue, a rhyme at the end to go along with the common given name.

For even the generations born decades later, the summer of '41, the last prewar season, is a mystical, logical and near-perfect line drawn between baseball epochs. It was the season Ted Williams hit .406, the last .400 season, yet did not win the American League MVP. That went to DiMaggio, the brother of Dom and Vince, who hit .357 to go along with 30 homers, 125 RBI, 122 runs and a .643 slugging average. But Williams hit 37 HRs, with 120 RBI and a .735 slugging average. So why did DiMaggio win out?

The Streak. Two months, from May 15 until July 17, 1956, straight games with a hit. Over the stretch DiMaggio went 91 for 223, a .408 clip. It took a pair of great snags at third base by Cleveland Indian Ken Keltner to stop him.

The stat is not the most unbreakable mark in the game, as it is often touted. Try besting Cy Young's 750 complete games or 7,356 innings pitched, or Walter Johnson's 110 shutouts, Ty Cobb's .367 lifetime average, Babe Ruth's .690 slugging percentage or Sam Crawford's 312 triples. It ain't gonna happen.

But 56 straight games with a hit—more than a third of a season of day games after night games and back ends of a rare twinbill and late games on the coast—is as close as we have to a modern reachable record that is patently unreachable (Pete Rose came closest, hitting in 44 straight in 1978). Unreachable, just as Joe DiMaggio was, and will always remain.

No. 7

TED WILLIAMS

It's back there, on the upper shelf, sandwiched between the latest *Star Wars* action figures: a GI Joe. But this one, in its Korean War leather flight jacket and officer's cap worn at a cocky angle, doesn't have the vacuous look of most of the traditional soldier dolls, with that same frozen face

Full Name: Theodore Samuel "The Thumper" Williams

Position: Outfield   Debut: April 1939, Boston Red Sox

Born: 8/30/1918, San Diego, California   Bats: Left

Height: 6'3"; Weight: 205   Throws: Right

BATTING SUMMARY STATISTICS

Year	Team	AVG	G	AB	R	H	HR	RBI	BB	SO	SB
1939	Boston-AL	.327	149	565	131	185	31	145	107	64	2
1940	Boston-AL	.344	144	561	134	193	23	113	96	54	4
1941	Boston-AL	.406	143	456	135	185	37	120	145	27	2
1942	Boston-AL	.356	150	522	141	186	36	137	145	51	3
1946	Boston-AL	.342	150	514	142	176	38	123	156	44	0
1947	Boston-AL	.343	156	528	125	181	32	114	162	47	0
1948	Boston-AL	.369	137	509	124	188	25	127	126	41	4
1949	Boston-AL	.343	155	566	150	194	43	159	162	48	1
1950	Boston-AL	.317	89	334	82	106	28	97	82	21	3
1951	Boston-AL	.318	148	531	109	169	30	126	144	45	1
1952	Boston-AL	.400	6	10	2	4	1	3	2	2	0
1953	Boston-AL	.407	37	91	17	37	13	34	19	10	0
1954	Boston-AL	.345	117	386	93	133	29	89	136	32	0
1955	Boston-AL	.356	98	320	77	114	28	83	91	24	2
1956	Boston-AL	.345	136	400	71	138	24	82	102	39	0
1957	Boston-AL	.388	132	420	96	163	38	87	119	43	0
1958	Boston-AL	.328	129	411	81	135	26	85	98	49	1
1959	Boston-AL	.254	103	272	32	69	10	43	52	27	0
1960	Boston-AL	.316	113	310	56	98	29	72	75	41	1
Career Totals:		.344	2292	7706	1798	2654	521	1839	2019	709	24

since the army doctor with the cold hands gave the first A-OK for the toy's tour of duty way back in 1964.

No, this GI Joe seems to have not a blank look but a vision. This GI Joe is Ted Williams.

Could you even imagine a GI Joe cast in the likeness of Babe Ruth? Maybe for the camp bowling league, but not as a true-life action hero. And that's what Ted Williams was. And will always be.

Fast forward to the 1999 All-Star Game at Fenway Park. There are enough future Hall of Famers there to make the bronze markets skyrocket. But all of them—including Mark McGwire, Ken Griffey, Jr., Cal Ripken, Jr., and Sammy Sosa—instantly went from multimillionaire legends, some with stamped tickets for Cooperstown, to disciples. To hopeful heirs. To fans. Ted Williams was in the house.

"I'm just happy he knows who I am, and he talked to me," said McGwire, who 10 months before crushed the single-season home run mark of Roger Maris. The game, with all those millions in national television time, all those newspaper deadlines ticking closer, and all those egos on the field, waited. Ten, 15 minutes passed as the current and future stars clamored for Williams's attention at the pitcher's mound.

Williams was 80 when baseball's present and future felt the power of its past. And after a couple of strokes and a broken hip, the man who relied on no one but himself for 18 all-star seasons sat in a golf cart and leaned on apostle Tony Gwynn's strong arm. But he still had those strong, piercing, unparalleled eyes, a vision that made him a success at the plate and in the cockpit. Those all-stars must have been thinking what Williams once said was his ultimate goal: "To have people say, 'There goes Ted Williams, the greatest hitter who ever lived.'"

Williams is the last man to hit .400. He hit .406 in 1941 and risked all the pressure of that season and the chase for .400 by refusing to sit out the final game of the year. It wasn't necessarily that Williams felt obligated to give a full day's pay for the paycheck; Williams was just that confident. Despite the rivalry with the popular Joe DiMaggio down the coast at Yankee Stadium, despite the indefensible boos and press bashing at his own Fenway Park (he didn't win the 1947 MVP because one Boston sportswriter didn't even give him a Top 10 vote—and Williams won the Triple Crown), Williams knew he was the best at getting wood on a ball. If you didn't think so, you were wrong. There goes Ted Williams.

Theodore Samuel Williams of San Diego, CA, played major league baseball from 1939 to 1960. But he didn't play 22 seasons. He had an even higher calling than the Boston Red Sox in 1943, and for three years he defended his country in World War II, not at hitting demonstrations at home to sell war bonds but in fighter planes. In combat.

He was 25 when he joined the fight. He was 28 when he came out. Prime years for anyone, crucial years if you play baseball for a living. In the early 1950s he lost most of another three years serving in the Korean War. He didn't complain.

By the time he was done with baseball he led the league six times in batting, hitting .406 in 1941, .356 a year later, .343 in 1947, .369 a year after that, .388 in 1957 and .328 in 1958 at age 40.

He finished his career with a .344 batting average, a near-record

number of walks, a .634 slugging percentage and 1,839 RBI. He also hit 521 home runs, including the one on his last at bat off a 1–1 pitch on September 28, 1960.

At 6-foot, 3-inches tall and 208 pounds he was larger than life for the era's baseball players—or, for that matter, its football players and professional wrestlers. Yet he glided, not just in stride but in the disciplined and unnatural confines of a baseball swing. It is the prettiest swing ever to grace the diamond.

He had it still at an Old Timers' Game 20 years after he retired, a 60-something Williams wearing his typical open-collared shirt (never a tie) and styleless, baggy suit that always seemed to say, "Hey, you invited me, you dress up." After he received his latest hardware and the lords of baseball went on blathering about how great the game is even at $20 a seat, there was Ted in the background, almost off camera.

He was swinging a bat. Pretty, too.

No. 8

Stan Musial

In the 1950s cars were big, suits were huge, and America was boundless. So, too, was baseball.

The game busted at the seams with talent, freer than ever of racial barriers and from military service and growing with the country that won

Opposite: Late into his career—heck, late into his sixties—Ted Williams gave people a more harmonious swing than Benny Goodman. Smooth, confident, his entire body in tune with one second of exertion. Everyone talks about the Splendid Splinter's eyes, how he could see the ball better than anyone because of his extraordinary eyesight. But perhaps his eyes were a more basic key: He kept them on the ball. Even as he nails another in this image, his perfect form giving him a step forward first, his eyes are on the ball. It's a lesson still being taught to players whose fathers weren't alive when Williams was in his prime. And what a prime.

Full Name: Stanley Frank "Stan the Man" Musial

Position: OF, 1B   Debut: September 1941,
                                                      St. Louis Cardinals

Born: 11/21/1920, Donora, Pennsylvania   Bats: Left
Height: 6'; Weight: 175   Throws: Left

BATTING SUMMARY STATISTICS

Year	Team	AVG	G	AB	R	H	HR	RBI	BB	SO	SB
1941	St. Louis-NL	.426	12	47	8	20	1	7	2	1	1
1942	St. Louis-NL	.315	140	467	87	147	10	72	62	25	6
1943	St. Louis-NL	.357	157	617	108	220	13	81	72	18	9
1944	St. Louis-NL	.347	146	568	112	197	12	94	90	28	7
1946	St. Louis-NL	.365	156	624	124	228	16	103	73	31	7
1947	St. Louis-NL	.312	149	587	113	183	19	95	80	24	4
1948	St. Louis-NL	.376	155	611	135	230	39	131	79	34	7
1949	St. Louis-NL	.338	157	612	128	207	36	123	107	38	3
1950	St. Louis-NL	.346	146	555	105	192	28	109	87	36	5
1951	St. Louis-NL	.355	152	578	124	205	32	108	98	40	4
1952	St. Louis-NL	.336	154	578	105	194	21	91	96	29	7
1953	St. Louis-NL	.337	157	593	127	200	30	113	105	32	3
1954	St. Louis-NL	.330	153	591	120	195	35	126	103	39	1
1955	St. Louis-NL	.319	154	562	97	179	33	108	80	39	5
1956	St. Louis-NL	.310	156	594	87	184	27	109	75	39	2
1957	St. Louis-NL	.351	134	502	82	176	29	102	66	34	1
1958	St. Louis-NL	.337	135	472	64	159	17	62	72	26	0
1959	St. Louis-NL	.255	115	341	37	87	14	44	60	25	0
1960	St. Louis-NL	.275	116	331	49	91	17	63	41	34	1
1961	St. Louis-NL	.288	123	372	46	107	15	70	52	35	0
1962	St. Louis-NL	.330	135	433	57	143	19	82	64	46	3
1963	St. Louis-NL	.255	124	337	34	86	12	58	35	43	2
Career Totals:		.331	3026	10972	1949	3630	475	1951	1599	696	78

The Good War. It was time to get down to some serious baseball. Working-class families flocked to cozy cathedrals named Forbes Field in Pittsburgh and Sportsman's Park in St. Louis. Radio gave millions of fans the best seat in these or any other house.

Yet, despite the Yankee glare, baseball's core in the 1950s wasn't really Manhattan. It was the Midwest. It wasn't Mantle. It was Musial.

So, as if to put a face on this gangly, proud country ready to forget war and revel in baseball again, God and Branch Rickey's pioneering farm system gave America Stan Musial, philanthropist and family man in the time of Mantle, Martin and Maris.

Before Stan was The Man he was the shy, hard-working son of an immigrant. After seven batting titles, three MVP awards, 3,630 hits, 475 home runs and three World Series rings, he was a shy, hard-working son of an immigrant.

In 1946, a year he hit .365 and was paid $13,000 (or about $20 an at bat), Musial was offered $50,000 to walk away from his contract and play in Mexico with other major leaguers lured by a rich man's gambit to get richer.

Stan said no. Not because of shaky finances (the pay was guaranteed). But he had made a promise to play in St. Louis. Case closed.

From 1941 to 1963 St. Louis and Musial kept their promises. Rarely outside of a "Goofus and Gallant" comic has loyalty paid off so well.

It's May 2, 1954. Musial has already hit two homers against the New York Giants in Sportsman's Park. Eighth inning, score tied 6–6, two men on. Jim Hearn fires one in and Musial fires it back—way back. That made three homers on the day—er, afternoon. Musial added two more in the second game of the double-header, setting a record and a country on its ear, for a while.

A year later the quiet Musial, who had simply hit .300 for a dozen years while slamming 20 or 30 homers most seasons, wasn't the fans' choice for the National League All-Stars' starting first baseman.

The long-dominant American League soon learned to watch out for those quiet ones. Musial entered the midsummer classic in Milwaukee as a left fielder and figured into the National League's emotional rally against the glitzy American League that led 5–0 in the top of the seventh inning. Two runs in the seventh inning then three more in the eighth created a tie that would be battled for three more innings. Then in the bottom of the twelfth Musial put the first pitch into the stands. Not bad for a guy who started out as a pitcher and had an odd stance from the back line of the batter's box, his back almost turned to the pitcher as he glared over his right shoulder.

Eye-catching, but back in the '50s there wasn't much spotlight left to go around, what with Mays, Williams, Mantle, Ford, Aaron and others casting such long shadows. But for Musial, playing baseball—playing hard and playing well—was enough.

It wasn't, however, enough for America, which over the next four decades would be drawn to the brightest stars like a moth with an autograph book. Baseball has since recoiled a bit from the hype and money.

And fans, through film and even stadium architecture, have begun long-ing for those days in the '50s when watching baseball played hard and well was enough.

More than enough.

No. 9

Josh Gibson

Before Bad Henry came along and dispersed some of the aura, 714 was the most mystical and alluring of baseball numbers. The number belonged to the Babe and it meant career home runs, and it seemed no one was going to come along and challenge it.

Aaron would break Ruth's record almost 40 years after it was set—but also decades after it was first shattered by Josh Gibson.

By maybe 248 homers.

Six-foot-one and 215 rock-hard pounds, the catcher called "the Babe Ruth of the Negro Leagues" died young, felled by a brain tumor at age 35. But for his 17-year pro career the right-hander produced unparalleled numbers with his compact, flat-footed swing, with some sources credit-ing him with 962 home runs and a .391 lifetime batting average.

His official Negro League stats credit him with only 146 career home runs, but remember, the league's official season would last only about 50 games, and most of the competitions were exhibitions. But no matter the competition, Gibson feasted: in 1936 Gibson was credited with 84 home runs in 170 games.

Catch that, Mac and Sammy. "A homer a day will boost my pay," Gibson said.

And when he was done hitting, Gibson would roll down his left sleeve; he would push up and squat behind the plate, equipped with one of the best arms in the game and quickness that was also apparent on the base paths. He had to work on his defense, but his contemporaries said that over the years he became one of the best defensive backstops in the game.

"Josh Gibson," baseball legend Bill Veeck once said, "was, at the minimum, two Yogi Berras."

Gibson played 16 years in the Negro Leagues; 13 seasons with the Homestead Grays and three with the Pittsburgh Crawfords. A nine-time starter in the East-West All-Star Game, Gibson won nine home run titles and four batting titles. In 1941 he jumped to the Mexican League, playing one season with Vera Cruz. Of course, he won the home run and RBI titles.

The native Georgian died Jan. 20, 1947, in his home in Pittsburgh, just months before Jackie Robinson would make his debut in a Brooklyn Dodger uniform. The second Negro Leaguer inducted into the Baseball Hall of Fame (after one-time teammate Satchel Paige) in 1972, Gibson certainly would have been called to the majors after Robinson broke the color barrier, even though his prime was probably past.

Would he have hit 900-plus home runs in the majors had he had a chance from the start? No.

But the legend of Josh Gibson would be even greater if people had a chance to see him try.

No. 10

WALTER JOHNSON

Little League coaches and big league managers all tell pitchers the same thing: don't go for strikeouts, throw the ball in the strike zone and make batters hit a bad one.

No one told Walter Johnson, or at least the lesson didn't stick. Instead, he found it was better to get the ball in the strike zone, but get it there so fast batters couldn't see it.

Like no other fireball before or since, it worked.

From 1907 to 1927 Johnson ruled the era of Cobb, Ruth and Gehrig. By the time he stepped from the mound for his last inning, Johnson was 417–279, with a 2.17 ERA, 531 complete games, 3,509 strikeouts and an astounding 110 shutouts.

Full Name: Walter Perry "The Big Train" Johnson

Position: Pitcher

Debut: August 1907,
Washington Senators

Born: 11/6/1887, Humboldt, Kansas

Bats: Right

Height: 6'1"; Weight: 200

Throws: Right

PITCHING SUMMARY STATISTICS

Year	Team	W	L	PCT	ERA	G	SV	IP	BB	SO
1907	Washington-AL	5	9	.357	1.88	14	0	110.1	20	71
1908	Washington-AL	14	14	.500	1.65	36	1	256.1	53	160
1909	Washington-AL	13	25	.342	2.22	40	1	296.1	84	164
1910	Washington-AL	25	17	.595	1.36	45	1	370.0	76	313
1911	Washington-AL	25	13	.658	1.90	40	1	322.1	70	207
1912	Washington-AL	33	12	.733	1.39	50	2	369.0	76	303
1913	Washington-AL	36	7	.837	1.14	48	2	346.0	38	243
1914	Washington-AL	28	18	.609	1.72	51	1	371.2	74	225
1915	Washington-AL	27	13	.675	1.55	47	4	336.2	56	203
1916	Washington-AL	25	20	.556	1.90	48	1	369.2	82	228
1917	Washington-AL	23	16	.590	2.21	47	3	326.0	68	188
1918	Washington-AL	23	13	.639	1.27	39	3	326.0	70	162
1919	Washington-AL	20	14	.588	1.49	39	2	290.1	51	147
1920	Washington-AL	8	10	.444	3.13	21	3	143.2	27	78
1921	Washington-AL	17	14	.548	3.51	35	1	264.0	92	143
1922	Washington-AL	15	16	.484	2.99	41	4	280.0	99	105
1923	Washington-AL	17	12	.586	3.48	42	4	261.1	73	130
1924	Washington-AL	23	7	.767	2.72	38	0	277.2	77	158
1925	Washington-AL	20	7	.741	3.07	30	0	229.0	78	108
1926	Washington-AL	15	16	.484	3.63	33	0	260.2	73	125
1927	Washington-AL	5	6	.455	5.10	18	0	107.2	26	48
Career Totals:		417	279	.599	2.17	802	34	5914.2	1363	3509

The statistics are good enough to be among the top six places in baseball history. The last one, shutouts, is the record.

Dominance. It transcends eras; it transcends generations. Walter Johnson had almost everyone's number when he played for the woeful Washington Senators. They won because he kept the other team from scoring. In 1913 he ran a string of 56 consecutive innings without giving up a run. That year he had 36 wins (11 shutouts) and 7 losses. Yes, 36 wins. His ERA was 1.14, and he had 29 complete games in a time when pitchers usually had to finish what they started.

From 1912 to 1913 he was 69–19, with an ERA less than a run and a half a game and 18 shutouts. The Senators won, at least when Johnson played, not because he seized the full responsibility of a game's outcome but because it usually fell to him.

In 1912 Johnson was in a showdown with Smokey Joe Wood, who was riding a 15-game win streak. Johnson had a 16-game winning run earlier in the year, and baseball built this up as a test of titans in Boston. After six scoreless innings, a Washington outfielder didn't get to a fly ball and a runner on second base scored. The outfielder apologized to Johnson profusely, crying, after the Senators, and Johnson, lost 1–0. "Don't feel badly," Johnson said. "I should have struck him out."

The fact is, he should have, because he usually had to. Johnson had 10 seasons with 20 or more wins, but not a few of them depended on his own bat (.236 career batting average, .433 in 36 games in 1925 at age 38, and .348 in 1927, his final season).

The farm boy who struck out more batters than there were voters back home in Humboldt, Kansas, had a fastball that he could put between any buttons on your shirt. Maybe even the ones back in the hotel. And in this era without helmets, he may have hit more batters than anyone, but no one charged his mound.

The players knew this gentleman and converted rube wouldn't bean them on purpose, but they knew, too, that the plate and its immediate environs belonged to The Big Train. Don't dig in, and although you probably wouldn't get a hit, you'd escape alive. For most with a passing acquaintance with his fastball, that was a bargain.

Ray Chapman, who would later be killed by a Carl Mays fastball, once walked away after two strikes. He figured the third would do him no good because he couldn't see the first two. The story in various forms has been attributed to others, but most seem to think it fits best with Johnson. He wasn't flamboyant on or off the field, but he was dominant in the small box where baseball is really played, the strike zone.

No. 11

ROGERS HORNSBY

1926. It was one of those years that God took a fungo bat and smacked humankind a bit, just to remind us that, in the scheme of things, we really belong in Double-A ball until He calls us up.

The Fall of Rome was one of those times; so was Disco. And so, too, was 1926.

An ornery guy from Texas was pretty much rewriting the National League record books, and some laws of probability along the way, after averaging better than .400 over the previous five years. Rogers Hornsby led the National League in batting average and slugging for six straight years, including a .722 slugging average in 1922.

Then he slumped, just like a real human being.

He hit .317.

Oh, and he also led the Cardinals to a major World Series upset of the Yankees in seven games.

Hornsby was so good that even his bad breaks worked out. He was traded—yes, traded—after the series to the Giants. But he had collected a big chunk of St. Louis Cardinals stock in his 12 years there, and in order for the Cards to trade Hornsby, they had to buy his stock (to avoid conflicts of interest). Hornsby settled for $120,000, triple his investment.

This is a guy who won the Triple Crown twice. He hit 42 homers, had 152 RBI and batted .401 in 1922. Three years later he had 39 homers, 143 RBI and hit .403.

And the Triple Crown has been accomplished 16 times since 1888, with Ted Williams being the only other player to wear the crown twice, and neither time did he hit .400.

Hornsby's career batting average makes his second to Ty Cobb. Hornsby hit .358 over 23 years, including the modern record .424 in 1924. In 1937 he hit .321, at 41 years old.

Opposite: **What is he thinking about? The answer to that question for Rogers Hornsby was usually "baseball," and not just from April to October. He was a student of the game before the phrase was coined. A rookie pitcher once argued that pitches he threw that were just a hair off the plate were strikes. The umpire advised the lad that when the pitch is a strike, Hornsby will let you know.**

But what a pain in the butt.

Like his historic rival, Cobb, he never met a man he couldn't tick off. "Rajah" Hornsby was traded five times, including three times in three years, while never hitting less than .361 and taking the league MVP once.

Fifty-five years after he retired as a player, he was resurrected in the best line of the movie *A League of Their Own* to show how baseball could be tougher than nails.

Tom Hanks's character scolds a player, saying his manager, Hornsby, shouted at him on a day he disappointed his parents, who drove hours to the game: "There's no crying in baseball!"

No. 12

Honus Wagner

Keep an eye on this Alex Rodriguez kid. Derek Jeter and Nomar Garciaparra, too. A-Rod and Co., along with phenom gloveman Rey Ordonez (the only one of the four with no stick), represent arguably the greatest crop of shortstops to ever come up at the same time.

But the best ever? They can dream, sure. And Alex, Derek and Nomar all have legitimate shots at immortality. But the best? No problem: Just hit over .300 for more than 15 straight seasons (16 overall), lead the league in hitting more than eight times, steal more than 722 bases and hit better than .327 for your career. And, by the way, be the best shortstop in the field.

Until then, let's not start comparing anybody to Honus Wagner.

When the name John Peter Wagner—Johannes to some, Hans to others, Honus to history—comes up today, it is usually associated with his baseball card, considered the most rare and valuable in existence. But the Pittsburgh Pirate put up numbers all the subsequent greats, from Cronin to Reese to Ripken, have never approached.

New York Giants skipper John McGraw called Wagner the best all-around player in the game. A bowlegged and squat 5-foot-11 and 200

Full Name: John Peter "The Flying Dutchman" Wagner

Position: SS, OF, 1B, 3B, 2B　　　　Debut: July 1897, Louisville Colonels

Born: 2/24/1874,　　　　　　　　　Bats: Right
　Mansfield, Pennsylvania

Height: 5'11"; Weight: 200　　　　Throws: Right

BATTING SUMMARY STATISTICS

Year	Team	AVG	G	AB	R	H	HR	RBI	BB	SO	SB
1897	Louisville-NL	.338	61	237	37	80	2	39	15	-	19
1898	Louisville-NL	.299	151	588	80	176	10	105	31	-	27
1899	Louisville-NL	.336	147	571	98	192	7	113	40	-	37
1900	Pittsburgh-NL	.381	135	527	107	201	4	100	41	-	38
1901	Pittsburgh-NL	.353	140	549	101	194	6	126	53	-	49
1902	Pittsburgh-NL	.330	136	534	105	176	3	91	43	-	42
1903	Pittsburgh-NL	.355	129	512	97	182	5	101	44	-	46
1904	Pittsburgh-NL	.349	132	490	97	171	4	75	59	-	53
1905	Pittsburgh-NL	.363	147	548	114	199	6	101	54	-	57
1906	Pittsburgh-NL	.339	142	516	103	175	2	71	58	-	53
1907	Pittsburgh-NL	.350	142	515	98	180	6	82	46	-	61
1908	Pittsburgh-NL	.354	151	568	100	201	10	109	54	-	53
1909	Pittsburgh-NL	.339	137	495	92	168	5	100	66	-	35
1910	Pittsburgh-NL	.320	150	556	90	178	4	81	59	47	24
1911	Pittsburgh-NL	.334	130	473	87	158	9	89	67	34	20
1912	Pittsburgh-NL	.324	145	558	91	181	7	102	59	38	26
1913	Pittsburgh-NL	.300	114	413	51	124	3	56	26	40	21
1914	Pittsburgh-NL	.252	150	552	60	139	1	50	51	51	23
1915	Pittsburgh-NL	.274	156	566	68	155	6	78	39	64	22
1916	Pittsburgh-NL	.287	123	432	45	124	1	39	34	36	11
1917	Pittsburgh-NL	.265	74	230	15	61	0	24	24	17	5
Career Totals:		.327	2792	10430	1736	3415	101	1732	963	327	722

pounds, he didn't look the part. Then again, Wagner thought his feats were no big thing.

"There ain't much to being a ballplayer, if you're a ballplayer," he said. Take out ballplayer (if you are not one), put in your profession or craft, and you have a humble philosophy to live by.

Not that Wagner didn't appreciate his value: he vowed not to play for a penny less than ... $1,500 a year (years after he retired, when it was learned Wagner was down on his luck, the Pirates gave him a coaching job, and teams around the league held "Honus Wagner" days). With eight

NL batting crowns between 1900 and 1911, he hit .300 or better between 1899 and 1913. Six-time league slugging champion, Wagner also led the league in doubles seven times, stolen bases five times, RBI four times, triples three times, hits twice.

After ending a 21-year career with the Pirates and Louisville, Wagner tied Babe Ruth for second (behind Ty Cobb) in votes cast for the introductory Hall of Fame balloting. But in voting for the best shortstop ever, he still ranks second to no one for now, and possibly forever.

No. 13

CHRISTY MATHEWSON

In Robert Louis Stevenson's "The Strange Case of Dr. Jekyll and Mr. Hyde," the upstanding, compassionate Dr. Jekyll writes in his journal: "I have more than once observed that, in my second character, my faculties seemed sharpened to a point and my spirits more tensely elastic; thus it came about that, where Jekyll perhaps might have succumbed, Hyde rose to the importance of the moment."

Baseball's equivalent of Stevenson's character was Christy Mathewson, the soft-spoken family man and glee club singer, who for fifty or so days a year intimidated, infuriated and ultimately humiliated hitters.

Between 1900 and 1916 he kept his ERA under 2.01 six of those years, including 1.14 in 1909 when he went 25–6. In four seasons he had 30 or more wins, and he ended his career with 80 shutouts with the mighty New York Giants.

He was a fearful presence on the mound, armed with an arsenal of pitches that the college-educated student of the game meticulously catalogued. The most famous, of course, was his fadeaway. It was a kind of reverse curve that broke in to a right-handed batter like a lefty's screwball breaks in on a left-hander. The pitch required an odd motion that took such a toll on his arm that he threw just a dozen a game, but that turned out to be not just a constant threat but a good chunk of the day's

Full Name: Christopher "Matty" Mathewson

Position: Pitcher   Debut: July 1900, New York Giants

Born: 8/12/1880,
   Factoryville, Pennsylvania   Bats: Right

Height: 6'1.5"; Weight: 195   Throws: Right

PITCHING SUMMARY STATISTICS

Year	Team	W	L	PCT	ERA	G	SV	IP	BB	SO
1900	New York-NL	0	3	.000	5.08	6	0	33.2	20	15
1901	New York-NL	20	17	.541	2.41	40	0	336.0	97	221
1902	New York-NL	14	17	.452	2.11	34	0	276.2	73	159
1903	New York-NL	30	13	.698	2.26	45	2	366.1	100	267
1904	New York-NL	33	12	.733	2.03	48	1	367.2	78	212
1905	New York-NL	31	9	.775	1.28	43	2	338.2	64	206
1906	New York-NL	22	12	.647	2.97	38	1	266.2	77	128
1907	New York-NL	24	12	.667	2.00	41	2	315.0	53	178
1908	New York-NL	37	11	.771	1.43	56	5	390.2	42	259
1909	New York-NL	25	6	.806	1.14	37	2	275.1	36	149
1910	New York-NL	27	9	.750	1.89	38	0	318.1	60	184
1911	New York-NL	26	13	.667	1.99	45	3	307.0	38	141
1912	New York-NL	23	12	.657	2.12	43	4	310.0	34	134
1913	New York-NL	25	11	.694	2.06	40	2	306.0	21	93
1914	New York-NL	24	13	.649	3.00	41	2	312.0	23	80
1915	New York-NL	8	14	.364	3.58	27	0	186.0	20	57
1916	New York-NL	3	4	.429	2.33	12	2	65.2	7	16
1916	Cincinnati-NL	1	0	1.000	8.00	1	0	9.0	1	3
1916	NL Totals	4	4	.500	3.01	13	2	74.2	8	19
Career Totals:		373	188	.665	2.13	635	28	4780.2	844	2502

pitches. He usually threw no more than 80 in an era when complete games were the expectation, leading the National League in strikeouts five years.

Umpire Jack Sheridan, who was behind the plate in the 1905 World Series when the Giants beat the Philadelphia A's four games to one, said Mathewson's fadeaway was the best pitch he ever called. It had lefties and right-handed batters bailing out of the box.

That series Mathewson pitched three complete games, won all three by shutout, gave up one walk, and had 18 strikeouts. But he wasn't perfect; he only batted .250.

Year in and year out, it was a tense cat-and-mouse battle from the batter's box, and the batter always knew who the mouse was.

But World War I prompted the man, taunted by some as a goody-goody, to enlist. He entered the army as an officer, was sent to Europe, and was gassed while training. The deadly gas warfare of the day left him with tuberculosis. At 40 his playing career was over. Seven years later he was dead.

Mathewson was inducted posthumously into the Baseball Hall of Fame in 1936 with the original class that included Ruth, Wagner, Cobb and Walter Johnson. A day after he died in October 1925, baseball's greatest celebration—the World Series—flew flags at half-staff.

No. 14

JIMMIE FOXX

Who was the second person to hit 60 home runs in a season? Well, the first was, obviously, The Babe. So the second was Roger Maris. Duh.

Well, yes and no. In 1932 Jimmie Foxx belted 60 home runs for the Philadelphia Athletics.

Why haven't you heard about this, especially after all the attention given to the McGwire-Sosa races? You see "Double X" lost two of those home runs to rain because they came in games that did not reach official duration. Fifty-eight is just not a number seared into our baseball consciousness.

Sort of the story of Foxx's career: so close, but so often forgotten. Foxx is overshadowed today by Ruth, Lou Gehrig, Hank Greenberg, Mel Ott and Joe DiMaggio, among others in his era. But for the 1930s no one had more home runs (415) or RBI (1,403), and only four players did better than Foxx's .336.

Opposite: **Christy Mathewson was teased for being a goody-goody. Hitters who faced him must have shuddered at what he'd be like if he was mean. Mathews ended his 17-year career with an ERA of 2.13. That's for the whole career, not for a month or a year. The only thing that ultimately knocked him off the mound was toxic gas that he was subjected to in World War I, where he had enlisted as an officer. He left the game and died at 47.**

Full Name: James Emory "Double X" Foxx

Position: 1B, 3B, C   Debut: May 1925, Philadelphia Athletics

Born: 10/22/1907,   Bats: Right
  Sudlersville, Maryland

Height: 6'; Weight: 195   Throws: Right

BATTING SUMMARY STATISTICS

Year	Team	AVG	G	AB	R	H	HR	RBI	BB	SO	SB
1925	Philadelphia-AL	.667	10	9	2	6	0	0	0	1	0
1926	Philadelphia-AL	.313	26	32	8	10	0	5	1	6	1
1927	Philadelphia-AL	.323	61	130	23	42	3	20	14	11	2
1928	Philadelphia-AL	.327	118	400	85	131	13	79	60	43	3
1929	Philadelphia-AL	.354	149	517	123	183	33	118	103	70	9
1930	Philadelphia-AL	.335	153	562	127	188	37	156	93	66	7
1931	Philadelphia-AL	.291	139	515	93	150	30	120	73	84	4
1932	Philadelphia-AL	.364	154	585	151	213	58	169	116	96	3
1933	Philadelphia-AL	.356	149	573	125	204	48	163	96	93	2
1934	Philadelphia-AL	.334	150	539	120	180	44	130	111	75	11
1935	Philadelphia-AL	.346	147	535	118	185	36	115	114	99	6
1936	Boston-AL	.338	155	585	130	198	41	143	105	119	13
1937	Boston-AL	.285	150	569	111	162	36	127	99	96	10
1938	Boston-AL	.349	149	565	139	197	50	175	119	76	5
1939	Boston-AL	.360	124	467	130	168	35	105	89	72	4
1940	Boston-AL	.297	144	515	106	153	36	119	101	87	4
1941	Boston-AL	.300	135	487	87	146	19	105	93	103	2
1942	Boston-AL	.270	30	100	18	27	5	14	18	15	0
1942	Chicago-NL	.205	70	205	25	42	3	19	22	55	1
1944	Chicago-NL	.050	15	20	0	1	0	2	2	5	0
1945	Philadelphia-NL	.268	89	224	30	60	7	38	23	39	0
Career Totals:		.325	2317	8134	1751	2646	534	1922	1452	1311	87

Simply put, Double X was the best player of the 1930s.

"Jimmie Foxx wasn't scouted," pitcher Lefty Gomez said of the man sometimes called "The Beast." "He was trapped."

En route to 534 career dingers from 1925 to 1945, Foxx hit at least

Opposite: **Before questionable muscle supplements, before the sculpted Sammy Sosa and the maxed Mark McGwire, there was Jimmie Foxx—and his biceps. A pitcher once said even Foxx's hair had muscles. But pitchers had more to worry about than Double X's physique. He once hit 58 homers in a season and left a lasting imprint on baseball. Sixty years after his playing days were over, he was the inspiration for Tom Hanks's character in the film *A League of Their Own*.**

30 for a record 12 seasons in a row (1929–40), including 58 in 1932 and 50 in 1938, while racking up at least 100 RBI for 13 straight campaigns (1929–41). The three-time American League MVP (1932, 1933, 1938) for the Philadelphia Athletics and Boston Red Sox won the Triple Crown in 1933.

Not overly massive at a shade under 6-foot and 190 pounds, the right-hand Foxx gripped the bat "as if I wanted to leave my fingerprints on the wood." And he did not just hit home runs but rather laser shots before lasers that sent fans scattering—not for the ball but to get out of the way. The man who once dented an upper-deck seat at Yankee Stadium with a home run was McGwire before McGwire, with a better batting average tacked on.

"When Neil Armstrong first set foot on the moon, he and all the space scientists were puzzled by an unidentifiable white object," Gomez said years later. "I knew immediately what it was. That was a home run ball hit off me in 1937 by Jimmie Foxx."

After baseball Foxx fell on hard times, just as fellow Hall of Famer Honus Wagner and many other ex–major leaguers did. "Baseball was mighty good to me," Foxx said, "but I was born 10 years too soon." Foxx did end up managing in baseball, for a team in the All-American Girls Baseball League (AAGBL), the woman's circuit formed during World War II.

It would have made a good movie; in fact, it did. Tom Hanks played a character based on Foxx in the 1992 gem *A League of Their Own*. Only the name of the Foxx character was changed, to Jimmy Dugan.

But you still knew who it was; Jimmie Foxx was someone you just can't, or at least shouldn't, overlook.

No. 15

MICKEY MANTLE

As much as Mickey Mantle's knees pained him, it's easy to imagine that the phrase "what if?" hurt much more.

Full Name: Mickey Charles "The Commerce Comet" Mantle

Position: OF, 1B   Debut: April 1951, New York Yankees

Born: 10/20/1931,
  Spavinaw, Oklahoma   Bats: Both

Height: 5'11"; Weight: 198   Throws: Right

BATTING SUMMARY STATISTICS

Year	Team	AVG	G	AB	R	H	HR	RBI	BB	SO	SB
1951	New York-AL	.267	96	341	61	91	13	65	43	74	8
1952	New York-AL	.311	142	549	94	171	23	87	75	111	4
1953	New York-AL	.295	127	461	105	136	21	92	79	90	8
1954	New York-AL	.300	146	543	129	163	27	102	102	107	5
1955	New York-AL	.306	147	517	121	158	37	99	113	97	8
1956	New York-AL	.353	150	533	132	188	52	130	112	99	10
1957	New York-AL	.365	144	474	121	173	34	94	146	75	16
1958	New York-AL	.304	150	519	127	158	42	97	129	120	18
1959	New York-AL	.285	144	541	104	154	31	75	93	126	21
1960	New York-AL	.275	153	527	119	145	40	94	111	125	14
1961	New York-AL	.317	153	514	132	163	54	128	126	112	12
1962	New York-AL	.321	123	377	96	121	30	89	122	78	9
1963	New York-AL	.314	65	172	40	54	15	35	40	32	2
1964	New York-AL	.303	143	465	92	141	35	111	99	102	6
1965	New York-AL	.255	122	361	44	92	19	46	73	76	4
1966	New York-AL	.288	108	333	40	96	23	56	57	76	1
1967	New York-AL	.245	144	440	63	108	22	55	107	113	1
1968	New York-AL	.237	144	435	57	103	18	54	106	97	6
Career Totals:		.298	2401	8102	1677	2415	536	1509	1733	1710	153

What if The Mick hadn't missed so many games? What if he could have played healthy? What if his swing's power and grace wasn't impaired by the nagging and shooting pains? But now that baseball is in its third century, maybe it's time we all just get a grip. Mantle missed games that cut deep into his prime like scalpels did so much to his muscular frame. Ted Williams and Christy Mathewson lost years to war, and many others had careers ended by injury.

But for Williams and Mathewson, the lost prime is an afterthought. For too many Mickey's injuries help define him. That's just wrong.

The man left Spavinaw, OK, with some of God's best work: Speed that shocked Casey Stengel and layers of muscles draping his back and arms that impressed everyone else.

He had two weaknesses that we know all about: injury and just about anything from a bottle. The first fed his belief that the second was OK: he figured he'd never live to 40 or so because his father, Elvin "Mutt" Mantle, didn't. And a locomotive couldn't stop Dad. So Mickey partied like it was an art, and he wanted to be the best at that, too.

So let's say he cut down his playing time, even his ability some days because he had some nights. Mickey into his 50s gave that smile whenever someone tried to get him to say he regretted the way he spent his seasons. Never ask a man in his declining years if he regrets his memories.

Want to see what Mickey Mantle meant to baseball? Go to a Little League practice when they hand out uniforms. See how fast number seven goes. If the kid is fuzzy on Mantle, Dad or Granddad are probably nearby, smiling, brimming with stories that begin, "I remember the time Mickey..."

Through his career it would have been easy for plenty to hate him (hating the Yankees is the nation's second leading pastime). In the years after, it would have been easy to denigrate him because of his excesses. But through it all and more Mickey has been loved.

And with baseball's affinity for purifying the great ones after death, the affair is likely to be without end.

Yet some still ask, "What if?" The only profound question about Mantle that should be started that way is: "What if we never had Mickey Mantle?"

No. 16

MIKE SCHMIDT

Philadelphia is a great sports town, one with a rich sports tradition dating back to the days of Connie Mack. But Philadelphians will have to answer to a fact that will perplex fans and historians for generations to come:

They booed Mike Schmidt.

Full Name: Michael Jack Schmidt

Position: 3B, 1B

Debut: September 1972,
Philadelphia Phillies

Born: 9/27/1949, Dayton, Ohio

Bats: Right

Height: 6'2"; Weight: 203

Throws: Right

BATTING SUMMARY STATISTICS

Year	Team	AVG	G	AB	R	H	HR	RBI	BB	SO	SB
1972	Philadelphia-NL	.206	13	34	2	7	1	3	5	15	0
1973	Philadelphia-NL	.196	132	367	43	72	18	52	62	136	8
1974	Philadelphia-NL	.282	162	568	108	160	36	116	106	138	23
1975	Philadelphia-NL	.249	158	562	93	140	38	95	101	180	29
1976	Philadelphia-NL	.262	160	584	112	153	38	107	100	149	14
1977	Philadelphia-NL	.274	154	544	114	149	38	101	104	122	15
1978	Philadelphia-NL	.251	145	513	93	129	21	78	91	103	19
1979	Philadelphia-NL	.253	160	541	109	137	45	114	120	115	9
1980	Philadelphia-NL	.286	150	548	104	157	48	121	89	119	12
1981	Philadelphia-NL	.316	102	354	78	112	31	91	73	71	12
1982	Philadelphia-NL	.280	148	514	108	144	35	87	107	131	14
1983	Philadelphia-NL	.255	154	534	104	136	40	109	128	148	7
1984	Philadelphia-NL	.277	151	528	93	146	36	106	92	116	5
1985	Philadelphia-NL	.277	158	549	89	152	33	93	87	117	1
1986	Philadelphia-NL	.290	160	552	97	160	37	119	89	84	1
1987	Philadelphia-NL	.293	147	522	88	153	35	113	83	80	2
1988	Philadelphia-NL	.249	108	390	52	97	12	62	49	42	3
1989	Philadelphia-NL	.203	42	148	19	30	6	28	21	17	0
Career Totals:		.267	2404	8352	1506	2234	548	1595	1507	1883	174

Remember, Yankee fans were wont to boo Mickey Mantle. But you must take into account that The Mick replaced a legend in Joe DiMaggio. But in 1973 Schmidt replaced … Don Money. Money went on to a nice career with the Milwaukee Brewers, but the closest thing he was to a legend was having the nickname "Brooks."

Meanwhile, all Schmidt did was go on to become the greatest third baseman of all time.

In fairness, Schmidt wasn't giving fans much to cheer about his rookie year, hitting a mere .196 in 1973, with 18 home runs and just 52 RBI.

"You're trying your damnedest, you strike out and they boo you," said Schmidt, who had also credited Philadelphia fans' passion and knowledge.

"I act like it doesn't bother me, like I don't hear anything the fans say, but the truth is I hear every word of it and it kills me."

But despite any echoing boos, Schmidt exploded in 1974, leading the league in home runs, RBI and slugging percentage. It was the first of three straight National League home run and RBI titles; he would win eight home run crowns, and seven RBI races in his career, which ended midway through the 1989 season.

In addition to his Top-10 career ranking in home runs (548), Schmidt won nine straight Gold Gloves at third base and 10 overall; in the field only Brooks Robinson played the hot corner better.

Still the boos continued through much of Schmidt's career—pitcher Bo Belinsky once said Philadelphians would boo a funeral—although toward the end, when Schmidt's status as not just a Hall of Famer but all-time best came into focus, cheers drowned out any critics.

There is history here. In 1932 two hometown fans, Bull and Eddie Kessler, would sit across the diamond from each other and hurl insults back and forth directed at another Philadelphia third baseman, the Athletics' Jimmy Dykes. Dykes was traded after the season, run out of town.

But Mike Schmidt played his whole career in the Town of Brotherly Love, quitting not because he was fed up with the fans but because he felt he had nothing left to give them. And he had given enough.

No. 17

Joe Jackson

Baseball is full of great stories of triumph and heroism and bombast and tragedy, but really there have been only two great dramatic figures to rise from its history to transcend sport. One is The Babe, despite the fact no one can make a good movie about him (see Chapter 1 for the complete rant). The other is Shoeless Joe Jackson.

Jackson has been the focus of two of the best baseball movies ever, *Eight Men Out* and *Field of Dreams*, and arguably the best-ever work of

Full Name: Joseph Jefferson "Shoeless Joe" Jackson

Position: Outfield   Debut: August 1908, Philadelphia Athletics

Born: 7/16/1889   Bats: Left
   Pickens Co., South Carolina

Height: 6'1"; Weight: 200   Throws: Right

BATTING SUMMARY STATISTICS

Year	Team	AVG	G	AB	R	H	HR	RBI	BB	SO	SB
1908	Philadelphia-AL	.130	5	23	0	3	0	3	0	-	0
1909	Philadelphia-AL	.176	5	17	3	3	0	3	1	-	0
1910	Cleveland-AL	.387	20	75	15	29	1	11	8	-	4
1911	Cleveland-AL	.408	147	571	126	233	7	83	56	-	41
1912	Cleveland-AL	.395	154	572	121	226	3	90	54	-	35
1913	Cleveland-AL	.373	148	528	109	197	7	71	80	26	26
1914	Cleveland-AL	.338	122	453	61	153	3	53	41	34	22
1915	Cleveland-AL	.327	83	303	42	99	3	45	28	11	10
1915	Chicago-AL	.272	45	158	21	43	2	36	24	12	6
1915	AL Totals	.308	128	461	63	142	5	81	52	23	16
1916	Chicago-AL	.341	155	592	91	202	3	78	46	25	24
1917	Chicago-AL	.301	146	538	91	162	5	75	57	25	13
1918	Chicago-AL	.354	17	65	9	23	1	20	8	1	3
1919	Chicago-AL	.351	139	516	79	181	7	96	60	10	9
1920	Chicago-AL	.382	146	570	105	218	12	121	56	14	9
Career Totals:		.356	1332	4981	873	1772	54	785	519	158	202

fiction centering on the game, *Shoeless Joe* by W. P. Kinsella, the basis for Kevin Costner's "Is-this-heaven?"/"No-it's-Iowa" film. Shoeless Joe (so named because he once played in a minor league game without his spikes, which were hurting him) was a great player, in fact the greatest player ... not in the Hall of Fame.

Jackson used a monstrous 48-ounce bat, "Black Betsy" he called it, which he wrapped around the side rather than over his left shoulder. And the man could swing it: While the 1920s were unquestionably the time of the Babe, the teens belonged to two hitters: Ty Cobb and Joe Jackson.

After two years of pine time with the Philadelphia Athletics in 1908 and 1909, Jackson moved to Cleveland in 1910, where he hit .387 in 20 games. Jackson was primed for prime time. In his first season as a regular, Jackson (a righty fielder and lefty hitter, unlike in *Field of Dreams*) hit .408—and did not lead the league; Cobb hit .420. But it was the first of Jackson's 10-straight seasons of hitting at least .300. In his final season in the majors, in 1920, Jackson hit .382 for the Chicago White Sox, with 42 doubles, 20 triples (his third time he led the league) and 105 runs scored.

He was 31, with maybe another 10 years to go, when he got the word in September 1920 that Commissioner Kenesaw Mountain Landis wanted to see him about the 1919 World Series against the Cincinnati Reds: Was there a fix?

Sadly, the answer would be "yes." Eight members of the Black Sox— named not because of the scandal but because Chicago owner Charles Comiskey was too cheap to pay for laundering uniforms—had received money to throw the series. Jackson was one of them, pocketing $5,000.

But Jackson, wracked by guilt, did not throw the series. Instead, the illiterate from Pickens County, SC, led all hitters with a .375, displaying a glove so good it was labeled "where triples go to die." But it was and always will be The Fix that follows his name, embodied by one of baseball's greatest quotes that may or may not have been said. It came from a kid on the courthouse steps, a simple plea: "Say it ain't so, Joe."

There has been an effort to get Jackson's name off the banned list and into the Hall, a drive that parallels the Pete Rose saga. Jackson, provoked by Comiskey's stinginess or not, duped as a result of his mental simplicity or not, did stain the game. But you must ask yourself, do we then take out the racists like Cap Anson and Cobb? The alcoholics? The druggies, wife beaters, neglectful husbands, charlatans and scum? It might get awful lonely up there in Cooperstown. Jackson's sin, taking the money, did not manifest itself on the field.

Put him in. He paid his price. Fans deserve to know the legacy of the player who hit a staggering .356 lifetime as much as the drama, and failure, of the man.

No. 18

Warren Spahn

Who?

You can almost hear the generation gap creak wider when you pick

Full Name: Warren Edward Spahn

Position: Pitcher   Debut: April 1942, Boston Braves

Born: 4/23/1921, Buffalo, New York   Bats: Left

Height: 6'; Weight: 175   Throws: Left

PITCHING SUMMARY STATISTICS

Year	Team	W	L	PCT	ERA	G	SV	IP	BB	SO
1942	Boston-NL	0	0	-	5.74	4	0	15.2	11	7
1946	Boston-NL	8	5	.615	2.94	24	1	125.2	36	67
1947	Boston-NL	21	10	.677	2.33	40	3	289.2	84	123
1948	Boston-NL	15	12	.556	3.71	36	1	257.0	77	114
1949	Boston-NL	21	14	.600	3.07	38	0	302.1	86	151
1950	Boston-NL	21	17	.553	3.16	41	1	293.0	111	191
1951	Boston-NL	22	14	.611	2.98	39	0	310.2	109	164
1952	Boston-NL	14	19	.424	2.98	40	3	290.0	73	183
1953	Milwaukee-NL	23	7	.767	2.10	35	3	265.2	70	148
1954	Milwaukee-NL	21	12	.636	3.14	39	3	283.1	86	136
1955	Milwaukee-NL	17	14	.548	3.26	39	1	245.2	65	110
1956	Milwaukee-NL	20	11	.645	2.78	39	3	281.1	52	128
1957	Milwaukee-NL	21	11	.656	2.69	39	3	271.0	78	111
1958	Milwaukee-NL	22	11	.667	3.07	38	1	290.0	76	150
1959	Milwaukee-NL	21	15	.583	2.96	40	0	292.0	70	143
1960	Milwaukee-NL	21	10	.677	3.50	40	2	267.2	74	154
1961	Milwaukee-NL	21	13	.618	3.02	38	0	262.2	64	115
1962	Milwaukee-NL	18	14	.563	3.04	34	0	269.1	55	118
1963	Milwaukee-NL	23	7	.767	2.60	33	0	259.2	49	102
1964	Milwaukee-NL	6	13	.316	5.29	38	4	173.2	52	78
1965	New York-NL	4	12	.250	4.36	20	0	126.0	35	56
1965	San Francisco-NL	3	4	.429	3.39	16	0	71.2	21	34
1965	NL Totals	7	16	.304	4.01	36	0	197.2	56	90
Career Totals:		363	245	.597	3.09	750	29	5243.2	1434	2583

Warren Spahn as one of the greatest baseball players ever. That's because he was a quiet man—yeah, like the one John Wayne played in the Irish movie of the same name, a quiet man who could lay you out cold. While that movie was on its way to becoming a St. Patrick's Day staple, Spahn was becoming the best left-handed pitcher ever, laying out batting orders, cold.

From just after World War II to just after the Beatles invaded America, Warren Edward Spahn collected 363 wins. He also managed to keep a career ERA at 3.09 despite some swelling as he pitched until he was 44 years old. For several years he led the National League in ERA, strikeouts, wins and shutouts. In 1948, 1957 and 1958 he led the Braves (first in Boston, then in Milwaukee) to the pennant and won the Cy Young in '57 when it was one award for both leagues.

In the Boston Braves' World Series loss to the Indians in six games back in '48, Spahn got 12 strikeouts in his one win and a loss. Cleveland's Lemon and Feller combined for 13 over four games. And Spahn inspired one of the more clever baseball chants along with fellow starter Johnny Sain: "Spahn and Sain and two days of rain!"

His 21 years in the majors included his no-hitter on September 15, 1960, and his second the following April, a week after he turned 40. Spahn, however, wasn't a fireballer. He was a pitcher. He put the ball in the strike zone, but that didn't mean you could hit it.

It's a shame pitchers rarely get credit for arguably the best play in baseball: the double play. Some sportscasters even say a pitcher just lucks out. Spahn knew better. He started 82 of them himself, more than any other major league pitcher. And a DP not only gets a team out of a jam but can put a hurting on an opponent desperately seeking momentum, a key to many games that doesn't end up on the back of bubble gum cards.

You know, the quiet stuff.

No. 19

Bob Gibson

On the mound Bob Gibson didn't have a sneer, really. It was meaner, colder. Jaw set, his face revealed nothing. He pitched in near perpetual motion like a windmill in San Francisco Bay, with edgy, flesh-ripping

Opposite: Even a picture of Bob Gibson's glare can make you uneasy. Imagine facing the real thing, with just a stick of wood in your hands. Intimidation was all part of pitching for Gibson. Opponents feared him and his teammates—well, they mostly feared him, too. Now turn the page, quickly.

Full Name: Robert Gibson

Position: Pitcher   Debut: April 1959, St. Louis Cardinals

Born: 11/9/1935, Omaha, Nebraska   Bats: Right

Height: 6'1.5"; Weight: 195   Throws: Right

PITCHING SUMMARY STATISTICS

Year	Team	W	L	PCT	ERA	G	SV	IP	BB	SO
1959	St. Louis-NL	3	5	.375	3.33	13	0	75.2	39	48
1960	St. Louis-NL	3	6	.333	5.61	27	0	86.2	48	69
1961	St. Louis-NL	13	12	.520	3.24	35	1	211.1	119	166
1962	St. Louis-NL	15	13	.536	2.85	32	1	233.2	95	208
1963	St. Louis-NL	18	9	.667	3.39	36	0	254.2	96	204
1964	St. Louis-NL	19	12	.613	3.01	40	1	287.1	86	245
1965	St. Louis-NL	20	12	.625	3.07	38	1	299.0	103	270
1966	St. Louis-NL	21	12	.636	2.44	35	0	280.1	78	225
1967	St. Louis-NL	13	7	.650	2.98	24	0	175.1	40	147
1968	St. Louis-NL	22	9	.710	1.12	34	0	304.2	62	268
1969	St. Louis-NL	20	13	.606	2.18	35	0	314.0	95	269
1970	St. Louis-NL	23	7	.767	3.12	34	0	294.0	88	274
1971	St. Louis-NL	16	13	.552	3.04	31	0	245.2	76	185
1972	St. Louis-NL	19	11	.633	2.46	34	0	278.0	88	208
1973	St. Louis-NL	12	10	.545	2.77	25	0	195.0	57	142
1974	St. Louis-NL	11	13	.458	3.83	33	0	240.0	104	129
1975	St. Louis-NL	3	10	.231	5.04	22	2	109.0	62	60
Career Totals:		251	174	.591	2.91	528	6	3884.1	1336	3117

scythes roaring by on each arm. But the key to his intimidation was nei-ther of those.

It was his eyes. Bob Gibson's eyes saw through hitters, their reputa-tions, their parents, their grandparents. And the look burned.

The man changed the definition of intimidation in baseball. It was no longer an act for nine innings, or a series. It was all intimidation, all the time.

Not even the World Series, where the biggest egos and biggest tough guys in baseball gather, could make him yield, seem vulnerable, or even human. Especially not in the World Series.

In three World Series for the St. Louis Cardinals—1964, 1967 and 1968—Gibson was 7-2. His ERA was 1.89. He was in the World Series' Top 10 for wins, complete games, strikeouts, and shutouts. He retired tops in strikeouts per nine World Series innings at 10.22.

But his last fall classic was the crowning jewel. He beat the Detroit Tigers 4–0 in the first game after striking out 17 batters, a new series record, and won the game facing just 32 batters. As for the "pitching duel of the century," Gibson sent 30-game-winner Denny McLain to the showers by the sixth inning. Over in the St. Louis locker room, the quote tacked to the bulletin board was McLain's "I want to humiliate the Cardinals."

Wrong move, like a movie character going into a haunted house because he heard "something."

And Gibson was something.

The one-time Harlem Globetrotter (loved playing, hated clowning) said at the time he never felt nervous before a game. He slept just fine before he pitched. Whether that was true or not is uncertain because it fit into his intimidation of batters who stayed awake nights, fearing a nightmare of Gibson's fastballs and sharp curves, and always inside. They didn't know if the intimidation was an act; Gibson refused to talk to hitters. He hated All-Star Games because he had to be teammates with the enemy. Before a game he even refused to talk to his own team.

When roommate Bill White was traded, Gibson's first pitch to the new enemy was right at him. David Halberstam, in *October 1964*, wrote that Gibson threw at Dodger Willie Crawford because he tried to talk to Gibson on an elevator.

His catcher, Tim McCarver, once went to the mound to talk over a tight situation. Once. McCarver says Gibson told him that unless he was going to pitch, go back and catch.

"I get a certain satisfaction out of getting a man out," Gibson said back then, "but I wouldn't call it fun."

Neither would anyone else on the field.

No. 20
CY YOUNG

You know the name, obviously, but have you seen the numbers? Forget Joe D's 56-game hitting streak: Denton True Young has the records that will never be broken.

Full Name: Denton True Young

Position: Pitcher   Debut: August 1890, Cleveland Spiders

Born: 3/29/1867, Gilmore, Ohio   Bats: Right

Height: 6'2"; Weight: 210   Throws: Right

PITCHING SUMMARY STATISTICS

Year	Team	W	L	PCT	ERA	G	SV	IP	BB	SO
1890	Cleveland-NL	9	7	.563	3.47	17	0	147.2	30	39
1891	Cleveland-NL	27	22	.551	2.85	55	2	423.2	140	147
1892	Cleveland-NL	36	12	.750	1.93	53	0	453.0	118	168
1893	Cleveland-NL	34	16	.680	3.36	53	1	422.2	103	102
1894	Cleveland-NL	26	21	.553	3.94	52	1	408.2	106	108
1895	Cleveland-NL	35	10	.778	3.26	47	0	369.2	75	121
1896	Cleveland-NL	28	15	.651	3.24	51	3	414.1	62	140
1897	Cleveland-NL	21	19	.525	3.78	46	0	335.2	49	88
1898	Cleveland-NL	25	13	.658	2.53	46	0	377.2	41	101
1899	St. Louis-NL	26	16	.619	2.58	44	1	369.1	44	111
1900	St. Louis-NL	19	19	.500	3.00	41	0	321.1	36	115
1901	Boston-AL	33	10	.767	1.62	43	0	371.1	37	158
1902	Boston-AL	32	11	.744	2.15	45	0	384.2	53	160
1903	Boston-AL	28	9	.757	2.08	40	2	341.2	37	176
1904	Boston-AL	26	16	.619	1.97	43	1	380.0	29	200
1905	Boston-AL	18	19	.486	1.82	38	0	320.2	30	210
1906	Boston-AL	13	21	.382	3.19	39	2	287.2	25	140
1907	Boston-AL	21	15	.583	1.99	43	2	343.1	51	147
1908	Boston-AL	21	11	.656	1.26	36	2	299.0	37	150
1909	Cleveland-AL	19	15	.559	2.26	35	0	295.0	59	109
1910	Cleveland-AL	7	10	.412	2.53	21	0	163.1	27	58
1911	Cleveland-AL	3	4	.429	3.88	7	0	46.1	13	20
1911	Boston-NL	4	5	.444	3.71	11	0	80.0	15	35
Career Totals:		511	316	.618	2.56	906	17	7356.2	1217	2803

Wins: 511. Starts: 815. Complete games: 749. These are just silly.

How do you get 815 starts? Start every third—or sometimes every other—day, and even both games of a double-header, as he did as a rookie in 1890. How do you complete 749 of them? Well, you better be good, and have an arm not found in nature.

Young's theory, as printed in *The Sporting News* in 1951, was that a pitcher gets better with less rest and more work, not the other way around.

"Too many pitchers, that's all, there are just too many pitchers," he said. "Don't see how any of them get enough work. Four starting pitchers and one relief man ought to be enough. Pitch them every three days and you'd find they'd get control and good strong arms."

Cy Young (the Cy was short for "Cyclone," a nickname tagged on him when a warm-up pitch splintered a fence), started his career in the nineteenth century, and by the time the 1900s arrived his most stellar seasons were mostly behind him. Still, in the first decade of the twentieth century, Young posted two 30-win seasons; four 20-win seasons; two 19-win seasons; two wins in the first World Series, in 1903, pitching for the Boston Pilgrims (later the Red Sox); and three no-hitters, including a perfect game.

Yeah, we think he qualifies.

Intimidating at 6-foot-2 and 210 pounds, Young had nine straight 20-win seasons and 15 overall in his 22-year career. A 1937 inductee into the Baseball Hall of Fame, Young is better remembered today as an award rather than a player. Take the time to look at the numbers, and you will know why the award got its name.

A story goes that some reporters were arguing over which siblings made the best pitching tandem in major-league history. There were Dizzy and Daffy Dean, Gaylord and Jim Perry, Christy and Henry Mathewson and Phil and Joe Niekro, among many others.

One of the journalists then put the debate to rest: "Cy Young and his sister have still got them all beat."

No. 21

JOHNNY BENCH

Most of us saw it, right there on TV, more than once. Man on first, Johnny Bench behind the plate catches the strike, pivots in his squat and throws out the runner, who was leading a stride off the bag when the ball hit the catcher's mitt.

What's most amazing is that it wasn't amazing. Not for Bench.

Full Name: Johnny Lee Bench

Position: C, 3B, 1B, OF   Debut: August 1967, Cincinnati Reds

Born: 12/7/1947,
  Oklahoma City, Oklahoma   Bats: Right

Height: 6'1"; Weight: 208   Throws: Right

BATTING SUMMARY STATISTICS

Year	Team	AVG	G	AB	R	H	HR	RBI	BB	SO	SB
1967	Cincinnati-NL	.163	26	86	7	14	1	6	5	19	0
1968	Cincinnati-NL	.275	154	564	67	155	15	82	31	96	1
1969	Cincinnati-NL	.293	148	532	83	156	26	90	49	86	6
1970	Cincinnati-NL	.293	158	605	97	177	45	148	54	102	5
1971	Cincinnati-NL	.238	149	562	80	134	27	61	49	83	2
1972	Cincinnati-NL	.270	147	538	87	145	40	125	100	84	6
1973	Cincinnati-NL	.253	152	557	83	141	25	104	83	83	4
1974	Cincinnati-NL	.280	160	621	108	174	33	129	80	90	5
1975	Cincinnati-NL	.283	142	530	83	150	28	110	65	108	11
1976	Cincinnati-NL	.234	135	465	62	109	16	74	81	95	13
1977	Cincinnati-NL	.275	142	494	67	136	31	109	58	95	2
1978	Cincinnati-NL	.260	120	393	52	102	23	73	50	83	4
1979	Cincinnati-NL	.276	130	464	73	128	22	80	67	73	4
1980	Cincinnati-NL	.250	114	360	52	90	24	68	41	64	4
1981	Cincinnati-NL	.309	52	178	14	55	8	25	17	21	0
1982	Cincinnati-NL	.258	119	399	44	103	13	38	37	58	1
1983	Cincinnati-NL	.255	110	310	32	79	12	54	24	38	0
Career Totals:		.267	2158	7658	1091	2048	389	1376	891	1278	68

He led the National League in RBI three times, in homers twice, was Most Valuable Player twice and for the 1976 World Series. Oh, and along the way he hit 389 home runs, most of which came during afternoons in the hot sun, mostly under thick padding, plastic and metal, squatting for three hours with careening 90 mph balls thrown at him. It's the only big league job that even the loudest guy in the loudest softball uniform doesn't want.

There are challengers, like Mike Piazza, a power-hitting catcher, but come back in a decade or so, don't slack off, and win a few World Series.

"He is the Babe Ruth of catchers," Piazza said on a New York Mets' pregame show in 1999. "It is not really fair to compare anyone to him."

At the toughest position in baseball, Bench excelled, winning every Gold Glove from 1969 through 1977. All-century balloting had him with better than 25 percent more votes than Yogi Berra, more than three times the votes of Carlton Fisk, and five times those for Roy Campanella.

"I can throw out any man alive," Bench said in the 1970s.

No one challenged the statement. Few challenged the arm, knowing they did so at their extreme peril. As fast as a pro athlete can run, there's no slower trip in sports than the three steps to second base when the infielder is holding Bench's peg.

He played 17 years in Cincinnati, but like other cogs in the Big Red Machine, Bench played his best in 45 postseason games. Twice in the league championship series and three times in the World Series he surpassed his career batting average, hitting .333 in the NLCS in 1972 and 1976. He had a World Series batting average of .279, including .533 in four games in 1976.

But Bench was a slugger. In five of six pennant series he out-lumbered his career slugging percentage of .476 and in the 1976 World Series posted a typo of a slugging average of 1.133.

If a player's greatness depends on great play in the greatest games, he set the mark for players behind the mask.

No. 22

KEN GRIFFEY, JR.

He was just a kid before he was The Kid. Drafted at 17, in the majors at 19, Ken Griffey, Jr., had all the expectations that went along with being a number-one pick, the son of an all-star and 19-year veteran *and* sharing the nickname of Ted Williams.

April 10, 1989: Griffey's first home game for the Seattle Mariners. Batting second, he swings at the first pitch in his first at bat and drives the ball the other way to left for a home run. So young.

So quickly it became so long ago. Where will Junior end up among

the all-time greats? Griffey says he doesn't care about the historical numbers that have gone along with his career. We do. We all do.

This book's subjects constitute an all-century team, but even though the 1900s are gone, we still haven't had enough time to grant us the depth perception to accurately gauge where some of the active all-timers belong. We are rolling the dice on Griffey, based on what he has done but also tinged with what we think he is primed to do.

Griffey might be the best center fielder to ever play the field, a man who swept the American League Gold Glove competition in the 1990s. There has never been a fielder who plays—and climbs—the wall better than The Kid.

Then there is his threat at the plate. In the past six years Griffey has hit 40 home runs (in strike-shortened 1994), 17 (in 1995, in which he missed more than half the season to injury), 49, 56, 56, and 48. In the past four seasons he has driven in 140, 147, 146 and 134 runs. His career batting average hovers around .300.

In 1993 Griffey homered in eight straight games, matching the record set by Dale Long and later tied by Don Mattingly. He was the youngest player to reach 350 home runs, at a shade past his twenty-eighth birthday. He was on schedule to early in the 2000 season hit his 400th home run, at age 30. In 11 seasons he has knocked in 1,152 runs, three RBI better than half way to Hank Aaron's record. It's time to discuss immortality.

If the center fielder, with that beautiful swing from the left side of the plate and instincts in the field that get him to balls no other outfielder could, decides to remain focused, he will be allotted a place in history beyond mere enshrinement in Cooperstown. But unlike players of past generations, Griffey is financially set for several lives. He doesn't need to do this. He has to want to.

But what if he has another six, seven, eight, ten or more Griffey-like seasons? Aaron's career marks of home runs (755) and RBI (2,297) would be in jeopardy if not shattered. "I think the candidate that has a good chance is Ken Griffey, Jr.," Aaron said after the 1999 season. "He's going to be around for a while."

Opposite: **Ken Griffey, Jr., writes a textbook on hitting with just about every swing: feet planted and balanced, arms extended and level, eye on the ball, and ball in the stands. Breaking into the majors at 19 years old the son of Big Red Machine star Ken Griffey, "Junior" quickly rose to superstar. As the twentieth century closed, Junior and his easy yet crushing swing and acrobatic play in the outfield earned him a description most never thought would be spoken: "He's Willie Mays in his prime."**

But what do these records mean to a millionaire? What does it mean to Ken Griffey, Sr.'s son, now that both are with the Cincinnati Reds?

It's up to him to care about his place among baseball's legends as much as we do. If he does, Ted Williams will someday be sharing the nickname of Ken Griffey, Jr.

No. 23

Grover Cleveland Alexander

The quiz for today: Who was president of the United States in 1915?

If the answer came to you right off the top of your head, you spent too many days listening to history lectures when you should have been listening to a baseball game.

Today, few can easily name that year's president (Woodrow Wilson) or the foreign country he propped up with his chosen leader (Mexico), or even the luxury liner sunk by a German submarine (*Lusitania*). But baseball fans have heard of Grover Cleveland Alexander, who started an amazing pitching career that year, one that outlasted top hitters of the day and the star power of the Seavers and Madduxes ever since. Check the all-century selections: Alexander tops Tom Seaver, Jim Palmer and Greg Maddux in most of them.

Having a rookie season of 28–13, later followed by three seasons *in a row* of 30 or more wins, and ending up with 373 career wins and 90 shutouts over 20 years will do that every time.

So why was someone with the impeccable timing needed to uncork a devastating pitcher's windup the victim of such lousy timing in birth?

Alexander's contemporaries included Christy Mathewson, Walter Johnson and Smokey Joe Wood, three of the very few pitchers in baseball history who could best "Old Pete."

Still, Alexander rose to the occasion. And thanks to a penchant for

Full Name: Grover Cleveland Alexander

Position: Pitcher

Debut: April 1911
Philadelphia Phillies

Born: 2/26/1887, Elba, Nebraska

Bats: Right

Height: 6'1"; Weight: 185

Throws: Right

PITCHING SUMMARY STATISTICS

Year	Team	W	L	PCT	ERA	G	SV	IP	BB	SO
1911	Philadelphia-NL	28	13	.683	2.57	48	3	367.0	129	227
1912	Philadelphia-NL	19	17	.528	2.81	46	3	310.1	105	195
1913	Philadelphia-NL	22	8	.733	2.79	47	2	306.1	75	159
1914	Philadelphia-NL	27	15	.643	2.38	46	1	355.0	76	214
1915	Philadelphia-NL	31	10	.756	1.22	49	3	376.1	64	241
1916	Philadelphia-NL	33	12	.733	1.55	48	3	389.0	50	167
1917	Philadelphia-NL	30	13	.698	1.83	45	0	388.0	56	200
1918	Chicago-NL	2	1	.667	1.73	3	0	26.0	3	15
1919	Chicago-NL	16	11	.593	1.72	30	1	235.0	38	121
1920	Chicago-NL	27	14	.659	1.91	46	5	363.1	69	173
1921	Chicago-NL	15	13	.536	3.39	31	1	252.0	33	77
1922	Chicago-NL	16	13	.552	3.63	33	1	245.2	34	48
1923	Chicago-NL	22	12	.647	3.19	39	2	305.0	30	72
1924	Chicago-NL	12	5	.706	3.03	21	0	169.1	25	33
1925	Chicago-NL	15	11	.577	3.39	32	0	236.0	29	63
1926	Chicago-NL	3	3	.500	3.46	7	0	52.0	7	12
1926	St. Louis-NL	9	7	.563	2.91	23	2	148.1	24	35
1926	NL Totals	12	10	.545	3.05	30	2	200.1	31	47
1927	St. Louis-NL	21	10	.677	2.52	37	3	268.0	38	48
1928	St. Louis-NL	16	9	.640	3.36	34	2	243.2	37	59
1929	St. Louis-NL	9	8	.529	3.89	22	0	132.0	23	33
1930	Philadelphia-NL	0	3	.000	9.14	9	0	21.2	6	6
Career Totals:		373	208	.642	2.56	696	32	5190.0	951	2198

baseball fans to revel even in the stars who flickered in our grandfather's day, Alexander remains appreciated today, as one of the greatest players in a century in which he played only the first third.

If only Woodrow Wilson had such a good career after 1915 ... (Oh, go look it up to see what we mean).

No. 24

Sandy Koufax

Pity Bob Hendley. He managed one winning season, his last in a seven-year career that saw him bounce from the Milwaukee Braves to the San Francisco Giants to the Chicago Cubs and finally the New York Mets.

But for one night, he was nearly perfect. On September 9, 1965, at Dodger Stadium, the 6-foot-2 left-hander held the Dodgers to just one hit, and one lousy unearned run. Great pitching. Bad timing.

Problem was, Sandy Koufax was perfect. Twenty-seven Cubs up, 27 down, and a 1–0 Dodger win. It was his (then-record) fourth and final no-hitter, coming in a 14-strikeout performance in which only seven balls left the infield.

The Society for American Baseball Research declared it the greatest pitched game of all time, a very debatable designation considering that in 1917, in the same game, Fred Toney of the Cincinnati Reds and Hippo Vaughn of the Chicago Cubs *both* threw no-hitters through nine (Vaughn lost his bid, and the game, in the tenth, while Toney held on to his no-no). But if there ever was one game to be won, and you had to choose one pitcher from across the annals, many experts would tap Koufax. Go ask Hendley.

Koufax called pitching the art of instilling fear. But he also said he only went for strikeouts when he was in a jam, like with runners in scoring position. You win with outs, he reasoned.

"I became a good pitcher when I stopped trying to make them miss the ball and started trying to make them hit it," Koufax said in Leonard Koppett's book, *A Thinking Man's Guide to Baseball.*

Man, talk about screwing up. Koufax led the National League in strikeouts four times, three of those times going over 300 Ks. From 1961 to 1966 Koufax was the most dominant player in the game, compiling three seasons of 25 or more wins (each with less than 10 losses) and five straight seasons with an ERA of 2.54 or less (including three years under 2.00). Of course there were the strikeouts, accidental and otherwise. He averaged better than a K per inning for his career.

Full Name: Sanford Koufax (b: Sanford Braun)

Position: Pitcher   Debut: June 1955, Brooklyn Dodgers

Born: 12/30/1935,   Bats: Right
   Brooklyn, New York

Height: 6'2"; Weight: 210   Throws: Left

PITCHING SUMMARY STATISTICS

Year	Team	W	L	PCT	ERA	G	SV	IP	BB	SO
1955	Brooklyn-NL	2	2	.500	3.02	12	0	41.2	28	30
1956	Brooklyn-NL	2	4	.333	4.91	16	0	58.2	29	30
1957	Brooklyn-NL	5	4	.556	3.88	34	0	104.1	51	122
1958	Los Angeles-NL	11	11	.500	4.48	40	1	158.2	105	131
1959	Los Angeles-NL	8	6	.571	4.05	35	2	153.1	92	173
1960	Los Angeles-NL	8	13	.381	3.91	37	1	175.0	100	197
1961	Los Angeles-NL	18	13	.581	3.52	42	1	255.2	96	269
1962	Los Angeles-NL	14	7	.667	2.54	28	1	184.1	57	216
1963	Los Angeles-NL	25	5	.833	1.88	40	0	311.0	58	306
1964	Los Angeles-NL	19	5	.792	1.74	29	1	223.0	53	223
1965	Los Angeles-NL	26	8	.765	2.04	43	2	335.2	71	382
1966	Los Angeles-NL	27	9	.750	1.73	41	0	323.0	77	317
Career Totals:		165	87	.655	2.76	397	9	2324.1	817	2396

But what of his career? Koufax has fewer career wins (165) than Jerry Reuss, Charlie Hough, or Mickey Lolich, among many others. And he had fewer career strikeouts than the likes of Jerry Koosman, Frank Tanana and Luis Tiant. Koufax pitched only 12 years in the majors and didn't become dominant until the second half of his career. He did retire as the best in the game, knocked out by arm troubles that he worried would leave him crippled, but was it enough for a Hall of Fame career?

Don't even bother arguing. Koufax is the exception to the longevity rule that could keep great players like Don Mattingly out of the Hall. In the era of the pitcher, there was no one close to him; not for a career, not for a season, not even for a night. Go ask Bob Hendley.

No. 25

MARK MCGWIRE

His exploits are subject to hyperbole, his impact on baseball seemingly prone to exaggeration. It's been said that Mark McGwire, with a great assist from costar Sammy Sosa, "saved" baseball with the dramatic Great Home Run Race of 1998 (all good shows should have a catchy title).

So leave it to a veteran sportswriter, columnist Sam Donnellon of the *Philadelphia Daily News,* to cut through the hagiographic haze. Really now, how important was McGwire in 1998 in the grand scheme of things?

"Walking into that season, baseball was in fourth place," Donnellon, who extensively covered McGwire-Sosa I and II, said in an interview. "People were never going back [to the ballpark]. You had the whole spectra of the [world-champion Florida] Marlins selling off their team. It looked like a sport with no relevance, a sport with no controls, incapable of renewing itself.

"With 70 swings of the bat, within one summer, that was all turned around."

To twist a tongue-in-cheek journalistic axiom, sometimes facts don't screw up a great story.

McGwire and Sosa (Sammy, sorry, but you were about one Sosa-like season from making it on this list) dueled in a barrage that captivated baseball and its fans, even the justifiably cynical still burned by the labor strife of 1994 and 1995. In the end McGwire was the first to break Roger Maris's mark of 61 and edged out Sosa for the season, 70–66. In the reprise McGwire again topped the National League with 66 home runs—he is the first player ever to hit 50 or more homers four straight seasons—although he needed a flurry to catch Sosa in the end.

Back to 1998. It was actually romantic—calm down, in a guy sort of

Opposite: Some home runs make fans say, "Oooh!" Mark McGwire's make many of us go, "Ouch!" McGwire's massive forearms and biceps have powered baseballs 400 feet or more through his career, but more importantly they have helped power baseball back into something worth watching, and loving, after seasons of ignoring and complaining. McGwire's home run race with Sammy Sosa has, for many fans, re-created the good old days of baseball. McGwire, especially, seemed to have not only located baseball's long unreachable plateau—he set up camp.

way—that home run race. But there was no denying the lovefest—between the fans and both players, the media and the players themselves—salved a lot of the raw wounds created by money issues.

"I wish every player could feel what I've felt visiting ballparks," said McGwire, whose 500-plus-foot fireworks display gets fans packing bleachers just for batting practice. "It's blown me away."

He doesn't just hit home runs; he hits ridiculously long and majestic home runs. He doesn't just hit scoreboards, he breaks them. McGwire stories of tomorrow, about his epic blasts and gentlemanly conduct as goodwill ambassador for the game, will probably not creep into myth because the truth already stretches the bounds of credibility.

(OK, so this seems like the place to get the author's name thing out of the way [check the cover]. First, I had it first by more than a month before the other McGwire. Second, I spell it right. Third, I've run out of original answers to being asked "How many home runs you hit today?" Fourth, besides, as did my 98-year-old grandmother and one guy at a book signing, no one should confuse us in person. Finally, if I'm going to share a name, I certainly got lucky: At last count there are at least eight "Hitlers" listed in phone books in the United States—MM).

In 1987 McGwire was the American League Rookie of the Year and home run champion with a rookie record 49 for the Oakland A's. A Gold Glove winner in 1990, McGwire won the American League home run title in 1996 and, of course, the National League titles in 1998 and 1999. And 1997? McGwire was traded midyear from the A's to the St. Louis Cardinals, so he didn't lead either league. He did lead baseball, though, with 58.

McGwire, who also set a National League record for walks in 1998, is an 11-time All-Star who lost nearly two seasons to a heel injury in the first half of the 1990s. Still, he remained relatively injury free (despite episodic back flareups) thereafter, and for his career has hit home runs at a greater clip based on at bats than anyone—including The Babe. The question begins to simmer...

Big Mac cracked the Top-10 home run list with 522 at the end of 1999. He will be 36 entering the 2000 season. Four straight 50-plus home run seasons, two straight 60-plus. Maybe, possibly—could he?—catch 755? Do the math for yourself.

"He could be knocking on Aaron's door," said Donnellon, noting that McGwire could do it as a DH in his last years. "I think he is having a second life."

Despite all the obits, so is baseball. And that, like McGwire, is not only a great story, but fact.

No. 26

BOB FELLER

What does a major leaguer do after tying the record for most strike-outs in a game? If you are 17-year-old Bob Feller, you finish high school.

What does a major leaguer do after a war breaks out? If you are 23-year-old Bob Feller, you enlist in the navy, sacrificing more than three and a half seasons of baseball during World War II and earning battle citations as a gun crew chief on a battleship.

And what do you do after all those lost seasons away from the game? If you are 26-year-old Bob Feller, you come back to the Cleveland Indians and remain the most dominating hurler in the game. Feller went from a boyhood phenom to a star to navy veteran to a Hall of Famer, armed with one of the best fastballs the game has ever seen.

Feller was legend throughout his native Iowa by the time he was 16, and the Indians soon came knocking on his door in Van Meter with a contract. The Detroit Tigers also came with an offer—despite its being against major league rules to sign kids before they finished high school. Feller was declared a free agent, but the 6-foot right-hander chose to stick with Cleveland.

By 1936, at the ridiculous age of 17, he was in the majors. He struck out 76 in 62 innings that season, doing what he always had done dating back to his days in the cornfields: rearing back and firing.

"Rapid Robert" wasn't sure if his fastball would find the plate or the backstop—he led the American League in walks four times and is fifth all-time in walks allowed—but he could be just as sure no one was going to touch it, leading the league in strikeouts seven times. To make it simple: He was Nolan Ryan before Nolan Ryan.

Full Name: Robert William Andrew "Rapid Robert" Feller

Position: Pitcher

Debut: July 1936,
Cleveland Indians

Born: 11/3/1918, Van Meter, Iowa

Bats: Right

Height: 6'; Weight: 185

Throws: Right

Pitching Summary Statistics

Year	Team	W	L	PCT	ERA	G	SV	IP	BB	SO
1936	Cleveland-AL	5	3	.625	3.34	14	1	62.0	47	76
1937	Cleveland-AL	9	7	.563	3.39	26	1	148.2	106	150
1938	Cleveland-AL	17	11	.607	4.08	39	1	277.2	208	240
1939	Cleveland-AL	24	9	.727	2.85	39	1	296.2	142	246
1940	Cleveland-AL	27	11	.711	2.61	43	4	320.1	118	261
1941	Cleveland-AL	25	13	.658	3.15	44	2	343.0	194	260
1945	Cleveland-AL	5	3	.625	2.50	9	0	72.0	35	59
1946	Cleveland-AL	26	15	.634	2.18	48	4	371.1	153	348
1947	Cleveland-AL	20	11	.645	2.68	42	3	299.0	127	196
1948	Cleveland-AL	19	15	.559	3.56	44	3	280.1	116	164
1949	Cleveland-AL	15	14	.517	3.75	36	0	211.0	84	108
1950	Cleveland-AL	16	11	.593	3.43	35	0	247.0	103	119
1951	Cleveland-AL	22	8	.733	3.50	33	0	249.2	95	111
1952	Cleveland-AL	9	13	.409	4.74	30	0	191.2	83	81
1953	Cleveland-AL	10	7	.588	3.59	25	0	175.2	60	60
1954	Cleveland-AL	13	3	.813	3.09	19	0	140.0	39	59
1955	Cleveland-AL	4	4	.500	3.47	25	0	83.0	31	25
1956	Cleveland-AL	0	4	.000	4.97	19	1	58.0	23	18
Career Totals:		266	162	.621	3.25	570	21	3827.0	1764	2581

Feller remains the only player to throw a no-hitter on Opening Day, blanking the Chicago White Sox, 1–0, to kick off the 1940 season. It was the first of his three no-hitters, a trifecta coupled with his 12 one-hitters that shows his true dominance.

A six-time 20-game winner who also won 19 for the Tribe's 1948 World Series championship team, Feller's fastball ranks with Ryan's and Walter Johnson's as legendary, flecked with an unpredictable wildness that would make batters not all that willing to dig in against him.

If you were a major leaguer—phenom, veteran or Hall of Famer—in the box against him, what would you do?

No. 27

TRIS SPEAKER

There once rode a cowboy into baseball's springtime. Tris Speaker was that Texan, and he rode a herd of legends from dusty ballfields where he nearly perfected the game before the twentieth century began.

One legend had it that he was thrown from horseback as a child and broke his right arm, then drove himself to excel as a lefty. Soon after he is said to have broken his left arm, so he just worked harder to become a double-threat. True or not, it doesn't really matter. They're great stories, and baseball breathes great stories.

Besides, once Speaker got to the big leagues, he rustled up a whole new pack of legends. And these are facts, witnessed by millions and filed in Cooperstown. Yet that doesn't make them any easier to believe:

Speaker was one of the greatest fielders responsible for the largest real estate in baseball. As a center fielder, he left the game tops in assists for all outfielders with 448, well ahead of Ty Cobb's 392. From the deepest part of ballparks, he also led all outfielders in double plays with 139 (by comparison, even at third base, Brooks Robinson had just 618).

Full Name: Tristram E. "The Grey Eagle" Speaker

Position: OF, PM

Born: 4/4/1888, Hubbard, Texas

Height: 5'11.5"; Weight: 193

Debut: September 1907, Boston Red Sox

Bats: Left

Throws: Left

BATTING SUMMARY STATISTICS

Year	Team	AVG	G	AB	R	H	HR	RBI	BB	SO	SB
1907	Boston-AL	.158	7	19	0	3	0	1	1	–	0
1908	Boston-AL	.224	31	116	12	26	0	9	4	–	3
1909	Boston-AL	.309	143	544	73	168	7	77	38	–	35
1910	Boston-AL	.340	141	538	92	183	7	65	52	–	35
1911	Boston-AL	.334	141	500	88	167	8	70	59	–	25
1912	Boston-AL	.383	153	580	136	222	10	90	82	–	52
1913	Boston-AL	.363	141	520	94	189	3	71	65	22	46

Year	Team	AVG	G	AB	R	H	HR	RBI	BB	SO	SB
1914	Boston-AL	.338	158	571	101	193	4	90	77	25	42
1915	Boston-AL	.322	150	547	108	176	0	69	81	14	29
1916	Cleveland-AL	.386	151	546	102	211	2	79	82	20	35
1917	Cleveland-AL	.352	142	523	90	184	2	60	67	14	30
1918	Cleveland-AL	.318	127	471	73	150	0	61	64	9	27
1919	Cleveland-AL	.296	134	494	83	146	2	63	73	12	15
1920	Cleveland-AL	.388	150	552	137	214	8	107	97	13	10
1921	Cleveland-AL	.362	132	506	107	183	3	75	68	12	2
1922	Cleveland-AL	.378	131	426	85	161	11	71	77	11	8
1923	Cleveland-AL	.380	150	574	133	218	17	130	93	15	8
1924	Cleveland-AL	.344	135	486	94	167	9	65	72	13	5
1925	Cleveland-AL	.389	117	429	79	167	12	87	70	12	5
1926	Cleveland-AL	.304	150	539	96	164	7	86	94	15	6
1927	Washington-AL	.327	141	523	71	171	2	73	55	8	9
1928	Philadelphia-AL	.267	64	191	28	51	3	30	10	5	5
Career Totals:		.345	2789	10195	1882	3514	117	1529	1381	220	432

But the most amazing thing about the fielding of Speaker is that it was his second-best talent. The guy hit over .350 nine different years.

In 1916 alone, playing for Cleveland, Speaker led the American League in hitting (.386), slugging percentage (.502), and hits (211), finishing second in total bases and doubles, fourth in RBI and fifth in stolen bases, beating the stats of a guy named Hornsby in the National League.

When Speaker was inducted into the Hall of Fame in 1937, most were sure no other center fielder would equal him. We know now that the assurances of the day were part illusion, one that depended on exclusion of a whole pool of talent that would later produce Willie Mays and a few others.

But the fact that The Grey Eagle isn't the game's best center fielder shouldn't cloud the fact that he was the best when baseball was young—when it needed someone to show what the best really meant. When it needed a legend.

No. 28

YOGI BERRA

For much of America in the 1950s through the 1980s, Yogi Berra was, perhaps foremost, a clown.

Then in the late 1990s, as America fell in love again with baseball, Yogi became a sage philosopher.

Sportswriters are still trying to decipher Yogi-isms to reveal the genius behind what were long simply considered his malaprops. "It ain't over 'til it's over" and "We made too many wrong mistakes" became prophetic.

Whether Yogi really should be considered a Kant with a can-do attitude and a catcher's mask or a simple guy with a simple, populist view of the world, one thing is for sure: he shouldn't be remembered primarily as either.

He was a baseball player. A great baseball player. But he was more because—to risk a Yogi-ism—he was less.

He didn't try to embellish his performance with analysis, with canned phrases delivered to sportswriters and talk show hosts. All he did was play the toughest position in baseball and play in more World Series than anyone.

If the true object of a game is winning, rather than personal glory, then Yogi might be the best who ever played.

Yogi was a Yankee with Mickey Mantle, Whitey Ford, Roger Maris, Joe DiMaggio and other greats. The Stadium was newly haunted with the ghosts of Ruth and Gehrig and up north was a guy named Ted Williams.

Still, one of the greatest of that time or any time, Jackie Robinson, said that if a big game came down to one hitter, he'd want Yogi in the batter's box. Robinson called Berra the best clutch hitter he ever saw, high praise from a guy who lost so many World Series games to the Yankees and played under unimaginable pressure.

So how did this guy, who was passed over by his hometown St. Louis Cardinals (not even given a minor-league gig), become one of the most remembered, beloved, and successful players of all time?

Full Name: Lawrence Peter "Yogi" Berra

Position: C, OF   Debut: September 1946, New York Yankees

Born: 5/12/1925,   Bats: Left
   St. Louis, Missouri

Height: 5'8"; Weight: 194   Throws: Right

Batting Summary Statistics

Year	Team	AVG	G	AB	R	H	HR	RBI	BB	SO	SB
1946	New York-AL	.364	7	22	3	8	2	4	1	1	0
1947	New York-AL	.280	83	293	41	82	11	54	13	12	0
1948	New York-AL	.305	125	469	70	143	14	98	25	24	3
1949	New York-AL	.277	116	415	59	115	20	91	22	25	2
1950	New York-AL	.322	151	597	116	192	28	124	55	12	4
1951	New York-AL	.294	141	547	92	161	27	88	44	20	5
1952	New York-AL	.273	142	534	97	146	30	98	66	24	2
1953	New York-AL	.296	137	503	80	149	27	108	50	32	0
1954	New York-AL	.307	151	584	88	179	22	125	56	29	0
1955	New York-AL	.272	147	541	84	147	27	108	60	20	1
1956	New York-AL	.298	140	521	93	155	30	105	65	29	3
1957	New York-AL	.251	134	482	74	121	24	82	57	24	1
1958	New York-AL	.266	122	433	60	115	22	90	35	35	3
1959	New York-AL	.284	131	472	64	134	19	69	43	38	1
1960	New York-AL	.276	120	359	46	99	15	62	38	23	2
1961	New York-AL	.271	119	395	62	107	22	61	35	28	2
1962	New York-AL	.224	86	232	25	52	10	35	24	18	0
1963	New York-AL	.293	64	147	20	43	8	28	15	17	1
1965	New York-NL	.222	4	9	1	2	0	0	0	3	0
Career Totals:		.285	2120	7555	1175	2150	358	1430	704	414	30

The answer must be back on The Hill in St. Louis, a scrappy Italian neighborhood where Berra insists he was, maybe, only the second-best ballplayer. Berra worked hard on baseball, knowing a guy 5-foot, 7-and-a-half inches tall and 185 pounds was no natural. So he seized each moment like it was his last. A bad pitch was still a major-league pitch, and who was he to let it go to waste?

He swatted at bad balls like he was back in the sandlot, as if he'd have to chase it if it got by him. That's funny to watch, especially when the guy's name is Yogi, but it is also how you score runs.

From 1946 to 1965, while usually taking 500 or so at bats a season, he never struck out more than 38 times in a year. Along the way he forced himself to be a solid catcher and collected three Most Valuable Player trophies. He played on 10 world champion teams, in 14 straight All-Star Games and retired with 19 major-league records.

Casey Stengel would later call Yogi, a guy with an eighth-grade education, his assistant manager. Yogi then went on to manage in his own right.

However tempting "I told you so" must have been for Yogi, he never said it publicly. Instead, he worked hard to prove—not merely say—that the rap against his intelligence was wrong.

Lawrence Peter Berra was a product of his times, but in many ways the best product. He worked hard to rise from a poor, working-class life that tested so many immigrants. He volunteered as a landing boat gunner on D-Day, then refused a Purple Heart because it would make his mother worry. He worked hard to play baseball for a living, then kept working hard to be great at it. Through it all he was not a Babe, or a Yankee Clipper or a Splendid Splinter. He was Yogi. Our Yogi. A guy who was thrilled to a rare display of emotion when a minor league park in New Jersey was named after him. A guy who refused to step in his beloved Yankee Stadium for 14 years because George Steinbrenner fired him as manager without doing so face to face, like a man. A guy who got Steinbrenner—Steinbrenner!—to apologize.

If you live in New York, that's plenty to make Yogi one of the best figures in baseball of all time.

But Yogi had an even better moment. Although he gets too little credit for it, he was perfect one World Series game in 1956. Oh, Don Larsen is the guy who pitched that only perfect game at the most important time to do so, but Berra called it, pitch by pitch. Only four batters that day had a chance for hits after the first hitter—one was foul, three were fly balls. No one ran the count to three balls. If that's not a testament to a catcher, nothing is.

But Yogi, being Yogi, even made a perfect World Series game better. His leap into Larsen's arms is ingrained in the national memory. It stands as proof through all the agents, lawsuits and money that some still play the game because they love it. Some even make the game more lovable.

No. 29

Roberto Clemente

He stood at second base, hands on hips, his face proud and dignified and maybe a tad defiant, in other words like it probably was after each of his 439 other doubles. Roberto Clemente then doffed his helmet, an image that seers nearly three decades later, a perfect moment to ensnare for memory.

Everyone knew right away that September 30, 1972, double at Three Rivers Stadium off of New York Met Jon Matlack was a milestone: Clemente's 3,000th hit. But who could know it would be his last? Three months and a day later the Pittsburgh Pirate would be dead at 38, a martyr for all of his native Puerto Rico, felled while trying to do good for fellow Latin Americans who revered him.

Clemente's plane went down on New Year's Eve just after takeoff from San Juan, a flight that was to take him to Managua, Nicaragua. That city had been rocked by a devastating earthquake that claimed more than 6,000 lives; the first Latin American to star in the majors felt it was his duty to be there.

The parallels to Lou Gehrig, another star taken late in his career but early in life, were so strong that Gehrig's eulogy was modified and read at Clemente's memorial service.

The body of Roberto Clemente y Walker was never found in the depths of the Atlantic Ocean. All that was left were snapshot memories— his rifle of an arm, his flailing but fluid running style, his ability to drive any pitch he could reach in or out of the strike zone. But standing on second, hands on hips, chin out and proud, well that was the scene to hand to the sculptor.

In a game of numbers Clemente's hold up well. The son of a sugar cane farmer and youngest of seven children was the National League batting champion four times in his 18-year career, all with the Pirates (before coming up as a 20-year-old, Clemente played one season in the minors in the Brooklyn Dodgers farm system). He hit better than .300 in 13 of his seasons and finished with a .317 mark in an era (1955–72) largely dominated by the pitcher. NL MVP in 1966 (.317, 29 HR, 119 RBI), he led the league twice in hits and once in triples.

Full Name: Roberto "Bob" Clemente (b: Clemente y Walker)

Position: Outfield   Debut: April 1955, Pittsburgh Pirates

Born: 8/18/1934, Carolina,   Bats: Right
   Puerto Rico

Height: 5'11"; Weight: 175   Throws: Right

BATTING SUMMARY STATISTICS

Year	Team	AVG	G	AB	R	H	HR	RBI	BB	SO	SB
1955	Pittsburgh-NL	.255	124	474	48	121	5	47	18	60	2
1956	Pittsburgh-NL	.311	147	543	66	169	7	60	13	58	6
1957	Pittsburgh-NL	.253	111	451	42	114	4	30	23	45	0
1958	Pittsburgh-NL	.289	140	519	69	150	6	50	31	41	8
1959	Pittsburgh-NL	.296	105	432	60	128	4	50	15	51	2
1960	Pittsburgh-NL	.314	144	570	89	179	16	94	39	72	4
1961	Pittsburgh-NL	.351	146	572	100	201	23	89	35	59	4
1962	Pittsburgh-NL	.312	144	538	95	168	10	74	35	73	6
1963	Pittsburgh-NL	.320	152	600	77	192	17	76	31	64	12
1964	Pittsburgh-NL	.339	155	622	95	211	12	87	51	87	5
1965	Pittsburgh-NL	.329	152	589	91	194	10	65	43	78	8
1966	Pittsburgh-NL	.317	154	638	105	202	29	119	46	109	7
1967	Pittsburgh-NL	.357	147	585	103	209	23	110	41	103	9
1968	Pittsburgh-NL	.291	132	502	74	146	18	57	51	77	2
1969	Pittsburgh-NL	.345	138	507	87	175	19	91	56	73	4
1970	Pittsburgh-NL	.352	108	412	65	145	14	60	38	66	3
1971	Pittsburgh-NL	.341	132	522	82	178	13	86	26	65	1
1972	Pittsburgh-NL	.312	102	378	68	118	10	60	29	49	0
Career Totals:		.317	2433	9454	1416	3000	240	1305	621	1230	83

In 15 of his 18 seasons Clemente had double digits in assists from right field (he led the league a record five straight years) and earned 12 Gold Gloves, testament to his strong and accurate right arm and ability to cover wide swaths of real estate.

"He didn't just play right field. He performed out there," fellow Hall of Famer Frank Robinson said of Clemente in a television documentary. "He would whirl like a ballet dancer. You started to watch to see what he would do next."

Clemente played in a pair of seven-game World Series, both victories, against the New York Yankees (1960) and the Baltimore Orioles (1971). Against the Orioles Clemente batted .414 (he averaged .362 for his Series appearances) and claimed MVP honors in one of the most dominating performances of his era. Clemente had at least one hit in every World Series game he played.

Had Clemente, a 5-foot-11, 175-pound right-hander, had more power than evidenced by the 240 home runs he produced, his play would have made him a Top-10 all-timer.

Now, forget all that for a moment and look at the man. Although he arrived eight seasons after Jackie Robinson, Clemente arguably had one of the toughest fights against racism faced by any player: he was black *and* Hispanic. Even Hank Aaron said Clemente had it tougher than he did. Clemente was often (and sometimes derisively) called Bob or Bobby by sportswriters and others; at least one of his Topps baseball cards had his name on the back also listed as "Robert Walker" in parentheses, as if a translation was needed.

Clemente was remote from teammates for much of his early career, separated as much by culture as by race and shackled with the reputation for "jaking" because he took time off for injuries. Only later, when more blacks and Latinos joined the team and Clemente matured and evolved into a leader, would he become comfortable and a cherished icon of the Iron City. He also grew to be more active in social justice affairs, the sting of the numerous affronts thrown at him in the 1950s Jim Crow era partially salved by his superstar position that afforded him a chance to make a difference.

But that superstar tag did not come until he was long into his career, as playing in Pittsburgh robbed him of the kind of fame bestowed on some of his contemporaries on each coast. Some national sportswriters were shocked by his performance in the 1971 World Series.

The Pittsburgh writers, by now in his corner, could merely smile. They had been seeing it for years: Clemente proud and a touch defiant, standing on second base.

No. 30

ERNIE BANKS

We all have a memory that goes something like this: School's out, you run with your glove to the sandlot, you share a bat and whack a dark brown, slightly water-logged baseball. The bases are cardboard, the warning track is a cracked sidewalk, foul territory is marked by Fords and Chevys, and nothing could be better.

Full Name: Ernest Banks

Position: 1B, SS

Born: 1/31/1931, Dallas, Texas

Height: 6'1"; Weight: 180

Debut: September 1953, Chicago Cubs

Bats: Right

Throws: Right

BATTING SUMMARY STATISTICS

Year	Team	AVG	G	AB	R	H	HR	RBI	BB	SO	SB
1953	Chicago-NL	.314	10	35	3	11	2	6	4	5	0
1954	Chicago-NL	.275	154	593	70	163	19	79	40	50	6
1955	Chicago-NL	.295	154	596	98	176	44	117	45	72	9
1956	Chicago-NL	.297	139	538	82	160	28	85	52	62	6
1957	Chicago-NL	.285	156	594	113	169	43	102	70	85	8
1958	Chicago-NL	.313	154	617	119	193	47	129	52	87	4
1959	Chicago-NL	.304	155	589	97	179	45	143	64	72	2
1960	Chicago-NL	.271	156	597	94	162	41	117	71	69	1
1961	Chicago-NL	.278	138	511	75	142	29	80	54	75	1
1962	Chicago-NL	.269	154	610	87	164	37	104	30	71	5
1963	Chicago-NL	.227	130	432	41	98	18	64	39	73	0
1964	Chicago-NL	.264	157	591	67	156	23	95	36	84	1
1965	Chicago-NL	.265	163	612	79	162	28	106	55	64	3
1966	Chicago-NL	.272	141	511	52	139	15	75	29	59	0
1967	Chicago-NL	.276	151	573	68	158	23	95	27	93	2
1968	Chicago-NL	.246	150	552	71	136	32	83	27	67	2
1969	Chicago-NL	.253	155	565	60	143	23	106	42	101	0
1970	Chicago-NL	.252	72	222	25	56	12	44	20	33	0
1971	Chicago-NL	.193	39	83	4	16	3	6	6	14	0
Career Totals:		.274	2528	9421	1305	2583	512	1636	763	1236	50

Ernie Banks gave us many memories that showed he loved this game, whether it was played on the street or in Wrigley Field. He was the National League MVP twice, despite playing on a team more comfortable in the cellar than a teenager with a basement bedroom. Through the Cubs' losses, Banks played his heart out and never looked to New York or Los Angeles for a World Series ring. Take 1958: with fifth-place Chicago, the shortstop led the league in homers with 47, slugging average at .614, and in RBI with 129.

But Ernie gave us so much more. He put a phrase to the feeling many of us have for baseball, and for life, when the sun shines bright on a warm afternoon: "Let's play two!"

Rarely has poetry captured an emotion so well.

Banks, however, not only gave life to the phrase, he lived it. Baseball was more than a game, more than a job for the former Negro Leaguer. He'd seen baseball's worst in his short time with the Kansas City Monarchs of the Negro American League; the dusty bus trips, the bad hotels, the adulation of fans followed by the disdain of bellboys. Yet Ernie Banks loved the game still.

He'd field 50 hard ones on each side, then beg the coach for more. He'd ask questions, learn a trick, then practice it until the ballpark lights flickered out.

There have been better shortstops since Banks (who played the bulk of his latter career at first base). There have been better hitters. There have even been more memorable power-hitting shortstops like Cal Ripken, Jr.

But all stars eventually fade. Poetry belongs to the ages.

No. 31

Tom Seaver

With pitchers, it appears it's all in the arm. They have strong arms, sore arms, loose arms, tight arms, live arms, dead arms. Pitchers ice, heat,

Full Name: George Thomas "Tom Terrific" Seaver

Position: Pitcher   Debut: April 1967, New York Mets

Born: 11/17/1944, Fresno, California   Bats: Right

Height: 6'1"; Weight: 206   Throws: Right

PITCHING SUMMARY STATISTICS

Year	Team	W	L	PCT	ERA	G	SV	IP	BB	SO
1967	New York-NL	16	13	.552	2.76	35	0	251.0	78	170
1968	New York-NL	16	12	.571	2.20	36	1	277.2	48	205
1969	New York-NL	25	7	.781	2.21	36	0	273.1	82	208
1970	New York-NL	18	12	.600	2.82	37	0	290.2	83	283
1971	New York-NL	20	10	.667	1.76	36	0	286.1	61	289
1972	New York-NL	21	12	.636	2.92	35	0	262.0	77	249
1973	New York-NL	19	10	.655	2.08	36	0	290.0	64	251
1974	New York-NL	11	11	.500	3.20	32	0	236.0	75	201
1975	New York-NL	22	9	.710	2.38	36	0	280.1	88	243
1976	New York-NL	14	11	.560	2.59	35	0	271.0	77	235
1977	New York-NL	7	3	.700	3.00	13	0	96.0	28	72
1977	Cincinnati-NL	14	3	.824	2.34	20	0	165.1	38	124
1977	NL Totals	21	6	.778	2.58	33	0	261.1	66	196
1978	Cincinnati-NL	16	14	.533	2.88	36	0	259.2	89	226
1979	Cincinnati-NL	16	6	.727	3.14	32	0	215.0	61	131
1980	Cincinnati-NL	10	8	.556	3.64	26	0	168.0	59	101
1981	Cincinnati-NL	14	2	.875	2.54	23	0	166.1	66	87
1982	Cincinnati-NL	5	13	.278	5.50	21	0	111.1	44	62
1983	New York-NL	9	14	.391	3.55	34	0	231.0	86	135
1984	Chicago-AL	15	11	.577	3.95	34	0	236.2	61	131
1985	Chicago-AL	16	11	.593	3.17	35	0	238.2	69	134
1986	Chicago-AL	2	6	.250	4.38	12	0	72.0	27	31
1986	Boston-AL	5	7	.417	3.80	16	0	104.1	29	72
1986	AL Totals	7	13	.350	4.03	28	0	176.1	56	103
Career Totals:		311	205	.603	2.86	656	1	4782.2	1390	3640

massage, soak, rub, wrap, nurse and otherwise pamper their wings, a collection of tendons, muscle and bone on which they make their living.

Tom Seaver was different. Sure he had one unbelievable right arm, but what made him one of the most dominating pitchers of his era, and helped propel the New York Mets from a national joke to world champions, were his legs.

Look at the photos, or better yet, the video: watch Seaver push off the rubber; maybe more than any other pitcher, that is where he generated his power. All those kids who came up with the New York Mets back in the 1960s pitched that way under the tutelage of coach Rube Walker: Seaver, Jerry Koosman, Gary Gentry, and that real young one, Nolan Ryan. Ryan and Seaver logged a lot of miles on their legs.

Seaver, the greatest New York Met ever, pitched his way to 311 wins and 3,640 strikeouts in his 20-year career, which also included stops with the Cincinnati Reds, Chicago White Sox and Boston Red Sox. In New York he tallied three Cy Youngs (1969, 1973, 1975), a record nine straight seasons of 200 or more strikeouts, a 19-strikeout game (including a record 10 in a row to close it out), two pennants and the most improbable of titles.

The late 1960s belonged to the youth, the antiestablishment that challenged the status quo, which looked down on the youngsters with either bemusement or disdain. In New York baseball the establishment resided in the Bronx with the Yankees, the counterculture in Queens with the Mets. And while much of baseball was (justifiably) laughing at the Mets, the "Amazin's" were building one of the best staffs in baseball. Seaver, the 1967 Rookie of the Year, was leading the way.

By the time the game woke up in the latter half of 1969, it was too late. First to fall were the Chicago Cubs in the East. Then Hank Aaron's Atlanta Braves were steam-rolled in three straight in the first-ever National League playoff. The Baltimore Orioles, after winning what would be the first of three straight American League pennants, were smug, especially after winning Game One of the World Series. The Mets then swept four.

A man landing on the moon, Woodstock, and now the Mets. Anything was possible. "If the Mets can win the World Series," Seaver said, "the United States can get out of Vietnam." It took another six years, but it did.

When Seaver was traded from the Mets in the middle of the 1977 season, the heart was ripped from the team, which suffered in dank mediocrity until 1984. Seaver returned to the Mets that year but was not much of a factor (he is now an announcer for the team, in addition to working with young pitchers in the spring).

Appropriately, Seaver's career ended in Shea Stadium. Oddly, it was as an opponent, as Seaver rode the bench for Boston, as the Red Sox lost the 1986 World Series to the Mets (the "Bill Buckner" Series). In the midst of the wild celebration Seaver should have had the opportunity to take one last victory lap, on legs that took him so far.

No. 32

STEVE CARLTON

Hot-dogging kids are sometimes told, "There's no 'I' in 'team.'" But like many of the lessons we are lectured about as kids, it's not always true. Because there once was a right-wing lefty who, perhaps more than anyone, turned a team sport into a one-man mission.

In 1972 Steve "Lefty" Carlton played for the Philadelphia Phillies that lost 97 games while winning only 59. They had no .300 hitters, no slugger with even 20 home runs.

But they had Carlton. He won 27 games that year, almost half of all the team's wins, a major league record. When he pitched, especially in 1972, he couldn't count on much support from the other eight guys in the lineup, so his mission was clear: keep the opponents from scoring, keep them even from hitting the ball.

This he did. He ended that year with 30 complete games (one of 15 years he'd have at least that many), 310 strikeouts, eight shutouts, and his first Cy Young Award.

Full Name: Steven Norman "Lefty" Carlton

Position: Pitcher   Debut: April 1965, St. Louis Cardinals

Born: 12/22/1944, Miami, Florida   Bats: Left

Height: 6'4"; Weight: 210   Throws: Left

PITCHING SUMMARY STATISTICS

Year	Team	W	L	PCT	ERA	G	SV	IP	BB	SO
1965	St. Louis-NL	0	0	-	2.52	15	0	25.0	8	21
1966	St. Louis-NL	3	3	.500	3.12	9	0	52.0	18	25
1967	St. Louis-NL	14	9	.609	2.98	30	1	193.0	62	168
1968	St. Louis-NL	13	11	.542	2.99	34	0	231.2	61	162
1969	St. Louis-NL	17	11	.607	2.17	31	0	236.1	93	210
1970	St. Louis-NL	10	19	.345	3.73	34	0	253.2	109	193
1971	St. Louis-NL	20	9	.690	3.56	37	0	273.1	98	172
1972	Philadelphia-NL	27	10	.730	1.97	41	0	346.1	87	310
1973	Philadelphia-NL	13	20	.394	3.90	40	0	293.1	113	223

Year	Team	W	L	PCT	ERA	G	SV	IP	BB	SO
1974	Philadelphia-NL	16	13	.552	3.22	39	0	291.0	136	240
1975	Philadelphia-NL	15	14	.517	3.56	37	0	255.1	104	192
1976	Philadelphia-NL	20	7	.741	3.13	35	0	252.2	72	195
1977	Philadelphia-NL	23	10	.697	2.64	36	0	283.0	89	198
1978	Philadelphia-NL	16	13	.552	2.84	34	0	247.1	63	161
1979	Philadelphia-NL	18	11	.621	3.62	35	0	251.0	89	213
1980	Philadelphia-NL	24	9	.727	2.34	38	0	304.0	90	286
1981	Philadelphia-NL	13	4	.765	2.42	24	0	190.0	62	179
1982	Philadelphia-NL	23	11	.676	3.10	38	0	295.2	86	286
1983	Philadelphia-NL	15	16	.484	3.11	37	0	283.2	84	275
1984	Philadelphia-NL	13	7	.650	3.58	33	0	229.0	79	163
1985	Philadelphia-NL	1	8	.111	3.33	16	0	92.0	53	48
1986	Philadelphia-NL	4	8	.333	6.18	16	0	83.0	45	62
1986	San Francisco-NL	1	3	.250	5.10	6	0	30.0	16	18
1986	Chicago-AL	4	3	.571	3.69	10	0	63.1	25	40
1986	NL Totals	5	11	.313	5.89	22	0	113.0	61	80
1987	Cleveland-AL	5	9	.357	5.37	23	1	109.0	63	71
1987	Minnesota-AL	1	5	.167	6.70	9	0	43.0	23	20
1987	AL Totals	6	14	.300	5.74	32	1	152.0	86	91
1988	Minnesota-AL	0	1	.000	16.76	4	0	9.2	5	5
Career Totals:		329	244	.574	3.17	741	2	5217.1	1833	4136

He'd win three more (1977, 1980 and 1982) in a career in which he led the National League in strikeouts five times, won 329 games, and won two games in the 1980 World Series to give the sports-crazy, championship-starved Phillie fans their first world championship.

Four Cy Youngs. You have to go to Sandy Koufax to find another record like that among lefties, and Koufax only had three.

Through it all Carlton used his all-out, every-game, every-pitch attitude and bested the enemy, which included Tom Seaver, Ferguson Jenkins, Don Sutton, Bob Gibson and sportswriters. Lefty's decidedly right—very right—political leanings left many sports commentators wondering how to handle the guy. Many dealt with it by ignoring him.

And that was fine with Carlton. He was used to being alone, depending on himself, a one-man team at times—not because he wanted to be but because he had to be.

No. 33

SATCHEL PAIGE

Do you know how many stories about Satchel Paige are actually true? Do you?

Oh, you were expecting an answer. Actually, we were hoping you knew.

Leroy "Satchel" Paige is a wellspring of folklore from the fountain of baseball legend, the Negro Leagues. Did he pull his outfielders in to sit behind the mound while he struck out the side? Did he intentionally walk the bases full to get to the usually feared Josh Gibson? Would he repeatedly strike out the first nine hitters of an exhibition game, as advertised (the answer to that one appears to be yes)? Maybe. Probably. At least it *could* have happened.

Satchel Paige is *the* legend of the Negro Leagues, a right-handed pitcher whose prowess was made readily apparent when directed on major leaguers in myriad barnstorming games he played that brought him renown.

In a 1930 exhibition game Paige struck out 22 major leaguers, including Babe Herman and Hack Wilson. Then there is the story of Paige battling another legend with an equally quick wit, Dizzy Dean, in an exhibition duel that was scoreless into the tenth inning. "I don't know what you are going to do, Mr. Dean," Paige told Dizzy, "but I'm not going to give up any runs if we have to stay here all night." Paige won in 13.

In 1932, pitching for the Pittsburgh Crawfords, Paige went 32–7. He followed up that season with a 31–4 mark the next year, which included a string of 62 straight scoreless innings and 21 consecutive wins. Paige jumped to the Dominican and then the Mexican League (he had repeated contract squabbles), developed a sore arm, and resurfaced with the Kansas City Monarchs in 1938, leading the team to four consecutive Negro American League pennants from 1939 to 1942, and another title in 1946. In the 1942 Negro League World Series, the Monarchs swept the Homestead Grays, with Paige winning three of the games.

On the heels of Jackie Robinson, Paige—who many thought should have been the man to crack the color barrier—was signed by the Cleveland Indians in 1948. *The Sporting News*, which railed against integration of the game (St. Louis, where the magazine was and is based, and its teams were among the most virulent supporters of the ban on blacks), editorialized that bringing a pitcher of Paige's age into the game as a rookie would "demean the standards of baseball."

So Paige went 6–1, with a 2.48 ERA, and helped the Tribe to a World Series title.

Paige had a few years in the bigs—he was the American League's leading relief pitcher for the St. Louis Browns in 1952—and bounced around the minors and Negro Leagues before resurfacing at the incredible age of 59 in 1965 to pitch three scoreless innings for the Kansas City Athletics. In 1971 he became the first player elected to the Hall of Fame based solely on his Negro League career. His major league record is a paltry 28–31. But exactly how many wins, shutouts and no-hitters he pitched in his colorful career will probably never be known.

"How old would you be if you didn't know how old you were?" Paige would repeatedly reply to the question of his age. Here is another: How good was Satchel Paige since we don't know, at least statistically, how good he was? Better than most, and on many days, all.

No. 34

Frank Robinson

Well, there was Manhattan Island for $24; that was a pretty bad one. And unloading Babe Ruth for $100,000 by the Boston Red Sox so owner Harry Frazee could finance a play not only gave New York a legend but also Broadway a hit. Finances, Frazee said, made him do it.

But for sheer boneheadedness, one need look no further than December 9, 1965, for the most lopsided, dumbest trade ever made, one between the Cincinnati Reds and Baltimore Orioles.

The Reds got three players: Milt Pappas, a solid pitcher who would win 209 games over his yeoman 17-year career but who was only one game over .500 in his two-plus years with the team; pitcher Jack Baldschun,

Full Name: Frank Robinson

Position: OF, DH, 1B

Born: 8/31/1935, Beaumont, Texas

Height: 6'1"; Weight: 195

Debut: April 1956, Cincinnati Reds

Bats: Right

Throws: Right

BATTING SUMMARY STATISTICS

Year	Team	AVG	G	AB	R	H	HR	RBI	BB	SO	SB
1956	Cincinnati-NL	.290	152	572	122	166	38	83	64	95	8
1957	Cincinnati-NL	.322	150	611	97	197	29	75	44	92	10
1958	Cincinnati-NL	.269	148	554	90	149	31	83	62	80	10
1959	Cincinnati-NL	.311	146	540	106	168	36	125	69	93	18
1960	Cincinnati-NL	.297	139	464	86	138	31	83	82	67	13
1961	Cincinnati-NL	.323	153	545	117	176	37	124	71	64	22
1962	Cincinnati-NL	.342	162	609	134	208	39	136	76	62	18
1963	Cincinnati-NL	.259	140	482	79	125	21	91	81	69	26
1964	Cincinnati-NL	.306	156	568	103	174	29	96	79	67	23
1965	Cincinnati-NL	.296	156	582	109	172	33	113	70	100	13
1966	Baltimore-AL	.316	155	576	122	182	49	122	87	90	8
1967	Baltimore-AL	.311	129	479	83	149	30	94	71	84	2
1968	Baltimore-AL	.268	130	421	69	113	15	52	73	84	11
1969	Baltimore-AL	.308	148	539	111	166	32	100	88	62	9
1970	Baltimore-AL	.306	132	471	88	144	25	78	69	70	2
1971	Baltimore-AL	.281	133	455	82	128	28	99	72	62	3
1972	Los Angeles-NL	.251	103	342	41	86	19	59	55	76	2
1973	California-AL	.266	147	534	85	142	30	97	82	93	1
1974	California-AL	.251	129	427	75	107	20	63	75	85	5
1974	Cleveland-AL	.200	15	50	6	10	2	5	10	10	0
1974	AL Totals	.245	144	477	81	117	22	68	85	95	5
1975	Cleveland-AL	.237	49	118	19	28	9	24	29	15	0
1976	Cleveland-AL	.224	36	67	5	15	3	10	11	12	0
Career Totals:		.294	2808	10006	1829	2943	586	1812	1420	1532	204

who went 1–5 for Cincy over two seasons; and Dick Simpson, who never hit more than .259 in a season for the Reds in limited duty.

What did the Orioles get? Only one player—and four pennants, two World titles and a Triple Crown/MVP season out of Frank Robinson.

There have been two-way players in sport, but Robinson was the greatest two-league player in baseball history. The outfielder is the only player to be elected MVP in both leagues (1961 with the Reds, 1966 with the O's), to hit at least 200 home runs in both leagues (on his way to 586 career dingers over a 21-year career) and the only player to hit home runs for both leagues in All-Star competition.

The 1956 National League Rookie of the Year added yet another first to his resume in 1975, becoming the first black manager when he took over the Cleveland Indians.

There was a knock against Robinson from his Reds days: that he only played well when he was mad and that he didn't get mad enough. Robinson was plenty mad in 1966 after the trade, and he took it out on the American League, winning the Triple Crown (.316, 49 HR, 122 RBI) and leading the league in slugging average, home run percentage and runs. The Orioles became World Champions that year, sweeping the Los Angeles Dodgers.

How sweet it would have been had it been against the Reds; too bad they finished seventh. But Robinson did get to face Cincinnati in the 1970 World Series: Frank Robinson hit a pair of home runs, as the Birds beat his old team in five.

And Frank Robinson wouldn't trade that moment for any in the world.

No. 35

BROOKS ROBINSON

Stars change the fortune of teams. Stars can even make fans switch allegiances, follow the game closer, or buy a different razor. But Brooks Robinson very quietly did something few of baseball's greats could ever hope to do: he changed the way kids play ball.

All of a sudden kids started to routinely dive for the ball, snatch an infield grounder barehanded and from a midair stride throw a runner out at first.

The thrill of fielding, not slugging, became another favorite fantasy and drew attention to the often overlooked but perhaps most artful part of the game. What Robinson instilled in kids wasn't just hustle; Pete Rose

Full Name: Brooks Calbert Robinson

Position: Third Base   Debut: September 1955, Baltimore Orioles

Born: 5/18/1937,   Bats: Right
   Little Rock, Arkansas

Height: 6'1"; Weight: 190   Throws: Right

B*ATTING* S*UMMARY* S*TATISTICS*

Year	Team	AVG	G	AB	R	H	HR	RBI	BB	SO	SB
1955	Baltimore-AL	.091	6	22	0	2	0	1	0	10	0
1956	Baltimore-AL	.227	15	44	5	10	1	1	1	5	0
1957	Baltimore-AL	.239	50	117	13	28	2	14	7	10	1
1958	Baltimore-AL	.238	145	463	31	110	3	32	31	51	1
1959	Baltimore-AL	.284	88	313	29	89	4	24	17	37	2
1960	Baltimore-AL	.294	152	595	74	175	14	88	35	49	2
1961	Baltimore-AL	.287	163	668	89	192	7	61	47	57	1
1962	Baltimore-AL	.303	162	634	77	192	23	86	42	70	3
1963	Baltimore-AL	.251	161	589	67	148	11	67	46	84	2
1964	Baltimore-AL	.317	163	612	82	194	28	118	51	64	1
1965	Baltimore-AL	.297	144	559	81	166	18	80	47	47	3
1966	Baltimore-AL	.269	157	620	91	167	23	100	56	36	2
1967	Baltimore-AL	.269	158	610	88	164	22	77	54	54	1
1968	Baltimore-AL	.253	162	608	65	154	17	75	44	55	1
1969	Baltimore-AL	.234	156	598	73	140	23	84	56	55	2
1970	Baltimore-AL	.276	158	608	84	168	18	94	53	53	1
1971	Baltimore-AL	.272	156	589	67	160	20	92	63	50	0
1972	Baltimore-AL	.250	153	556	48	139	8	64	43	45	1
1973	Baltimore-AL	.257	155	549	53	141	9	72	55	50	2
1974	Baltimore-AL	.288	153	553	46	159	7	59	56	47	2
1975	Baltimore-AL	.201	144	482	50	97	6	53	44	33	0
1976	Baltimore-AL	.211	71	218	16	46	3	11	8	24	0
1977	Baltimore-AL	.149	24	47	3	7	1	4	4	4	0
Career Totals:		.267	2896	10654	1232	2848	268	1357	860	990	28

had the corner on that. What Robinson gave kids was a lesson in how hustle, combined with imagination and hours and hours of practice, could lead not just to a bounding, head-first slide, but to something beautiful.

Rose put it best. He said Robinson "belongs in a higher league."

High praise from a guy you'd expect would put only himself at that level.

In 1970 Rose and America had all the evidence they needed to prove that statement as true as a Robinson throw to first.

The Baltimore Orioles were a great team, ready and expected to become a dynasty. Only the New York Mets and God stopped it in 1969, but that only made the lineup of Baltimore stars—Palmer, Frank Robinson, Belanger and more—hungry in addition to dangerously talented.

A year later the Orioles dismantled a team beginning to build its own dynasty, the Cincinnati Reds. Brooks Robinson would have six RBI, but that wasn't the beauty of it. He dove, he bare-handed, he leaped, he slid and took away eight key World Series hits, including two by Johnny Bench, another by Tony Perez, and a couple by Lee May. The man who would collect 16 Gold Gloves hit .429 that series, with two homers and a slugging average of .810.

The incredible performance came during one of baseball's darkest hours—before we knew there would be many. Sports pages were filled with Curt Flood's battle over the reserve clause; revelations of drug use; continued racial conflict, alcohol and womanizing; owners threatening to take their marbles (what was left of them) and go home, as if the rich owned baseball. Players and fans were split by the Vietnam War and the national unrest that somehow we never thought could affect The Game.

Society's problems would never leave baseball after 1970, but neither will memories of pure performances like Robinson's. That may not be perfect, but on the whole, we'll take it.

No. 36

ROY CAMPANELLA

To understand Roy Campanella, you have to understand the Negro Leagues, Brooklyn, and Jackie Gleason.

In eight years with the Negro Leagues' Baltimore Elite Giants, he learned to be a catcher with reflexes a cat would give a half-dozen lives for. Back there, pitchers threw spitballs, scuffed balls and just about anything they could get away with—and they got away with a lot. Not knowing what a 90-mph pitch would do for 60 feet, 6 inches gives you fast hands, or brain damage.

Eight years. Campy was almost 27 when Branch Rickey and Jackie Robinson broke the color barrier in the majors. Campanella could have been bitter and stayed comfortably in black baseball. But he didn't think much of the status quo. Instead he signed with Rickey before Robinson's first major league season was complete back in 1947.

Campanella would go on to win three MVP awards, set the home run mark for catchers at 41 in 1953 (since broken), and become a major figure in the history of the game that banned his race.

Brooklyn, the home of every race and racial tension on the planet, embraced him. More than 62,000 fans jammed Yankee Stadium over in the Bronx for that seventh game of the 1955 series, even though "Dem Bums" had lost seven Series, including the last five they played the Yankees. Still, the New York Stock Exchange, after a busy morning, saw trading almost stop through the game. And Jackie Gleason, the biggest man in television, stopped in the middle of filming an episode of "The Honeymooners" in Manhattan to shout that the Dodgers had won the World Series. The show was stopped, as was the baseball world.

Campanella was 36 when a car accident ended his unparalleled career behind and at the plate. Generations of fans have only seen the Hall-of-Famer in a wheelchair. And that's the tragedy.

No. 37

RICKEY HENDERSON

In a flurry of moves made by the New York Mets front office prior to the 1999 season—including the re-signings of Mike Piazza and Al Leiter and the acquisition of free agent Robin Ventura—the signing of a 40-year-old outfielder was somewhat of an afterthought. Nice pickup, but no big deal.

Everyone should have known better. The physical specimen that is Rickey Henderson has always been a big deal, even in his twenty-first season. In 121 regular-season games in 1999, Henderson hit .315, with 82 walks, 89 runs and a .423 on-base percentage. Of course, his age limited him once he was on the base paths: Henderson stole only—only—37 bases.

Rickey Henderson is the greatest leadoff man ever, not only the most dangerous man who ever took a mincing lead off of first but a sculpted athlete who has led off games with home runs a record 75 times. He has 278 regular season dingers overall through 1999, a rare combination of speed and power at the top of the lineup.

But his legend is built on the base paths. The "Man of Steal" is the all-time stolen base leader with 1,334: only four other active players have as many stolen bases as Henderson is ahead of Lou Brock on the all-time list—396. Henderson also holds the modern record for most steals in a season; his record 1982 year with the Oakland A's of 130 thefts is one of three seasons he had 100-plus steals. From 1980 to 1991 he led the American League every year in steals except for 1987, in which he missed 57 games because of injuries.

Of the Top 25 stolen base marks for a season in the twentieth century, Henderson holds six of the slots. These feats reflect Henderson's most prominent places in the record book but are far from his only ones.

The 1990 American League MVP—who was also the playoff and World Series Most Valuable Player the previous postseason for the Oakland A's—is fifth all-time in runs (2,103), and has a shot to catch Ty Cobb's record of 2,245. He is also third in walks, just 90 free passes behind Babe Ruth. But there is more.

Games played, twentieth all-time. At bats, twenty-third all-time. Hits, thirty-ninth. Years of served, tied for fifty-second. Doubles, fifty-third. He even has another distinction: Henderson was Nolan Ryan's five-thousandth strikeout victim in 1989.

"It's an honor," Henderson said at the time. "I'll have another paragraph in all the baseball books. I'm already in the books three or four times."

And, as the century closed, still counting.

No. 38

OSCAR CHARLESTON

Physically, he looked like Tony Gwynn, roundish and almost out of place on the diamond, yet possessed with the sweetest of swings from the left side of the plate. He was also armed with power, one of the several Negro League players to be compared to Babe Ruth.

But on the bases, he was Ty Cobb, spikes and fists at the ready, dropping drag bunts and using his speed and mean streak to intimidate anyone in his way.

And in the field the comparisons veer toward Tris Speaker, an outfielder with a cannon for an arm and speed who played a shallow center field, daring hitters all the while to poke one over his head.

There were better power hitters in the Negro Leagues, and one-time pitcher Oscar Charleston certainly wasn't the best hurler. But Charleston was the best player in the Negro Leagues in the 1920s and maybe its best all-around player ever. "[The] greatest outfielder that ever lived," teammate Ben Taylor called him.

In terms of years in the game, Charleston had a little Nolan Ryan in him, playing from 1915 to 1944 as an outfielder, first baseman and sometimes player-manager with a host of teams: Indianapolis ABCs, Chicago American Giants, St. Louis Giants, Harrisburg Giants, Philadelphia Hilldales, Homestead Grays, Pittsburgh Crawfords, Toledo Crawfords and Philadelphia Cuban Yankees.

In 1921, for St. Louis, he hit .434 with 34 stolen bases while leading the league in doubles, triples and home runs. As a player-manager for Harrisburg (PA) in the Eastern Colored League, Charleston won batting titles in 1924 and 1925. In 1931 he played with Josh Gibson on one of the best Negro League teams ever, the Homestead Grays.

His name doesn't come up as often as fellow Negro Leaguers Satchel Paige or Gibson or Buck Leonard or Cool Papa Bell. Still, one source gives Charleston a .376 lifetime average, with undeniable power and speed. As said earlier, Negro League statistics are suspect at best. But there was no disputing that at the plate, on the bases or in the field, Oscar Charleston was one of the greats. Maybe we should start comparing other players to him.

No. 39

TONY GWYNN

Tony Gwynn is one of the most beloved players in baseball, as solid a family man as he is a hitter. But it is one fan's adulation among the millions that certifies him one as of the best hitters of the twentieth century. That's because the fan is Ted Williams.

Williams and Gwynn have been a bit of a touring company for hitting in the 1990s, the great master and the gifted protégé. Ted Williams, remember, is the guy who openly referred to himself as the best hitter in baseball (and, of course, he was), and he has, through most of his life, been noticeably stingy when it comes to praising other hitters. But listen to Williams, the guy baseball treats as a favorite if cranky uncle, when he talks to Gwynn:

"I still think as good as you are, everybody wants to know, 'Well, is he going to hit .400?' I said, well, if … [there's] anybody I got to bet on now, I got to bet on you, Tony. You can hit with two strikes."

As the 1999 All-Star Game showed, baseball's biggest stars were giddy even to be near Williams (Mark McGwire gushed when Williams just knew who he was). But there was Williams, in an ESPN television interview, laying it on thick over the chunky San Diego Padre.

There is no better endorsement for a ballplayer. Gwynn earned it by winning seven NL batting titles in his first 16 seasons (all .300 or better in full seasons, a league record), hitting around .340 for his career as the century drew to a close, and often flirting with The Number so closely associated with Williams, hitting .394 in 1997.

But Gwynn is more. The man who hit his 2,000th and 3,000th hits on his mother's birthday is a much, much-needed bridge from the game's golden era. In a television documentary Williams once asked Gwynn an easy question about his own stance, something a Little Leaguer would shout out in a second. Gwynn hesitated, not because he didn't know the answer, but "because I didn't want to be wrong." He respects—and is intimidated by—Williams that much.

The Splendid Splinter helped Gwynn build that bridge to the next century, a critical feat of engineering. Now it's up to Gwynn, the new honors student in hitting, to see where it takes him.

No. 40

LEFTY GROVE

Lefty Grove had a great arm, a must-win attitude ... and perhaps the worst timing in baseball history. To become one of the best pitchers of all time, he'd have to face, several times a season, the dynasty-in-progress Yankees among notable others in the eight-team American League. Guys like Ruth, Gehrig, Charlie Gehringer and Heinie Manush

Full Name: Robert Moses "Lefty" Grove

Position: Pitcher

Born: 3/6/1900,
  Lonaconing, Maryland

Height: 6'3"; Weight: 190

Debut: April 1925, Philadelphia Athletics

Bats: Left

Throws: Left

PITCHING SUMMARY STATISTICS

Year	Team	W	L	PCT	ERA	G	SV	IP	BB	SO
1925	Philadelphia-AL	10	12	.455	4.75	45	1	197.0	131	116
1926	Philadelphia-AL	13	13	.500	2.51	45	6	258.0	101	194
1927	Philadelphia-AL	20	13	.606	3.19	51	9	262.1	79	174
1928	Philadelphia-AL	24	8	.750	2.58	39	4	261.2	64	183
1929	Philadelphia-AL	20	6	.769	2.81	42	4	275.1	81	170
1930	Philadelphia-AL	28	5	.848	2.54	50	9	291.0	60	209
1931	Philadelphia-AL	31	4	.886	2.06	41	5	288.2	62	175
1932	Philadelphia-AL	25	10	.714	2.84	44	7	291.2	79	188
1933	Philadelphia-AL	24	8	.750	3.20	45	6	275.1	83	114
1934	Boston-AL	8	8	.500	6.50	22	0	109.1	32	43
1935	Boston-AL	20	12	.625	2.70	35	1	273.0	65	121
1936	Boston-AL	17	12	.586	2.81	35	2	253.1	65	130
1937	Boston-AL	17	9	.654	3.02	32	0	262.0	83	153
1938	Boston-AL	14	4	.778	3.08	24	1	163.2	52	99
1939	Boston-AL	15	4	.789	2.54	23	0	191.0	58	81
1940	Boston-AL	7	6	.538	3.99	22	0	153.1	50	62
1941	Boston-AL	7	7	.500	4.37	21	0	134.0	42	54
Career Totals:		300	141	.680	3.06	616	55	3940.2	1187	2266

weren't heroes, they were the enemy. Most of us would just roll over and leave calls for the National League, or the next decade.

Yet Grove, the fiercest of competitors, who tore up locker rooms, his uniforms and teammates when he lost, wasn't about to be intimidated. Instead he put up incredible numbers made more incredible by the era: late 1920s through the 1930s.

From 1929 to 1931 he won 79 games and lost 15—ruing every one in a maelstrom like it was the end of the world. Connie Mack (who bought Grove from the minors for more than the Red Sox's $100,000 price for Babe Ruth) tore up the American League that most people figured was dominated by the Yankees. Yet his Philadelphia Athletics won the league each of those years and the World Series twice.

As for Grove, his lowest number of wins in a year from 1927 to 1933 was 20. In 1930 and 1931 he won 59 and lost nine. His first seven years in the majors he led the American League in strikeouts, and in his 17-year career he had the lowest ERA nine seasons. His World Series ERA is 1.75, and he finished with a 300–141 record that inspired a sportswriter at the time to say Grove could throw a lamb chop past a wolf.

If, as the understatement goes, all a pitcher has to do is win, Robert Moses "Lefty" Grove was all a pitcher could be. Despite the lousy timing. Or maybe because of it.

No. 41

Nap Lajoie

Nap Lajoie may be the best baseball player most baseball fans today never heard of.

Need a hint? Check him out among some of the American League's career and season leaders in hits, batting average, doubles, triples, RBI, and batting average. He hit .426 in 1901, the second best single-season mark of the twentieth century, and .002 more than Rogers Hornsby's modern record.

Full Name: Napoleon "Larry" Lajoie

Position: 2B, 1B, SS   Debut: August 1896, Philadelphia Phillies

Born: 9/5/1874,   Bats: Right
   Woonsocket, Rhode Island

Height: 6'1"; Weight: 195   Throws: Right

BATTING SUMMARY STATISTICS

Year	Team	AVG	G	AB	R	H	HR	RBI	BB	SO	SB
1896	Philadelphia-NL	.326	39	175	36	57	4	42	1	11	7
1897	Philadelphia-NL	.361	127	545	107	197	9	127	15	-	20
1898	Philadelphia-NL	.324	147	608	113	197	6	127	21	-	25
1899	Philadelphia-NL	.378	77	312	70	118	6	70	12	-	13
1900	Philadelphia-NL	.337	102	451	95	152	7	92	10	-	22
1901	Philadelphia-AL	.426	131	544	145	232	14	125	24	-	27
1902	Philadelphia-AL	.250	1	4	0	1	0	1	0	-	1
1902	Cleveland-AL	.379	86	348	81	132	7	64	19	-	19
1902	AL Totals	.378	87	352	81	133	7	65	19	-	20
1903	Cleveland-AL	.344	125	485	90	167	7	93	24	-	21
1904	Cleveland-AL	.376	140	553	92	208	6	102	27	-	29
1905	Cleveland-AL	.329	65	249	29	82	2	41	17	-	11
1906	Cleveland-AL	.355	152	602	88	214	0	91	30	-	20
1907	Cleveland-AL	.299	137	509	53	152	2	63	30	-	24
1908	Cleveland-AL	.289	157	581	77	168	2	74	47	-	15
1909	Cleveland-AL	.324	128	469	56	152	1	47	35	-	13
1910	Cleveland-AL	.384	159	591	94	227	4	76	60	-	26
1911	Cleveland-AL	.365	90	315	36	115	2	60	26	-	13
1912	Cleveland-AL	.368	117	448	66	165	0	90	28	-	18
1913	Cleveland-AL	.335	137	465	66	156	1	68	33	17	17
1914	Cleveland-AL	.258	121	419	37	108	0	50	32	15	14
1915	Philadelphia-AL	.280	129	490	40	137	1	61	11	16	10
1916	Philadelphia-AL	.246	113	426	33	105	2	35	14	26	15
Career Totals:		.338	2480	9589	1504	3242	83	1599	516	85	380

What about that Cobb fella? The Georgia creep is a couple of spots below Nap. And it must have burned like a rusty spike in a shortstop's shin.

Ty Cobb hated everyone, of course, but Napolean Lajoie got an extra dose. Especially in 1910. Cleveland's very popular Lajoie (for a time the club was known as The Naps in his honor) had won the league batting championship in the Cobb era three times. Nap went eight for eight in his last doubleheader to nearly steal the crown from Cobb, but apparently a bit of a fix was in among the legion that Ty rubbed, and spiked, the wrong way. Nap benefited from a rookie third bagger who was instructed to play deep (against the deadly force of Nap's liners), despite giving up bunt single after bunt single.

Still, Cobb won the title and, more important it seemed, a Chalmers motor car, by .001 of a point. Nap hit .384, and it was only good enough for second-best in the eight-team league. Tough room.

But what a season the runner-up had. He collected the most bases, the most hits, the most doubles, and took second behind Cobb in runs and slugging average. Along the way Lajoie played the best second base in the league, fielding at a .966 clip that year. He'd finish his 21 years with a .339 batting average, 3,251 hits and a staggering 648 doubles.

Nap didn't end up besting Cobb overall; no one really did. But Lajoie, 12 years Cobb's senior, pushed Cobb and made him better. That kind of statement would have infuriated Cobb and been suicidal for a writer earlier in that century, but there's almost no chance today that he will rise from the dead to lance one more calf muscle.

Still, for Nap it must have been a source of pride to be perhaps Cobb's most serious rival. Nap was certainly a thorn in Cobb's side, and that's plenty reason to remember him 40 years after his death at age 85. Cobb, by the way, only posted 74.

No. 42

Jackie Robinson

No one will wear the number again. No journeyman relief pitcher or borderline power hitter or some rook trying to stick with the club out of spring training.

Satchel Paige, looking over to a runner on first that he had walked, shouted, "There you is and there you is going to stay." Well, there is only one number 42 in the Hall of Fame, and that is the way it is going to stay.

Full Name: Jack Roosevelt Robinson

Position: 2B, 1B, 3B, OF   Debut: April 1947, Brooklyn Dodgers

Born: 1/31/1919, Cairo, Georgia   Bats: Right

Height: 5'11"; Weight: 204   Throws: Right

BATTING SUMMARY STATISTICS

Year	Team	AVG	G	AB	R	H	HR	RBI	BB	SO	SB
1947	Brooklyn-NL	.297	151	590	125	175	12	48	74	36	29
1948	Brooklyn-NL	.296	147	574	108	170	12	85	57	37	22
1949	Brooklyn-NL	.342	156	593	122	203	16	124	86	27	37
1950	Brooklyn-NL	.328	144	518	99	170	14	81	80	24	12
1951	Brooklyn-NL	.338	153	548	106	185	19	88	79	27	25
1952	Brooklyn-NL	.308	149	510	104	157	19	75	106	40	24
1953	Brooklyn-NL	.329	136	484	109	159	12	95	74	30	17
1954	Brooklyn-NL	.311	124	386	62	120	15	59	63	20	7
1955	Brooklyn-NL	.256	105	317	51	81	8	36	61	18	12
1956	Brooklyn-NL	.275	117	357	61	98	10	43	60	32	12
Career Totals:		.311	1382	4877	947	1518	137	734	740	291	197

So decreed Major League Baseball in making it the only number officially retired by every club in both leagues.

Even without the benediction, there really would be only one number 42: Jackie Roosevelt Robinson.

But the only number Robinson is usually associated with is 1, as in first. In 1947, of course, he broke the color barrier. But Robinson was not the first black major leaguer, as is commonly believed. Moses Fleetwood Walker played catcher with major league Toledo in 1884 and was later joined on the team by his brother, Weldy W. Walker, an outfielder. But management and some players, including Hall of Famer Cap Anson, wanted to keep this "element" out. So by the end of the 1880s a ban was born in the Civil War residue of Jim Crow, one that survived into the new century and through two World Wars.

It has been well chronicled what the 28-year-old Robinson had to endure that first season with the Brooklyn Dodgers, how he was tough enough *not* to fight back with his fists against the racists. He was the right man in the right place.

What is sometimes overlooked because of his epic place in baseball is that he was one of the finest and grittiest players of his era—even though

baseball may have been his third-best sport; Robinson was also a legendary football and track star at UCLA. He came up as a first baseman—he played shortstop in his one Negro League season for the Kansas City Monarchs—before moving to second base, where he played the majority of his career. But he also played more than 150 games each at third, first and in the outfield, and all with the Dodgers. In December of 1956 he was traded to the New York Giants. He retired rather than don the hated black and orange.

Robinson led the Dodgers to six World Series in 10 years, winning the 1955 crown (ironically, his worst season). He posted a .311 lifetime batting average, led the National League once in hitting and twice in steals.

But those are mere numbers. Robinson, the one and only 42, was about much more than that.

No. 43

GREG MADDUX

Christy Mathewson slandered all his brethren, well, definitely at least one, in a single, sharp sentence: "A pitcher is not a ballplayer."

Greg Maddux is certainly a ballplayer, even if he doesn't look like one. He was the best pitcher of the 1990s—Maddux has won no less than 15 games every season since 1988—and to many the decade's best player, period.

Let's talk about Maddux the player as opposed to the pitcher. The Gold Glove competition has been anything but competitive for National

Opposite: **Out! Jackie Robinson the great hitter, the great base stealer, the great man, performed aspects of the game so well under pressure unimaginable before or after that it threatens to overshadow the complete ballplayer. Using a stick to hit a little ball traveling 90 mph in anything but a straight line in front of 30,000 people is hard enough. Getting notice on a regular basis that one of them has a gun pointed at you, or back home at your family, was the added burden Robinson carried in Major League Baseball. He resolved, however, that neither he nor his race would ever be out again.**

League pitchers, as Maddux won the award every season in the 1990s. Considering how many ground balls back to the box he induces, it's clear that Maddux is as much a weapon after he releases the ball as when he is throwing it.

Maddux won his first of four straight Cy Young Awards (the only such streak in history) in 1992 while pitching for the Chicago Cubs (20–11, 2.18 ERA). After signing with the Atlanta Braves the next season, Maddux went 20–10 in 1993, followed by a 16–6 mark with a 1.56 ERA in strike-shortened 1994.

But Maddux was at his most dominating in 1995, the year the Braves won their first world title in Atlanta. Maddux went 19–2 in 28 starts, posting a 1.63 ERA. It was the last of three-straight ERA titles and among his four overall.

But dominating is not the right word for this pitcher, who closed 1999 with a career record of 221–126 with a 2.81 ERA. In only one of his 13 full seasons, 1998, has Maddux rung up more than 200 strikeouts (although he also had seasons of 199, 198 and 197 Ks). None of the pitches in his arsenal would be considered the absolute best in the game.

No, Maddux nibbles at the plate, using uncanny accuracy rather than a blazing fastball or nasty slider or curve. He's averaged about two walks per nine innings for his career yet is constantly working off the strike zone, enticing hitters to swing at a ball an inch off the plate, then two, then five, eventually getting a ground ball back to the mound. Some pitchers are athletic specimens; Maddux is a craftsman, an artist. And, most of all, a ballplayer.

No. 44

George Brett

You're George Brett, and you have a choice on how you will be most remembered: (a) For having a highly public bout with hemorrhoids during the 1980 World Series or (b) for a bug-eyed, arm-waving, anger-fueled

Full Name: George Howard Brett

Position: 3B, DH, 1B   Debut: August 1973, Kansas City Royals

Born: 5/15/1953,   Bats: Left
  Glen Dale, West Virginia

Height: 6'; Weight: 200   Throws: Right

Batting Summary Statistics

Year	Team	AVG	G	AB	R	H	HR	RBI	BB	SO	SB
1973	Kansas City-AL	.125	13	40	2	5	0	0	0	5	0
1974	Kansas City-AL	.282	133	457	49	129	2	47	21	38	8
1975	Kansas City-AL	.308	159	634	84	195	11	89	46	49	13
1976	Kansas City-AL	.333	159	645	94	215	7	67	49	36	21
1977	Kansas City-AL	.312	139	564	105	176	22	88	55	24	14
1978	Kansas City-AL	.294	128	510	79	150	9	62	39	35	23
1979	Kansas City-AL	.329	154	645	119	212	23	107	51	36	17
1980	Kansas City-AL	.390	117	449	87	175	24	118	58	22	15
1981	Kansas City-AL	.314	89	347	42	109	6	43	27	23	14
1982	Kansas City-AL	.301	144	552	101	166	21	82	71	51	6
1983	Kansas City-AL	.310	123	464	90	144	25	93	57	39	0
1984	Kansas City-AL	.284	104	377	42	107	13	69	38	37	0
1985	Kansas City-AL	.335	155	550	108	184	30	112	103	49	9
1986	Kansas City-AL	.290	124	441	70	128	16	73	80	45	1
1987	Kansas City-AL	.290	115	427	71	124	22	78	72	47	6
1988	Kansas City-AL	.306	157	589	90	180	24	103	82	51	14
1989	Kansas City-AL	.282	124	457	67	129	12	80	59	47	14
1990	Kansas City-AL	.329	142	544	82	179	14	87	56	63	9
1991	Kansas City-AL	.255	131	505	77	129	10	61	58	75	2
1992	Kansas City-AL	.285	152	592	55	169	7	61	35	69	8
1993	Kansas City-AL	.266	145	560	69	149	19	75	39	67	7
Career Totals:		.305	2707	10349	1583	3154	317	1595	1096	908	201

charge at an umpire in 1983 after a home run he hit was disallowed—and he was called out—because he used too much pine tar.

Tough choice. Brett once said he would choose the latter (the home run was later reinstated on appeal in what became known as The Great Pine Tar Incident). But neither is fair. The most legendary Kansas City Royal, who subscribed to the quaint notion of loyalty to a city and played his entire 21-year career in K.C., should be remembered for one other thing more than any other: he was one of the handful of best third basemen in the history of the game.

Brett is the only player to win a batting crown in three different decades: 1976, 1980 and 1991. In 1980 he flirted seriously with .400—he would have been the first player to reach the mythical mark since Ted Williams in 1941—before settling on .390. He hit .305 for his career, with 3,154 hits.

Brett not only manned the hot corner but was the cornerstone of a team that won six divisional crowns, two pennants and one world title (1985) between 1976 and 1985. And as good as he was during the regular season, he was even better in the playoffs (.340 in 27 playoff games, with nine homers and 22 RBI) and World Series (.373 in 13 games).

Brett's brother Ken was a major league pitcher, and he had two other brothers who played in the minors. "I was never as good as my brothers growing up—ever," he said during his 1999 Hall of Fame induction. A great line, but George Brett has done too much to be remembered for that.

No. 45

George Sisler

Sometimes the trailblazer gets run over by those who follow. Such could be said of George Sisler. Joe DiMaggio broke Sisler's consecutive hit streak (Sisler's was 41). Gorgeous George hit .407 in 1920 and .420 in 1922. That last mark is surpassed just twice in the twentieth century, by Rogers Hornsby in 1924 (.424) and Nap Lajoie in 1901 (.422).

Ty Cobb, who criticized everyone, said Sisler was as close to a perfect ballplayer as there was. Sisler's collecting 200 or more hits a season for six years impressed even Cobb. But Sisler in 1922 impressed everyone.

Playing solid first base for the St. Louis Browns, Sisler led the American League in the days of Ruth and Cobb with 246 hits, 18 doubles, 134 runs, and 51 stolen bases. It won him the AL Most Valuable Player award.

Full Name: George Harold "Gorgeous George" Sisler

Position: First Base   Debut: June 1915, St. Louis Browns

Born: 3/24/1893, Manchester, Ohio   Bats: Left

Height: 5'11"; Weight: 170   Throws: Left

BATTING SUMMARY STATISTICS

Year	Team	AVG	G	AB	R	H	HR	RBI	BB	SO	SB
1915	St. Louis-AL	.285	81	274	28	78	3	29	7	27	10
1916	St. Louis-AL	.305	151	580	83	177	4	76	40	37	34
1917	St. Louis-AL	.353	135	539	60	190	2	52	30	19	37
1918	St. Louis-AL	.341	114	452	69	154	2	41	40	17	45
1919	St. Louis-AL	.352	132	511	96	180	10	83	27	20	28
1920	St. Louis-AL	.407	154	631	137	257	19	122	46	19	42
1921	St. Louis-AL	.371	138	582	125	216	12	104	34	27	35
1922	St. Louis-AL	.420	142	586	134	246	8	105	49	14	51
1924	St. Louis-AL	.305	151	636	94	194	9	74	31	29	19
1925	St. Louis-AL	.345	150	649	100	224	12	105	27	24	11
1926	St. Louis-AL	.290	150	613	78	178	7	71	30	30	12
1927	St. Louis-AL	.327	149	614	87	201	5	97	24	15	27
1928	Washington-AL	.245	20	49	1	12	0	2	1	2	0
1928	Boston-NL	.340	118	491	71	167	4	68	30	15	11
1929	Boston-NL	.326	154	629	67	205	2	79	33	17	6
1930	Boston-NL	.309	116	431	54	133	3	67	23	15	7
Career Totals:		.340	2055	8267	1284	2812	102	1175	472	327	375

But the one-time engineering major for the University of Michigan (coached by a young Branch Rickey) played all the angles. He played hard and was in the lineup just about every day, and for 44 games he hit safely. When Joe DiMaggio surpassed his record, Sisler sent a simple and supportive telegram, leading the cheer for Joe D. to keep the streak alive.

Sisler had 257 hits in 1920, enough to hold the single-season record ahead of his rival, Cobb. Sisler's 246 hits two years later sealed the eighth spot all-time. No one else held down two Top-10 spots in this most basic of baseball categories.

It took such giants to overshadow Sisler as the century closed, but Sisler helped lead the way.

No. 46

Carl Hubbell

James Thurber once said that 95 percent of American men put themselves to sleep striking out the heart of the Yankees lineup. Carl Hubbell was not one of them. In real life he did the dream one better.

July 10, 1934: 50,000 people jam New York's Polo Grounds before the gates have to be locked against the crush 15 minutes before game time. It's the second All-Star Game, and fans now understand this isn't just a

Full Name: Carl Owen "The Mealticket" Hubbell

Position: Pitcher

Born: 6/22/1903, Carthage, Missouri

Height: 6'; Weight: 170

Debut: July 1928, New York Giants

Bats: Right

Throws: Left

Pitching Summary Statistics

Year	Team	W	L	PCT	ERA	G	SV	IP	BB	SO
1928	New York-NL	10	6	.625	2.83	20	1	124.0	21	37
1929	New York-NL	18	11	.621	3.69	39	1	268.0	67	106
1930	New York-NL	17	12	.586	3.87	37	2	241.2	58	117
1931	New York-NL	14	12	.538	2.65	36	3	248.0	67	155
1932	New York-NL	18	11	.621	2.50	40	2	284.0	40	137
1933	New York-NL	23	12	.657	1.66	45	5	308.2	47	156
1934	New York-NL	21	12	.636	2.30	49	8	313.0	37	118
1935	New York-NL	23	12	.657	3.27	42	0	302.2	49	150
1936	New York-NL	26	6	.813	2.31	42	3	304.0	57	123
1937	New York-NL	22	8	.733	3.20	39	4	261.2	55	159
1938	New York-NL	13	10	.565	3.07	24	1	179.0	33	104
1939	New York-NL	11	9	.550	2.75	29	2	154.0	24	62
1940	New York-NL	11	12	.478	3.65	31	0	214.1	59	86
1941	New York-NL	11	9	.550	3.57	26	1	164.0	53	75
1942	New York-NL	11	8	.579	3.95	24	0	157.1	34	61
1943	New York-NL	4	4	.500	4.91	12	0	66.0	24	31
Career Totals:		253	154	.622	2.98	535	33	3590.1	725	1677

midseason exhibition for charity. It is a rare moment, the kind that you realize even as it happens that it's one for the books.

Pitching at home, the New York Giants' Carl Hubbell took the mound. Charlie Gehringer immediately lined a single into right center then took second when the ball was bobbled. Heinie Manush drew a walk. With two on and no outs, the National League infield met at the mound.

Whatever they said should be required reading at West Point.

Most of us wouldn't even dare dream what happened next: Babe Ruth is called out on strikes after four pitches; Lou Gehrig fans on a 3–2 pitch; Jimmie Foxx, "The Beast," strikes out on five pitches.

The screwballer would also strike out Al Simmons and Joe Cronin in the next inning. Five Hall of Famers up, five struck out.

For many players, a single statistic, season or even a single game unfairly overshadows the man's life work. To be sure, Hubbell had a whale of a career on his way to Cooperstown. He'd finish 16 years with 253 wins and a 2.97 ERA against some of the game's greatest players. He once won 24 straight decisions, threw a no-hitter, and was 4–2 in three World Series with a 1.79 ERA.

Hubbell may disagree, but fans know that those career marks can't make us think more of him—couldn't make us think more of him—after July 10, 1934. The dominating American League went on to win that All-Star Game 9–7 after Hubbell left in the third inning with the NL up 4–0. But Hubbell, in 23 pitches in an inning and two-thirds, won a piece of history and the hearts of everyone who falls asleep in mid-windup.

No. 47

BARRY BONDS

Barry Bonds was just four when he first started running around Candlestick Park. In less than another two decades he would make the entire National League his playground.

The son of All-Star San Francisco Giant Bobby Bonds—and the

godson of Willie Mays—grew from that kid hanging around the clubhouse to *The Sporting News* player of the 1990s, a Gold Glove winner and power hitter (hitting at least 33 home runs in 9 of 10 seasons) with speed (28 or more steals 9 of 10 seasons) who also hits for average (six .300 seasons).

Bonds is the only player in major league history to hit at least 350 home runs and steal 350 bases, as well as earn three Most Valuable Player awards in a four-year span (1990 and 1992 with the Pittsburgh Pirates, and 1993 with the San Francisco Giants). He is one of only eight players to win the Most Valuable Player award three times. All this despite playing home games in two of the worst hitters' parks in baseball—Candlestick Park in San Francisco and Three Rivers Stadium in Pittsburgh.

At the end of the century Bonds had nearly as many career home runs (445) as steals (460), to go along with a .288 career batting average and 1,299 RBI. Although far from an MVP in 1999, his numbers were impressive: 34 home runs and 83 RBI. What made the stats remarkable was that an elbow injury limited Bonds to 102 games.

Bonds, who has shed some of his early bad-boy image, will be hard-pressed to reach 3,000 hits—he had 2,010 at the end of 1999—primarily because he regularly draws more than 100 walks a season.

But a fanatical off-season training regimen, coupled with a strong desire to improve on his lackluster individual and team postseason performances (Pirates fans are still irked he did not throw out Atlanta's Sid Bream at the plate in the 1992 playoffs) could drive Bonds, 35 at the end of the 1999 season, to push himself harder, longer. It's no longer child's play; it's work. But Barry Bonds is among the best ever at the job.

No. 48

Hank Greenberg

When you talk about first basemen, all conversation begins with Lou Gehrig. Then you can move on to Jimmie Foxx and probably jump right to Mark McGwire or maybe Harmon Killebrew.

But, please, don't forget Hank Greenberg. The Detroit Tiger who lost almost five years to a fractured wrist and World War II military service led the league in home runs and RBI four times each in his 13-year career (which included only nine full seasons). The right-hander challenged three legendary season records, doubles (63 in 1934), home runs (58 in 1938) and RBI (183 in 1937), only to fall just short.

He put up four of the most outstanding seasons on record: 1935 (.328, 36 home runs and 170 RBI, 51 more than runner-up Lou Gehrig); 1937 (.337, 40, 183), 1938 (.315, 58, 146) and 1940 (.340, 41, 150).

Full Name: Henry Benjamin "Hammerin' Hank" Greenberg

Position: 1B, OF   Debut: September 1930, Detroit Tigers

Born: 1/1/1911, New York, New York Bats: Right

Height: 6'3.5"; Weight: 210   Throws: Right

BATTING SUMMARY STATISTICS

Year	Team	AVG	G	AB	R	H	HR	RBI	BB	SO	SB
1930	Detroit-AL	.000	1	1	0	0	0	0	0	0	0
1933	Detroit-AL	.301	117	449	59	135	12	87	46	78	6
1934	Detroit-AL	.339	153	593	118	201	26	139	63	93	9
1935	Detroit-AL	.328	152	619	121	203	36	170	87	91	4
1936	Detroit-AL	.348	12	46	10	16	1	16	9	6	1
1937	Detroit-AL	.337	154	594	137	200	40	183	102	101	8
1938	Detroit-AL	.315	155	556	144	175	58	146	119	92	7
1939	Detroit-AL	.312	138	500	112	156	33	112	91	95	8
1940	Detroit-AL	.340	148	573	129	195	41	150	93	75	6
1941	Detroit-AL	.269	19	67	12	18	2	12	16	12	1
1945	Detroit-AL	.311	78	270	47	84	13	60	42	40	3
1946	Detroit-AL	.277	142	523	91	145	44	127	80	88	5
1947	Pittsburgh-NL	.249	125	402	71	100	25	74	104	73	0
Career Totals:		.313	1394	5193	1051	1628	331	1276	852	844	58

But the two-time MVP (1935 and 1940, the later year as an outfielder), who won four pennants and two world titles with the Bengals, remained an afterthought; he did not even get selected to the American League All-Star team in 1935, his MVP season. In fact, he did not make the squad until 1937, the first of four straight seasons he was selected (he also made the team in 1945), perennially stuck behind Gehrig and Foxx.

Greenberg, a native New Yorker, was one of the biggest Jewish sports stars of his day and, along with Sandy Koufax, of all-time in baseball. His faith became an issue when he anguished over playing on Jewish holidays in the latter part of the season. A rabbi later decreed that Greenberg's playing on Rosh Hashanah (New Year) was all right, but on Yom Kippur (Day of Atonement) it was not. Greenberg abided, and fans mostly understood.

More lost days, among the lost years, among the lost attention and recognition. Greenberg, who was elected to the Hall of Fame in 1956 and died in 1986, was quoted in the 1988 *Baseball Card Engagement Book* as saying that the times his brilliance was recognized gained importance as the years rolled by.

"When you're playing, awards don't seem like much," he said. "Then you get older and all of it becomes more precious. It is nice to be remembered."

And we should.

No. 49
JOE MORGAN

In a city that for generations of boom and bust just kept its head down and kept plugging, Johnny Bench and Pete Rose were an odd fit for Cincinnati's Big Red Machine of the 1970s. Bench was the most brilliant man to play catcher, period, with astonishing power; Rose was less gifted but more flashy, drawing attention on the field and off.

Yet it was Joe Morgan, all five feet, seven inches and 150 pounds of him, who personified the city. He just kept his head down, and kept plugging. It's easy to forget his numbers decades later—it's enough for most that he was just part of that dynasty. But Morgan's numbers are as surprising, to too many, as they are staggering, to everyone. En route to eight consecutive All-Star Games, the second baseman was named the NL MVP in 1975 and 1976 (hitting a minimum of .320 with 60 stolen bases), when Cincy fans might not have made him the second or third choice for team MVP. In the Reds' hottest years, 1972–77, Morgan scored more than 100

Full Name: Joe Leonard Morgan

Position: Second Base   Debut: September 1963, Houston Colt .45s

Born: 9/19/1943, Bonham, Texas   Bats: Left

Height: 5'7"; Weight: 160   Throws: Right

BATTING SUMMARY STATISTICS

Year	Team	AVG	G	AB	R	H	HR	RBI	BB	SO	SB
1963	Houston-NL	.240	8	25	5	6	0	3	5	5	1
1964	Houston-NL	.189	10	37	4	7	0	0	6	7	0
1965	Houston-NL	.271	157	601	100	163	14	40	97	77	20
1966	Houston-NL	.285	122	425	60	121	5	42	89	43	11
1967	Houston-NL	.275	133	494	73	136	6	42	81	51	29
1968	Houston-NL	.250	10	20	6	5	0	0	7	4	3
1969	Houston-NL	.236	147	535	94	126	15	43	110	74	49
1970	Houston-NL	.268	144	548	102	147	8	52	102	55	42
1971	Houston-NL	.256	160	583	87	149	13	56	88	52	40
1972	Cincinnati-NL	.292	149	552	122	161	16	73	115	44	58
1973	Cincinnati-NL	.290	157	576	116	167	26	82	111	61	67
1974	Cincinnati-NL	.293	149	512	107	150	22	67	120	69	58
1975	Cincinnati-NL	.327	146	498	107	163	17	94	132	52	67
1976	Cincinnati-NL	.320	141	472	113	151	27	111	114	41	60
1977	Cincinnati-NL	.288	153	521	113	150	22	78	117	58	49
1978	Cincinnati-NL	.236	132	441	68	104	13	75	79	40	19
1979	Cincinnati-NL	.250	127	436	70	109	9	32	93	45	28
1980	Houston-NL	.243	141	461	66	112	11	49	93	47	24
1981	San Francisco-NL	.240	90	308	47	74	8	31	66	37	14
1982	San Francisco-NL	.289	134	463	68	134	14	61	85	60	24
1983	Philadelphia-NL	.230	123	404	72	93	16	59	89	54	18
1984	Oakland-AL	.244	116	365	50	89	6	43	66	39	8
Career Totals:		.271	2649	9277	1650	2517	268	1133	1865	1015	689

runs a year while hitting an average .301 with more than 20 homers, 60 stolen bases and 80 RBI. He was a Gold Glove winner from 1973 to 1977.

And when it counted most, Joe was there. In 23 World Series games over four years he had seven stolen bases, good for ninth best when he retired in 1984, and three homers.

All the way, the man who today is one of the game's high-profile television commentators quietly led by example rather than by highlight reel or sound bite. The Reds won four pennants and two World Series while Joe was in town, a town he reflected so well—then helped magnify as a championship city.

No. 50

Cal Ripken, Jr.

The story of Cal Ripken, Jr., can be told in a story from Rochester, NY—as unexpected a setting as the power-hitting shortstop is paradoxical on the field. In Rochester a little kid was gravely ill. His hero was Ripken. The star showed up and spent hours with the kid in the hospital. But while nurses and doctors held back tears, Ripken shared laughs and enjoyed life with the child who had so little of each.

Months later a call comes to Ripken's home in Maryland, during his own daughter's birthday. It's the terminally ill child's doctor. The kid has only hours. Could Cal talk to the boy on the phone? Ripken does, laughing and joking; the child can't speak but smiles long after the call is over.

This story took years to become public, and then surfaced only in the local Rochester newspaper, when the family was the focus of a Ripken tribute as the Orioles played their Triple-A farm team, for which Ripken once played, in a 1999 exhibition.

Ripken doesn't talk about these things; it's just the right thing to do. It's like playing baseball the way no one thought it could be played. For Ripken, it's just the right thing to do.

On the field Ripken holds perhaps the safest record in sports. He played in 2,632 straight games, blowing away Lou Gehrig's record that few could halve. Even the ghosts of the Crusades who forever guard the Holy Grail were scratching their armor over that one.

Setting the record may also have been a big mistake.

The Streak will forever define Ripken, but the definition is severely lacking if, in the long term, it overshadows his historic play during those games and hundreds more. For starters, at the end of 1999 he was only nine hits short of 3,000 for his career, to go along with 402 home runs, outslugging shortstops like Honus Wagner and Ernie Banks. In the field he held or shared 12 major league and American League fielding records. In 1990 he made three errors in 161 games. He ended the season with a fielding percentage of .996—as a shortstop.

But numbers, as we mentioned, fail to capture Ripken. No achievement matches what he did for that little boy in Rochester and for countless others. We'd love him anyway, and he knows that, but it was just the right thing to do.

No. 51
REGGIE JACKSON

After watching Reggie Jackson in the sixth and final game of the 1977 World Series in New York, pitcher Bill Lee said: "I think there are going to be a lot of Reggies born in this town."

Jackson had just hit three consecutive home runs against the Los Angeles Dodgers, the finale a blast off of Charlie Hough that landed in the black-painted abyss beyond the center field wall, to clinch the Yankees' first World Series in 15 seasons. Since Jackson walked in his first at bat in Game Six, and homered in his last at bat in Game Five, Jackson homered in four straight official at bats, off four different pitchers. Any question why he was called "Mr. October"?

Full Name: Reginald Martinez Jackson

Position: OF, DH   Debut: June 1967, Kansas City Athletics

Born: 5/18/1946,   Bats: Left
   Wyncote, Pennsylvania

Height: 6'; Weight: 200   Throws: Left

BATTING SUMMARY STATISTICS

Year	Team	AVG	G	AB	R	H	HR	RBI	BB	SO	SB
1967	Kansas City-AL	.178	35	118	13	21	1	6	10	46	1
1968	Oakland-AL	.250	154	553	82	138	29	74	50	171	14
1969	Oakland-AL	.275	152	549	123	151	47	118	114	142	13
1970	Oakland-AL	.237	149	426	57	101	23	66	75	135	26
1971	Oakland-AL	.277	150	567	87	157	32	80	63	161	16
1972	Oakland-AL	.265	135	499	72	132	25	75	59	125	9
1973	Oakland-AL	.293	151	539	99	158	32	117	76	111	22
1974	Oakland-AL	.289	148	506	90	146	29	93	86	105	25
1975	Oakland-AL	.253	157	593	91	150	36	104	67	133	17
1976	Baltimore-AL	.277	134	498	84	138	27	91	54	108	28
1977	New York-AL	.286	146	525	93	150	32	110	74	129	17
1978	New York-AL	.274	139	511	82	140	27	97	58	133	14
1979	New York-AL	.297	131	465	78	138	29	89	65	107	9
1980	New York-AL	.300	143	514	94	154	41	111	83	122	1

Year	Team	AVG	G	AB	R	H	HR	RBI	BB	SO	SB
1981	New York-AL	.237	94	334	33	79	15	54	46	82	0
1982	California-AL	.275	153	530	92	146	39	101	85	156	4
1983	California-AL	.194	116	397	43	77	14	49	52	140	0
1984	California-AL	.223	143	525	67	117	25	81	55	141	8
1985	California-AL	.252	143	460	64	116	27	85	78	138	1
1986	California-AL	.241	132	419	65	101	18	58	92	115	1
1987	Oakland-AL	.220	115	336	42	74	15	43	33	97	2
Career Totals:		.262	2820	9864	1551	2584	563	1702	1375	2597	228

"The only reason I don't like playing in the World Series," Jackson once said, "is I can't watch myself play."

So he was brash, and arrogant, and sometimes a liability if not a danger to himself in right field. He could be insufferable, which is why he and manager Billy Martin got into a brawl in the dugout in Boston in 1978. He was a quote machine and said "I" more often than an optometrist, but as the equally colorful Dizzy Dean once observed, "It ain't bragging if you can do it."

Jackson could do it. He was a four-time American League leader in home runs, and as was the 1973 MVP, he led the Oakland A's to a world title. Jackson's bragging put him in the spotlight, often with a bull's-eye on his back. The man who craved attention—he left the Baltimore Orioles after one season; "Not enough reporters around," he said—was at his best when all of baseball was watching.

In 27 games in five World Series (two with Oakland, three with the Yankees), Jackson hit .357, with 10 home runs and 24 RBI. His World Series slugging average of .755 ranks first all-time. He is a two-time series MVP (1973 and, of course, 1977).

Jackson is in the Top 10 in home runs, with 563—and number one in strikeouts, with 2,597. When the left-hander with arguably the strongest legs in baseball swung, something worth watching happened, even when he whiffed. One of the more loved—and hated—ballplayers of the day, Jackson knew he was an attraction for fans on both sides of the debate. "Fans don't boo nobodies," he noted.

And they don't name their kids after just anybody, either.

No. 52

CHARLIE GEHRINGER

Baseball players of every age are told a secret to being great that almost every one of them forgets: always hustle, and strive for consistency.

From 1924 to 1942 Charlie Gehringer was hustling consistency for the Detroit Tigers. He shined when these qualities were the expectation, not the exception. Maybe that's because in recent decades, unless hustle becomes sideshow, like Pete "Charlie Hustle" Rose's head-first slides or his bone-shattering collision at home during an All-Star Game, hustle does little for the individual—except win games.

A double can be a good gauge. For a non–power hitter, it means good wood, better wheels. Hustle. Gehringer had 574 of them to put him in the Top 10 in history and four more in his first two World Series. He averaged 30 a year. Rose, with the corner on hustle, averaged 31, Ty Cobb 30.

Full Name: Charles Leonard "The Mechanical Man" Gehringer

Position: Second Base   Debut: September 1924, Detroit Tigers

Born: 5/11/1903,   Bats: Left
   Fowlerville, Michigan

Height: 5'11"; Weight: 180   Throws: Right

BATTING SUMMARY STATISTICS

Year	Team	AVG	G	AB	R	H	HR	RBI	BB	SO	SB
1924	Detroit-AL	.462	5	13	2	6	0	1	0	2	1
1925	Detroit-AL	.167	8	18	3	3	0	0	2	0	0
1926	Detroit-AL	.277	123	459	62	127	1	48	30	42	9
1927	Detroit-AL	.317	133	508	110	161	4	61	52	31	17
1928	Detroit-AL	.320	154	603	108	193	6	74	69	22	15
1929	Detroit-AL	.339	155	634	131	215	13	106	64	19	27
1930	Detroit-AL	.330	154	610	144	201	16	98	69	17	19
1931	Detroit-AL	.311	101	383	67	119	4	53	29	15	13
1932	Detroit-AL	.298	152	618	112	184	19	107	68	34	9
1933	Detroit-AL	.325	155	628	103	204	12	105	68	27	5
1934	Detroit-AL	.356	154	601	134	214	11	127	99	25	11

Year	Team	AVG	G	AB	R	H	HR	RBI	BB	SO	SB
1935	Detroit-AL	.330	150	610	123	201	19	108	79	16	11
1936	Detroit-AL	.354	154	641	144	227	15	116	83	13	4
1937	Detroit-AL	.371	144	564	133	209	14	96	90	25	11
1938	Detroit-AL	.306	152	568	133	174	20	107	113	21	14
1939	Detroit-AL	.325	118	406	86	132	16	86	68	16	4
1940	Detroit-AL	.313	139	515	108	161	10	81	101	17	10
1941	Detroit-AL	.220	127	436	65	96	3	46	95	26	1
1942	Detroit-AL	.267	45	45	6	12	1	7	7	4	0
Career Totals:		.320	2323	8860	1774	2839	184	1427	1186	372	181

Now, take the All-Star Game. Rose is remembered for when he broke Cleveland catcher Ray Fosse's collarbone in 1970. Gehringer broke the batting average record. In his six straight All-Star starts, he became the event's leading batter with a .500 average. He went 10 for 20 in the midsummer classic that didn't exist until his 10th season, when he was 30 years old.

His opponents spoke of him glowingly, noting the qualities that players and managers hold high but that may not attract much notice on sports pages. They said he hated losing more than anyone, that he started the season hot and stayed that way, that he quietly said "Hello" in April and "Good-bye" in October, and in between hit .350.

The Mechanical Man, they called him. In 1929 it didn't refer simply to his perpetual motion of solid play. His performance was almost more than human, even in a league dominated by Ruth, Gehrig and Foxx. Gehringer tied for first in the American League in hits (215), doubles (45) and led outright in stolen bases (27), runs (131) and triples (19). He also hit .339.

But perhaps the best stat to illustrate the steadiness of the 1937 MVP (he hit .371 that year) is his career batting average: .320. His average in his three World Series: .321.

That might not grab a lot of headlines, but it goes a long way to grabbing a lot of wins.

No. 53

ROGER CLEMENS

ESPN recently awarded Roger Clemens its Comeback Player of the Year award. Clemens stood at the podium, looked at the audience, and said he didn't know what he was supposed to have come back from.

That's Clemens.

The moment showed both his confidence and the rest of the world's expectation of him. Early on he was the next Nolan Ryan, another hard-throwing righty from Texas. Now he's being compared to Tom Seaver, with the same powerful and prominent leg drive in his wind-up.

By the number of Cy Young Awards, at least, he's better than both of them. Under that criterion, he's also better than Sandy Koufax, Bob Gibson, and Jim Palmer among Cy Young Award–era pitchers.

Hey, you don't have to like him.

But five Cy Youngs (1986–87, '91, '97–'98), the most of anyone at any time, demands respect. One season Clemens struck out 20 guys in a game, a feat matched by himself—10 years later.

At age 35 in 1997, the Rocket led the AL in wins, strikeouts and ERA and won his fourth Cy Young. He did it all again a year later and won his fifth—a figure that is very subject to change.

It just always seems Clemens is the best pitcher not winning a fistful of World Series rings. Even in 1986, at 24–4 and winning the MVP and AL Cy Young, his Red Sox lost the series—although hitching up late with one of the winningest Yankees teams of all-time should make his jewelry box a bit more crowded. Winning the final game of the 1999 series sweep of Atlanta is a good start.

As an individual, though, few can match what Clemens does year in and year out, be it in Boston, Toronto or New York. What may infuriate some fans most is that the Rocket doesn't seem to particularly mind where he pitches. He just wins. And that's his job, one he's done better than anyone in recent memory.

You don't have to like it. It's just a fact.

No. 54

MICKEY COCHRANE

The man many considered the best catcher in baseball built a lifetime batting average of .320, led his teams to five pennants, and hit over .300 nine times in 13 years.

His name isn't Mike Piazza, Johnny Bench, Yogi Berra or Roy Campanella. It's Mickey Cochrane.

Cochrane doesn't come to mind to most for a few reasons. He played before TV, from 1925 to 1937. He was just one of many stars on Connie Mack's Philadelphia A's that included Jimmie Foxx and Al Simmons. And he played in an era when monumental names already dominated the American League, many of them on the Yankees, names that ate up sports page columns as fast as wins.

Here's a glimpse at what "Black Mike" faced: In 1930 Cochrane hit .357, but it wasn't even the best batting average on his team. Simmons hit

Full Name: Gordon Stanley Cochrane

Position: C, P/M   Debut: April 1925, Philadelphia Athletics

Born: 4/6/1903, Bridgewater,   Bats: Left
  Massachusetts

Height: 5'10.5"; Weight: 180   Throws: Right

BATTING SUMMARY STATISTICS

Year	Team	AVG	G	AB	R	H	HR	RBI	BB	SO	SB
1925	Philadelphia-AL	.331	134	420	69	139	6	55	44	19	7
1926	Philadelphia-AL	.273	120	370	50	101	8	47	56	15	5
1927	Philadelphia-AL	.338	126	432	80	146	12	80	50	7	9
1928	Philadelphia-AL	.293	131	468	92	137	10	57	76	25	7
1929	Philadelphia-AL	.331	135	514	113	170	7	95	69	8	7
1930	Philadelphia-AL	.357	130	487	110	174	10	85	55	18	5
1931	Philadelphia-AL	.349	122	459	87	160	17	89	56	21	2
1932	Philadelphia-AL	.293	139	518	118	152	23	112	100	22	0
1933	Philadelphia-AL	.322	130	429	104	138	15	60	106	22	8
1934	Detroit-AL	.320	129	437	74	140	2	76	78	26	8

Year	Team	AVG	G	AB	R	H	HR	RBI	BB	SO	SB
1935	Detroit-AL	.319	115	411	93	131	5	47	96	15	5
1936	Detroit-AL	.270	44	126	24	34	2	17	46	15	1
1937	Detroit-AL	.306	27	98	27	30	2	12	25	4	0
Career Totals:		.320	1482	5169	1041	1652	119	832	857	217	64

.381, Lou Gehrig hit .379, and Babe Ruth and Chicago's Carl Reynolds hit .359.

He got his nickname because whenever a critical at bat turned into a pop out or a call went the other way, he always saw the worst. He grew gloomy and melancholy, waiting for the other shoe to drop. In 1937 with the Detroit Tigers, he was batting .306 after an injury-plagued year and things were looking up. Then he was beaned in the head, almost fatally. He was unconscious for 10 days and never batted again. He was 34.

No. 55

CARL YASTRZEMSKI

Yaz.

Rarely has a nickname brought to mind so much: brilliant hitter, strong fielder, a gifted athlete who moved with the stride of a sprinter but with the strength of a butt-busting farmhand.

So why is the first name in the text of his Hall of Fame plaque "Ted Williams"? Yaz never seemed bothered by it or by constant reminders that he was carrying on Williams' Boston Red Sox tradition rather than blazing his own.

Carl Yastrzemski, respectful of the game and its masters, knew better. In fact, as an overpaid rookie on a team that reminded him of the fact he was hitting .220 and was lost, he asked for help; he asked for Ted Williams.

"Can we get a hold of him?" he recalled at his Hall of Fame induction speech. "I need help. I don't think I can play in the big leagues."

Whatever Williams told him, it worked.

Yaz took the lesson and made a legend. He seized the sure-fire yet rarely used combination of great talent and hard work to make a name for himself. And despite 23 years in which he landed in the Top 10 of all time in games, hits, doubles, and RBI, it was one season—1967—that set him apart.

Full Name: Carl Michael "Yaz" Yastrzemski

Position: OF, 1B, DH   Debut: April 1961, Boston Red Sox

Born: 8/22/1939, Southampton,   Bats: Left
    New York

Height: 5'11"; Weight: 182   Throws: Right

BATTING SUMMARY STATISTICS

Year	Team	AVG	G	AB	R	H	HR	RBI	BB	SO	SB
1961	Boston-AL	.266	148	583	71	155	11	80	50	96	6
1962	Boston-AL	.296	160	646	99	191	19	94	66	82	7
1963	Boston-AL	.321	151	570	91	183	14	68	95	72	8
1964	Boston-AL	.289	151	567	77	164	15	67	75	90	6
1965	Boston-AL	.312	133	494	78	154	20	72	70	58	7
1966	Boston-AL	.278	160	594	81	165	16	80	84	60	8
1967	Boston-AL	.326	161	579	112	189	44	121	91	69	10
1968	Boston-AL	.301	157	539	90	162	23	74	119	90	13
1969	Boston-AL	.255	162	603	96	154	40	111	101	91	15
1970	Boston-AL	.329	161	566	125	186	40	102	128	66	23
1971	Boston-AL	.254	148	508	75	129	15	70	106	60	8
1972	Boston-AL	.264	125	455	70	120	12	68	67	44	5
1973	Boston-AL	.296	152	540	82	160	19	95	105	58	9
1974	Boston-AL	.301	148	515	93	155	15	79	104	48	12
1975	Boston-AL	.269	149	543	91	146	14	60	87	67	8
1976	Boston-AL	.267	155	546	71	146	21	102	80	67	5
1977	Boston-AL	.296	150	558	99	165	28	102	73	40	11
1978	Boston-AL	.277	144	523	70	145	17	81	76	44	4
1979	Boston-AL	.270	147	518	69	140	21	87	62	46	3
1980	Boston-AL	.275	105	364	49	100	15	50	44	38	0
1981	Boston-AL	.246	91	338	36	83	7	53	49	28	0
1982	Boston-AL	.275	131	459	53	126	16	72	59	50	0
1983	Boston-AL	.266	119	380	38	101	10	56	54	29	0
Career Totals:		.285	3308	11988	1816	3419	452	1844	1845	1393	168

After several years in which mediocrity would be a step up, the Red Sox hired Dick Williams to manage. Soon the Sox started to play the way their individual stats indicated they should.

The Sox won 10 straight road games in July and kept winning to knot the American League with the White Sox, the Twins and the Tigers, all in a position to win through August.

Yaz led the Sox to the "Impossible Dream" pennant, giving life to one of baseball's most storied and disappointed cities.

Despite hitting three homers and batting .400 in the World Series, the Sox couldn't beat Bob Gibson's St. Louis Cardinals, and Boston had to refill its Valium prescription.

But Yaz ended the season with a league-leading 189 hits, 44 home runs, 112 runs, 121 RBI and .326 batting average. Those who were around for it were lucky: it was the last Triple Crown. Maybe the last ever.

But Yastrzemski was more than that. There was a way he went about the task of playing baseball. It wasn't a game, although he loved it so, and it wasn't a show. It was a job, one he worked at twice as hard as anyone around him. It was a job he felt lucky to have, a dream his dad had given up for himself so his family could survive during the Depression.

In his stirring Hall of Fame induction speech, Yaz repeated the question thrown at him many times, about the pressure of the major leagues: "Pressure, what pressure? Pressure is what faces millions and millions of fathers and mothers trying to earn a living every day to support a family, to give it comfort, devotion and love. That's what pressure really is."

For baseball, Yaz and the memories he gave us still provide comfort, instill devotion for the game, and love for a star who was lovable.

No. 56

MIKE PIAZZA

Future all-stars don't get drafted in the 62nd round of the free agent draft. Future bartenders get drafted in the 62nd round. Salesmen of tomorrow get drafted that late or, if a club is lucky, maybe a grounds-keeper.

Or a batboy. Los Angeles Dodger manager Tommy Lasorda, a long-time friend with a car dealer back East, drafted the man's son, a skinny first baseman from Miami-Dade Community College who was once a bat-boy back in Pennsylvania. It was a favor, but when you are at pick No. 1,390, what difference does it make?

The 1988 pick was converted to catcher and initially struggled in the low minors. The whispers of "Tommy's Boy" could be heard in the club-house (Lasorda was even the godfather of the kid's brother). Then some-thing clicked, from all the extra work with coaches, playing winter ball, the hours upon weeks of weight-lifting, or just plain fate. And Tommy's Boy, that favor of a late-late-late draft pick, merely turned into the great-est hitting catcher to play the game this side of Josh Gibson.

Mike Piazza is the only major league catcher with two 40–home run seasons (Johnny Bench hit some of his homers while playing other posi-tions). With the exception of the strike year of 1994, Piazza has hit at least 32 home runs in each of his first seven seasons, 240 in all by the end of 1999.

Not only does the 1993 National League Rookie of the Year, one of the strongest players in the game, hit with power and consistently drive in 100-plus runs every year, but at the end of 1999 his career batting aver-age (.328) was second among active players to only Tony Gwynn.

Piazza, who was traded to the New York Mets in mid–1998 after a very brief stint with the Florida Marlins, hit .362 in 1997, with 40 homers and 124 RBI. With the Mets in 1999 he hit .303, but again with 40 home runs and 124 RBI (the latter a club record), despite missing several weeks early in the season to injury.

Home run hitters tend to be pull hitters or at least hit their home runs that way (think of the Williams shift, or a McGwire blast landing in the upper deck in left). But when the righty Piazza, who has hit his share of 450-foot moonshots to left, is in his groove, his power alley is right center and even right field.

And those taters are not the "It is high/it is far/it is gone" variety; bleacher denizens—bartenders and salesmen and groundskeepers and maybe some of the 1,389 players drafted ahead of Mike Piazza—are advised to scramble, not to catch a souvenir, but to get out of the way.

No. 57

PETE ROSE

Drunks, wife beaters, deadbeat dads, drug addicts and racists. The Baseball Hall of Fame is full of them. Some are as bad as the motley crew of "thugs, pugs and mugs" signing up for an evil posse in *Blazing Saddles*. So why isn't Pete Rose in the Hall of Fame?

Because he's a stubborn knucklehead who won't admit he messed up. Once he does, and once he does his penance, Rose should be able to claim a place in Cooperstown outside of a signing booth.

But what's really important here is what Rose did for 24 head-first seasons: beat everyone. In the 1970s, when tradition was out and bad fashion and worse music were in, Pete Rose made hustle cool again.

He was derisively called Charlie Hustle by Mickey Mantle and Whitey Ford during a spring training game in 1963. Typical Rose response: he loved it.

The self-proclaimed "Hit King" ended his days on the field first in hits (Ty Cobb's spikes are still gnawing at his coffin over that one), at bats and games; second in doubles; fourth in runs and walks. He led the National League in batting average three times (.348 in 1969), and in hits seven times (230 in 1973).

He collected more than 200 hits 10 times. He also was the nitro injection in Cincinnati's Big Red Machine that rolled over most teams from 1970 to 1976.

He finished his career with a .303 batting average; granted, many were singles on a hard carpet. But, also granted, singles win more games than home runs. So does an almost maniacal drive to do whatever it takes to win.

Rose switched positions more than a congressman seeking reelection. He was a second baseman who became a solid outfielder, then an All-Star third baseman, then a fixture at first base.

Photographs on the next two pages: **Players slid headfirst before Pete Rose, but it's hard to remember any of them. The self-named Hit King found a lot of ways to beat you, and like an ancient torture, he did it a little bit at a time: a single here, a steal there, then a broken double play that grabs the game's momentum. Rose's quest to overcome a lifetime ban from baseball for gambling is aimed at getting him into the Hall of Fame. If he does, it won't be a walk into the hall, but a full-bore, headfirst slide. It's a tough way to get there but fitting for Charlie Hustle.**

Full Name: Peter Edward "Charlie Hustle" Rose

Position: OF, 1B, 2B, 3B, P/M   Debut: April 1963, Cincinnati Reds

Born: 4/14/1941, Cincinnati, Ohio   Bats: Both

Height: 5'11"; Weight: 200   Throws: Right

BATTING SUMMARY STATISTICS

Year	Team	AVG	G	AB	R	H	HR	RBI	BB	SO	SB
1963	Cincinnati-NL	.273	157	623	101	170	6	41	55	72	13
1964	Cincinnati-NL	.269	136	516	64	139	4	34	36	51	4
1965	Cincinnati-NL	.312	162	670	117	209	11	81	69	76	8
1966	Cincinnati-NL	.313	156	654	97	205	16	70	37	61	4
1967	Cincinnati-NL	.301	148	585	86	176	12	76	56	66	11
1968	Cincinnati-NL	.335	149	626	94	210	10	49	56	76	3
1969	Cincinnati-NL	.348	156	627	120	218	16	82	88	65	7
1970	Cincinnati-NL	.316	159	649	120	205	15	52	73	64	12
1971	Cincinnati-NL	.304	160	632	86	192	13	44	68	50	13
1972	Cincinnati-NL	.307	154	645	107	198	6	57	73	46	10
1973	Cincinnati-NL	.338	160	680	115	230	5	64	65	42	10
1974	Cincinnati-NL	.284	163	652	110	185	3	51	106	54	2
1975	Cincinnati-NL	.317	162	662	112	210	7	74	89	50	0
1976	Cincinnati-NL	.323	162	665	130	215	10	63	86	54	9
1977	Cincinnati-NL	.311	162	655	95	204	9	64	66	42	16
1978	Cincinnati-NL	.302	159	655	103	198	7	52	62	30	13
1979	Philadelphia-NL	.331	163	628	90	208	4	59	95	32	20
1980	Philadelphia-NL	.282	162	655	95	185	1	64	66	33	12
1981	Philadelphia-NL	.325	107	431	73	140	0	33	46	26	4
1982	Philadelphia-NL	.271	162	634	80	172	3	54	66	32	8
1983	Philadelphia-NL	.245	151	493	52	121	0	45	52	28	7
1984	Montreal-NL	.259	95	278	34	72	0	23	31	20	1
1984	Cincinnati-NL	.365	26	96	9	35	0	11	9	7	0
1984	NL Totals	.286	121	374	43	107	0	34	40	27	1
1985	Cincinnati-NL	.264	119	405	60	107	2	46	86	35	8
1986	Cincinnati-NL	.219	72	237	15	52	0	25	30	31	3
Career Totals:		.303	3562	14053	2165	4256	160	1314	1566	1143	198

Sure, to some he was always an all-star pain in the butt.

But sometimes being a pain wins games, too. Ask opposing players he rattled. Ask teammates he inspired.

He said the kind of things players' agents would later spoon-feed to millionaire stars to curry attention, but Rose meant every word. "I'd walk through hell in a gasoline suit to play baseball," is an eye-grabber in the tome by Geoffrey C. Ward and Ken Burns, *Baseball: An Illustrated History*. Rose also committed a bit of treason in the big-time labor movement in the big leagues: "Playing baseball for a living is like a license to steal."

He should have stuck with that crime. Instead gambling, including—the evidence indicates—on major league games, led to Rose's lifetime ban from baseball. It was, perhaps, the only sentence he couldn't handle. He's steadfastly refused to say he's sorry, to make amends. America embraces repentant fallen heroes, but Rose fails to assure new generations of fans when they repeat the plea asked so long after a similar black mark in baseball: Say it ain't so. Think of the game, Pete. Think of the kids.

No. 58

OZZIE SMITH

Listen up everybody. In 30 or so years, when we are the old-timers, we are going to have a very important job to do: pass along the Legend of Ozzie Smith. The best part is that no embellishment will be needed.

There will be doubters, to be sure, but unlike the greats of the 19th and early 20th centuries, we will have enough videotaped history to win over even the most stubborn skeptics.

You can even point to one play: April 20, 1978, fourth inning, two outs, Jeff Burroughs at the plate. The Atlanta Brave sends a hopper up the middle, sending Ozzie—then with the San Diego Padres—diving toward the hole. The ball takes a bad hop; no problem, as Smith snags it bare-handed and guns Burroughs out at first.

If you've seen it, you may well say it is the best you ever saw. And whether you saw him or not, Ozzie Smith was the best ever to field at shortstop or any other position.

Thirteen consecutive Gold Gloves (1980–92), a career total second only to Brooks Robinson's 16. Best fielding percentage in a season. Least errors in a season by a shortstop. Most assists in a season. Throw in 16 consecutive seasons of at least 20 steals and a bat that improved steadily throughout his career (average: .262), MVP of the 1985 National League Championship Series, a World Series title, and Smith, who started with the Padres but became an icon as a St. Louis Cardinal, emerges as one of the best all-around players ever.

If you don't believe it, ask anyone who saw him.

No. 59

EDDIE MATHEWS

The hot corner. Have a weak third basemen and plan on a lot of losses. Extra base hits will snake up the line in half a second and change the two hours of baseball before it. Double plays that could have ended opponents' momentum will be lost.

So a third baseman must be solid. If he can hit for power, too, that's a bonus. Eddie Mathews, then, was about the biggest bonus a manager could get. He ended the century tied with Ernie Banks for 13th in career home runs. That's ahead of Lou Gehrig and Stan Musial. At 512 dingers,

Full Name: Edwin Lee Mathews

Position: Third Base   Debut: April 1952, Boston Braves

Born: 10/13/1931, Texarkana, Texas   Bats: Left

Height: 6'1"; Weight: 200   Throws: Right

BATTING SUMMARY STATISTICS

Year	Team	AVG	G	AB	R	H	HR	RBI	BB	SO	SB
1952	Boston-NL	.242	145	528	80	128	25	58	59	115	6
1953	Milwaukee-NL	.302	157	579	110	175	47	135	99	83	1
1954	Milwaukee-NL	.290	138	476	96	138	40	103	113	61	10
1955	Milwaukee-NL	.289	141	499	108	144	41	101	109	98	3

Year	Team	AVG	G	AB	R	H	HR	RBI	BB	SO	SB
1956	Milwaukee-NL	.272	151	552	103	150	37	95	91	86	6
1957	Milwaukee-NL	.292	148	572	109	167	32	94	90	79	3
1958	Milwaukee-NL	.251	149	546	97	137	31	77	85	85	5
1959	Milwaukee-NL	.306	148	594	118	182	46	114	80	71	2
1960	Milwaukee-NL	.277	153	548	108	152	39	124	111	113	7
1961	Milwaukee-NL	.306	152	572	103	175	32	91	93	95	12
1962	Milwaukee-NL	.265	152	536	106	142	29	90	101	90	4
1963	Milwaukee-NL	.263	158	547	82	144	23	84	124	119	3
1964	Milwaukee-NL	.233	141	502	83	117	23	74	85	100	2
1965	Milwaukee-NL	.251	156	546	77	137	32	95	73	110	1
1966	Atlanta-NL	.250	134	452	72	113	16	53	63	82	1
1967	Houston-NL	.238	101	328	39	78	10	38	48	65	2
1967	Detroit-AL	.231	36	108	14	25	6	19	15	23	0
1968	Detroit-AL	.212	31	52	4	11	3	8	5	12	0
Career Totals:		.271	2391	8537	1509	2315	512	1453	1444	1487	68

Mathews is, along with Mike Schmidt, the best power hitting third bagger ever.

In his 15 years with the Braves—from 1952 to 1966 in Boston, Milwaukee and Atlanta (the only man to play for the team in all three cities)—he was also something more. He was half of the greatest home-run hitting duo on one team in history. Mathews and Henry Aaron hit 60 more than Ruth and Gehrig. It must have been frustrating to hit 30 homers in a season (he did it 10 times) or even 40 homers in a season (he did it four times) and still be the second-best slugger on the team. But Mathews earned a special place in baseball, with or without Aaron.

No. 60

NOLAN RYAN

Nolan Ryan's fastballing brilliance emerged with New York, but he is not really a Met. He started throwing no-hitters with California, but he is not really an Angel. The bulk of his career was spent in Houston,

Full Name: Lynn Nolan Ryan

Position: Pitcher   Debut: September 1966, New York Mets

Born: 1/31/1947, Refugio, Texas   Bats: Right

Height: 6'2"; Weight: 195   Throws: Right

PITCHING SUMMARY STATISTICS

Year	Team	W	L	PCT	ERA	G	SV	IP	BB	SO
1966	New York-NL	0	1	.000	15.00	2	0	3.0	3	6
1968	New York-NL	6	9	.400	3.09	21	0	134.0	75	133
1969	New York-NL	6	3	.667	3.53	25	1	89.1	53	92
1970	New York-NL	7	11	.389	3.42	27	1	131.2	97	125
1971	New York-NL	10	14	.417	3.97	30	0	152.0	116	137
1972	California-AL	19	16	.543	2.28	39	0	284.0	157	329
1973	California-AL	21	16	.568	2.87	41	1	326.0	162	383
1974	California-AL	22	16	.579	2.89	42	0	332.2	202	367
1975	California-AL	14	12	.538	3.45	28	0	198.0	132	186
1976	California-AL	17	18	.486	3.36	39	0	284.1	183	327
1977	California-AL	19	16	.543	2.77	37	0	299.0	204	341
1978	California-AL	10	13	.435	3.72	31	0	234.2	148	260
1979	California-AL	16	14	.533	3.60	34	0	222.2	114	223
1980	Houston-NL	11	10	.524	3.35	35	0	233.2	98	200
1981	Houston-NL	11	5	.688	1.69	21	0	149.0	68	140
1982	Houston-NL	16	12	.571	3.16	35	0	250.1	109	245
1983	Houston-NL	14	9	.609	2.98	29	0	196.1	101	183
1984	Houston-NL	12	11	.522	3.04	30	0	183.2	69	197
1985	Houston-NL	10	12	.455	3.80	35	0	232.0	95	209
1986	Houston-NL	12	8	.600	3.34	30	0	178.0	82	194
1987	Houston-NL	8	16	.333	2.76	34	0	211.2	87	270
1988	Houston-NL	12	11	.522	3.52	33	0	220.0	87	228
1989	Texas-AL	16	10	.615	3.20	32	0	239.1	98	301
1990	Texas-AL	13	9	.591	3.44	30	0	204.0	74	232
1991	Texas-AL	12	6	.667	2.91	27	0	173.0	72	203
1992	Texas-AL	5	9	.357	3.72	27	0	157.1	69	157
1993	Texas-AL	5	5	.500	4.88	13	0	66.1	40	46
Career Totals:		324	292	.526	3.19	807	3	5386.0	2795	5714

but he is not really an Astro. He set his final strikeout and no-hit milestones in Texas, the cap he wears on his plaque in Cooperstown, but he is not really a Ranger.

Ryan belongs to baseball. The awe of his fastball was only overshadowed by the awe watchers had as he continued to bring it hard to the plate well into his 40s, an unparalleled display of power and endurance. Ryan certainly is not the winningest pitcher the game has seen—twelfth all-time in wins (324),but third all-time in losses (292)—and his one World Series ring was earned way back in 1969, as a relief pitcher for the Mets. Yet fans continue to rate him among the best ever, because he was the home-run hitter of pitchers, bringing all to their feet with the strike-out.

Like many power pitchers, Ryan had to overcome early wildness. But after his trade from the Mets to the Angels, Ryan and his "express" fast-ball became scary-dominant. In one three-game stretch in 1972 Ryan struck out 47 hitters. The next year he fanned a modern record 383, one of his six 300-K seasons.

Ryan's seven no-hitters are three more than those by Sandy Koufax, whose record he eclipsed. When Ryan broke Walter Johnson's strikeout record, few would have thought that Ryan had another 12 seasons left in him. The K's kept coming, rookies and Hall of Famers alike.

The victim for number 5,000 was Rickey Henderson, who called it "an honor." A lot of players shared it.

No. 61

EDDIE COLLINS

Eddie Collins is one of those names in Cooperstown that you glance quickly at before moving on.

Yeah, yeah, old dead guy, not as good as Cobb. What else?

What else? Well, then you don't know that Collins:

- Hit .340 or more in 10 different seasons.
- Hit .300 or better from 1909 to 1916, and again from 1919 to 1928.
- Led the AL in at least one fielding category from 1909 to 1922.
- Racked up 744 stolen bases, including nine straight seasons of at least 38 steals, and ranks first all-time in World Series thefts.

Full Name: Edward Trowbridge "Cocky" Collins, Sr.
  (a.k.a. Edward T. Sullivan in 1906)

Position: 2B, P/M	Debut: September 1906, Philadelphia Athletics
Born: 5/2/1887,	Bats: Left
Millerton, New York	
Height: 5'9"; Weight: 175	Throws: Right

Batting Summary Statistics

Year	Team	AVG	G	AB	R	H	HR	RBI	BB	SO	SB
1906	Philadelphia-AL	.200	6	15	2	3	0	0	0	-	0
1907	Philadelphia-AL	.250	14	20	0	5	0	2	0	-	0
1908	Philadelphia-AL	.273	102	330	39	90	1	40	16	-	8
1909	Philadelphia-AL	.346	153	572	104	198	3	56	62	-	67
1910	Philadelphia-AL	.322	153	583	81	188	3	81	49	-	81
1911	Philadelphia-AL	.365	132	493	92	180	3	73	62	-	38
1912	Philadelphia-AL	.348	153	543	137	189	0	64	101	-	63
1913	Philadelphia-AL	.345	148	534	125	184	3	73	85	37	55
1914	Philadelphia-AL	.344	152	526	122	181	2	85	97	31	58
1915	Chicago-AL	.332	155	521	118	173	4	77	119	27	46
1916	Chicago-AL	.308	155	545	87	168	0	52	86	36	40
1917	Chicago-AL	.289	156	564	91	163	0	67	89	16	53
1918	Chicago-AL	.276	97	330	51	91	2	30	73	13	22
1919	Chicago-AL	.319	140	518	87	165	4	80	68	27	33
1920	Chicago-AL	.372	153	602	117	224	3	76	69	19	20
1921	Chicago-AL	.337	139	526	79	177	2	58	66	11	12
1922	Chicago-AL	.324	154	598	92	194	1	69	73	16	20
1923	Chicago-AL	.360	145	505	89	182	5	67	84	8	48
1924	Chicago-AL	.349	152	556	108	194	6	86	89	16	42
1925	Chicago-AL	.346	118	425	80	147	3	80	87	8	19
1926	Chicago-AL	.344	106	375	66	129	1	62	62	8	13
1927	Philadelphia-AL	.336	95	226	50	76	1	15	56	9	6
1928	Philadelphia-AL	.303	36	33	3	10	0	7	4	4	0
1929	Philadelphia-AL	.000	9	7	0	0	0	0	2	0	0
1930	Philadelphia-AL	.500	3	2	1	1	0	0	0	0	0
Career Totals:		.333	2826	9949	1821	3312	47	1300	1499	286	744

- Hit .333 for his career that included 3,312 hits over 25 years (1906–1930), the longest career for a position player and second only to Nolan Ryan.

And to think this second baseman for the Philadelphia Athletics and Chicago White Sox went by the nickname "Cocky."

Collins, along with first baseman Stuffy McInnis, shortstop Jack Barry and third baseman Frank "Home Run" Baker formed the "$100,000 Infield," since financially plagued Connie Mack wouldn't take that astronomical sum for all of them (five more bucks and cash-strapped Connie probably would have dumped them all). That unit would help the A's win four pennants and three World Series crowns between 1910 and 1914.

After Collins' MVP season of 1914, he was in fact sold to the Chicago White Sox, whom he led to pennants in 1917 and 1919. He also managed and at the end of his career became the best pinch hitter in the game. What else? What, that isn't enough?

No. 62

WHITEY FORD

In 1961 one of Babe Ruth's most amazing records was broken by a new breed of Yankee, a record no one figured any mortal could touch, a mark for the eons.

But Whitey Ford did.

Yes, Whitey Ford, not Roger Maris, who hit his 61 homers that year.

Ford, a lefty and native New Yorker, was in the World Series again, his second of four in a row. The year before he won two games without giving up a run in the Yankees' eventual loss to the Pittsburgh Pirates in seven games. In the '61 series, Ford again won two games, this time against the Cincinnati Reds, as the Yankees won in five games. Ford went nine innings in the first game and threw a two-hitter for a 2–0 win. He started Game Four with New York up two games to one and threw five scoreless innings before an ankle injury knocked him out.

Add those two years up and Ford, the greatest of all World Series pitchers, had 33 and two-thirds consecutive scoreless innings in world championship play. He surpassed Ruth's 43-year-old record set with the Boston Red Sox by four innings, a mark even older than the single-season homer mark Maris broke.

Full Name: Edward Charles "Chairman of the Board" Ford

Position: Pitcher　　　　　　　　　　Debut: July 1950, New York Yankees

Born: 10/21/1928, New York, New York　Bats: Left

Height: 5'10"; Weight: 181　　　　　　Throws: Left

PITCHING SUMMARY STATISTICS

Year	Team	W	L	PCT	ERA	G	SV	IP	BB	SO
1950	New York-AL	9	1	.900	2.81	20	1	112.0	52	59
1953	New York-AL	18	6	.750	3.00	32	0	207.0	110	110
1954	New York-AL	16	8	.667	2.82	34	1	210.2	101	125
1955	New York-AL	18	7	.720	2.63	39	2	253.2	113	137
1956	New York-AL	19	6	.760	2.47	31	1	225.2	84	141
1957	New York-AL	11	5	.688	2.57	24	0	129.1	53	84
1958	New York-AL	14	7	.667	2.01	30	1	219.1	62	145
1959	New York-AL	16	10	.615	3.04	35	1	204.0	89	114
1960	New York-AL	12	9	.571	3.08	33	0	192.2	65	85
1961	New York-AL	25	4	.862	3.21	39	0	283.0	92	209
1962	New York-AL	17	8	.680	2.90	38	0	257.2	69	160
1963	New York-AL	24	7	.774	2.74	38	1	269.1	56	189
1964	New York-AL	17	6	.739	2.13	39	1	244.2	57	172
1965	New York-AL	16	13	.552	3.24	37	1	244.1	50	162
1966	New York-AL	2	5	.286	2.47	22	0	73.0	24	43
1967	New York-AL	2	4	.333	1.64	7	0	44.0	9	21
Career Totals:		236	106	.690	2.75	498	10	3170.1	1086	1956

"It was a tough year for the Babe," laughed Ford.

And a tough 16 years for every other player in baseball.

Ford would end his career with 236 wins and 106 losses, third-best winning percentage in history when he retired, and a 2.75 ERA. But forget that. Whitey Ford was a money pitcher. In 11 World Series he won 10 games—a record—and lost eight; started 22 games—a record; pitched 146 innings—a record; struck out 94—a record; and had three shutouts—second best.

Ford, however, was not the strongest hurler of his day nor did he have the most action on the ball. So he studied, hard. He owes much to Ed Lopat, a Yankee pitcher from 1944 to 1952 who won 166 games for New York but who gave the dynasty much more in his tutelage of Ford and how to keep a batter off balance. Weaknesses, always watch for the hitter's weaknesses, Lopat lectured.

In the end Ford would forever be known as the man who did the most when his team needed it the most. For a ballplayer, there's no greater achievement.

No. 63

EDDIE MURRAY

He was one of the greatest switch-hitting power hitters of all time. At different times he led the American League in RBI, home runs and walks, finishing his career with a batting average in the neighborhood of .300, while slamming 500 homers and 3,000 hits.

He isn't Mickey Mantle.

Outside of Baltimore, Eddie Murray might not immediately spring to mind when you read stats like that. But you'll quickly remember the powerful build, the mustache and glower that gave him that Apollo Creed look from *Rocky*—a look that told you the Oriole was ready and anxious for a fight.

Like in the 1983 World Series. Murray hit two homers in Game Five against the Phillies, accounting for three of the Orioles' five runs, to win the world title in Philadelphia. That's the kind of battling that put Murray into the 3,000/500 Club. And that's one exclusive club: Just two others in baseball history have more than 500 home runs and 3,000 hits—Henry Aaron and Willie Mays.

Enough said?

No. 64

JIM PALMER

OK, the first rule of this chapter is: No reference to Jim Palmer's underwear commercials.

That said, there's much to add about Jim Palmer. But perhaps the most telling moment of the three-time Cy Young winner, the winner of 20 or more games in eight seasons, was when he put his career on the line—and failed.

March 1991. Palmer was 47 years old and recently enshrined in the Hall of Fame as the winningest pitcher in the 1970s, during which he had 186 wins for the Baltimore Orioles. So why is he pitching in spring training? To play again, to win again. Doctors said a hammy tear ended that, but age may have pulled the strings. He was already, understandably, sinking to a lower level. But remarkably he still had major league stuff, if only briefly. However, the man who started more than 520 games wouldn't accept an offer to pitch in relief.

Full Name: James Alvin Palmer

Position: Pitcher   Debut: April 1965, Baltimore Orioles

Born: 10/15/1945, New York,   Bats: Right
    New York

Height: 6'3"; Weight: 196   Throws: Right

PITCHING SUMMARY STATISTICS

Year	Team	W	L	PCT	ERA	G	SV	IP	BB	SO
1965	Baltimore-AL	5	4	.556	3.72	27	1	92.0	56	75
1966	Baltimore-AL	15	10	.600	3.46	30	0	208.1	91	147
1967	Baltimore-AL	3	1	.750	2.94	9	0	49.0	20	23
1969	Baltimore-AL	16	4	.800	2.34	26	0	181.0	64	123
1970	Baltimore-AL	20	10	.667	2.71	39	0	305.0	100	199
1971	Baltimore-AL	20	9	.690	2.68	37	0	282.0	106	184
1972	Baltimore-AL	21	10	.677	2.07	36	0	274.1	70	184
1973	Baltimore-AL	22	9	.710	2.40	38	1	296.1	113	158

Year	Team	W	L	PCT	ERA	G	SV	IP	BB	SO
1974	Baltimore-AL	7	12	.368	3.27	26	0	178.2	69	84
1975	Baltimore-AL	23	11	.676	2.09	39	1	323.0	80	193
1976	Baltimore-AL	22	13	.629	2.51	40	0	315.0	84	159
1977	Baltimore-AL	20	11	.645	2.91	39	0	319.0	99	193
1978	Baltimore-AL	21	12	.636	2.46	38	0	296.0	97	138
1979	Baltimore-AL	10	6	.625	3.30	23	0	155.2	43	67
1980	Baltimore-AL	16	10	.615	3.98	34	0	224.0	74	109
1981	Baltimore-AL	7	8	.467	3.75	22	0	127.1	46	35
1982	Baltimore-AL	15	5	.750	3.13	36	1	227.0	63	103
1983	Baltimore-AL	5	4	.556	4.23	14	0	76.2	19	34
1984	Baltimore-AL	0	3	.000	9.17	5	0	17.2	17	4
Career Totals:		268	152	.638	2.86	558	4	3948.0	1311	2212

Jim Palmer is a starter who didn't know when to stop. Or maybe how to stop. He led the league in wins three times, in ERA twice and finished his 19 years 268–152 with a 2.86 ERA. Tack on another six league championship series where he went 4–1 with a 1.96 ERA, and six World Series, where he was 4–2 with a 3.20 ERA, and it begins to become clear why Palmer figured he couldn't be stopped. He was right.

No. 65

MEL OTT

Baseball has the Splendid Splinter, the Bambino, the Commerce Comet, and the Human Vacuum Cleaner. Baseball also had Master Melvin. While that moniker might not draw attention, its bearer did. And the numbers he left behind are positively riveting.

Mel "Master Melvin" Ott played for the New York Giants from 1926 to 1947 and for nine of those seasons collected 100 RBI or more. He also was the first National Leaguer to hit 500 homers.

You got a hint of it his rookie year. He batted .383 with a couple of doubles in 60 at bats. He had just turned 17 years old that spring.

Full Name: Melvin Thomas "Master Melvin" Ott

Position: OF, 3B, P/M   Debut: April 1926, New York Giants

Born: 3/2/1909, Gretna, Louisiana   Bats: Left

Height: 5'9"; Weight: 170   Throws: Right

BATTING SUMMARY STATISTICS

Year	Team	AVG	G	AB	R	H	HR	RBI	BB	SO	SB
1926	New York-NL	.383	35	60	7	23	0	4	1	9	1
1927	New York-NL	.282	82	163	23	46	1	19	13	9	2
1928	New York-NL	.322	124	435	69	140	18	77	52	36	3
1929	New York-NL	.328	150	545	138	179	42	151	113	38	6
1930	New York-NL	.349	148	521	122	182	25	119	103	35	9
1931	New York-NL	.292	138	497	104	145	29	115	80	44	10
1932	New York-NL	.318	154	566	119	180	38	123	100	39	6
1933	New York-NL	.283	152	580	98	164	23	103	75	48	1
1934	New York-NL	.326	153	582	119	190	35	135	85	43	0
1935	New York-NL	.322	152	593	113	191	31	114	82	58	7
1936	New York-NL	.328	150	534	120	175	33	135	111	41	6
1937	New York-NL	.294	151	545	99	160	31	95	102	69	7
1938	New York-NL	.311	150	527	116	164	36	116	118	47	2
1939	New York-NL	.308	125	396	85	122	27	80	100	50	2
1940	New York-NL	.289	151	536	89	155	19	79	100	50	6
1941	New York-NL	.286	148	525	89	150	27	90	100	68	5
1942	New York-NL	.295	152	549	118	162	30	93	109	61	6
1943	New York-NL	.234	125	380	65	89	18	47	95	48	7
1944	New York-NL	.288	120	399	91	115	26	82	90	47	2
1945	New York-NL	.308	135	451	73	139	21	79	71	41	1
1946	New York-NL	.074	31	68	2	5	1	4	8	15	0
1947	New York-NL	.000	4	4	0	0	0	0	0	0	0
Career Totals:		.304	2730	9456	1859	2876	511	1860	1708	896	89

Crusty manager John McGraw was so afraid the minor leagues would ruin Ott's swing that he made the Louisianian ride the pine for a couple of years. Ott spent it learning much more than how to chew tobacco.

By the time he retired, the six-time NL home run leader had played in 16 World Series games, leaving with a .295 average, four homers and 10 RBI. His career bottom line includes 511 home runs while hitting .300 or better 10 times.

Among the majors' Top 10 in RBI and runs, Master Melvin earned the nickname.

No. 66

AL KALINE

Al Kaline was not the greatest power hitter, or on-base man, or RBI guy, or fielder (he was close on that one). But Al Kaline was very good at a lot of things. And that is what made him great.

"He's in a very rare category," said the late Billy Martin, a teammate who later managed for and against Kaline. "There are a lot of good hitters in baseball and a lot of good baserunners and a lot of good outfielders. But there are very few who combine everything with a good throwing arm. Al Kaline could do all those things."

And that made Kaline a first-ballot Hall of Famer in 1980. A .297 hitter with 3,007 hits over his 22-year career, the Detroit Tiger never won an MVP award, did not win a batting title after shocking the baseball world with a .340 average in 1955 as a 20-year-old to top the American League, and never won a home run title despite 399 career dingers.

Full Name: Albert William Kaline

Position: OF, DH, DH

Born: 12/19/1934, Baltimore, Maryland

Height: 6'2"; Weight: 180

Debut: June 1953, Detroit Tigers

Bats: Right

Throws: Right

BATTING SUMMARY STATISTICS

Year	Team	AVG	G	AB	R	H	HR	RBI	BB	SO	SB
1953	Detroit-AL	.250	30	28	9	7	1	2	1	5	1
1954	Detroit-AL	.276	138	504	42	139	4	43	22	45	9
1955	Detroit-AL	.340	152	588	121	200	27	102	82	57	6
1956	Detroit-AL	.314	153	617	96	194	27	128	70	55	7
1957	Detroit-AL	.295	149	577	83	170	23	90	43	38	11
1958	Detroit-AL	.313	146	543	84	170	16	85	54	47	7
1959	Detroit-AL	.327	136	511	86	167	27	94	72	42	10
1960	Detroit-AL	.278	147	551	77	153	15	68	65	47	19
1961	Detroit-AL	.324	153	586	116	190	19	82	66	42	14
1962	Detroit-AL	.304	100	398	78	121	29	94	47	39	4

Year	Team	AVG	G	AB	R	H	HR	RBI	BB	SO	SB
1963	Detroit-AL	.312	145	551	89	172	27	101	54	48	6
1964	Detroit-AL	.293	146	525	77	154	17	68	75	51	4
1965	Detroit-AL	.281	125	399	72	112	18	72	72	49	6
1966	Detroit-AL	.288	142	479	85	138	29	88	81	66	5
1967	Detroit-AL	.308	131	458	94	141	25	78	83	47	8
1968	Detroit-AL	.287	102	327	49	94	10	53	55	39	6
1969	Detroit-AL	.272	131	456	74	124	21	69	54	61	1
1970	Detroit-AL	.278	131	467	64	130	16	71	77	49	2
1971	Detroit-AL	.294	133	405	69	119	15	54	82	57	4
1972	Detroit-AL	.313	106	278	46	87	10	32	28	33	1
1973	Detroit-AL	.255	91	310	40	79	10	45	29	28	4
1974	Detroit-AL	.262	147	558	71	146	13	64	65	75	2
Career Totals:		.297	2834	10116	1622	3007	399	1583	1277	1020	137

But Kaline, who once turned down a raise to the $100,000 mark because he felt he didn't deserve it (that makes him, with the utmost respect, a lug), was *among* the best for so very long: a 16-time All-Star, including 10 starts; 20 or more home runs nine times and .300 or better eight times. Kaline was even better in the field, the winner of 10 Gold Gloves who once went 242 straight games without an error. Among Hall of Famers only Roberto Clemente could be considered an equal in right field.

Kaline, who in his first few days in the majors threw out runners at second, third and home in successive innings against the Chicago White Sox, was a two-time winner of *The Sporting News* Player of the Year (1955 and 1963). He was the key to the Tigers' rally from three games to one in the 1968 World Series, leading the Bengals to an improbable comeback and title over the St. Louis Cardinals with a .379 average and eight RBI.

Pitcher Johnny Podres said of Kaline that "you almost have to watch him play every day to appreciate what he does." Al Kaline was not the best of his day. But he was one of the best ever.

No. 67

JUAN MARICHAL

July 13, 1965—the All-Star Game in Bloomington, MN. The National League puts up the dream rotation that includes Sandy Koufax, Don Drysdale, and Bob Gibson.

One NL pitcher throws three scoreless innings, gives up one hit, and is named Most Valuable Player.

He's Juan Marichal.

True, the All-Star Game is an exhibition, and its most important numbers increasingly seem to be the TV ad revenue it generates. But not for the players. Given a chance for a much-sought-after midseason break or a long weekend with the family and friends, the vast majority of players ignore injuries and fatigue to get an at bat, an inning of pitching.

The San Francisco Giant earned his place nine times in the game during one of the eras most crowded with Hall of Fame–bound pitchers. His eight appearances tie him for first all-time with Drysdale, Tom Seaver and Jim Bunning. Marichal's windup with a high kick—his foot directly overhead like it was planted against a ceiling—made many batters shift uneasily, just a bit. And that's usually enough. For the two All-Star Games he won (1963 and 1965) it was enough against the best.

Full Name: Juan Antonio "Manito" Marichal
   (b: Marichal y Sanchez)

Position: Pitcher   Debut: July 1960, San Francisco Giants

Born: 10/20/1937, Laguna Verde,   Bats: Right
   Dominican Rep.

Height: 6'; Weight: 185   Throws: Right

PITCHING SUMMARY STATISTICS

Year	Team	W	L	PCT	ERA	G	SV	IP	BB	SO
1960	San Francisco-NL	6	2	.750	2.66	11	0	81.1	28	58
1961	San Francisco-NL	13	10	.565	3.89	29	0	185.0	48	124
1962	San Francisco-NL	18	11	.621	3.36	37	1	262.2	90	153

Year	Team	W	L	PCT	ERA	G	SV	IP	BB	SO
1963	San Francisco-NL	25	8	.758	2.41	41	0	321.1	61	248
1964	San Francisco-NL	21	8	.724	2.48	33	0	269.0	52	206
1965	San Francisco-NL	22	13	.629	2.13	39	1	295.1	46	240
1966	San Francisco-NL	25	6	.806	2.23	37	0	307.1	36	222
1967	San Francisco-NL	14	10	.583	2.76	26	0	202.1	42	166
1968	San Francisco-NL	26	9	.743	2.43	38	0	326.0	46	218
1969	San Francisco-NL	21	11	.656	2.10	37	0	299.2	54	205
1970	San Francisco-NL	12	10	.545	4.12	34	0	242.2	48	123
1971	San Francisco-NL	18	11	.621	2.94	37	0	279.0	56	159
1972	San Francisco-NL	6	16	.273	3.71	25	0	165.0	46	72
1973	San Francisco-NL	11	15	.423	3.82	34	0	207.1	37	87
1974	Boston-AL	5	1	.833	4.87	11	0	57.1	14	21
1975	Los Angeles-NL	0	1	.000	13.50	2	0	6.0	5	1
Career Totals:		243	142	.631	2.89	471	2	3507.1	709	2303

The Dominican Dandy (OK, so he didn't have a great nickname) threw fairly basic pitches—fastball, slider, screwball—but the batter never knew where it was coming from. Sidearm, overhand, submarine and somewhere in between. It was enough to make a batter hesitate just that much more and shake his head on the way back to the dugout.

Marichal had 191 wins in the 1960s (best in the NL and 27 more than Gibson) including six years with 20 or more wins and an ERA always lower than 3.00. In his first game as a major leaguer, back in midseason 1960, Marichal pitched a one-hitter against the Philadelphia Phillies. Baseball people at the time said they were impressed by the rookie with the odd windup somewhat akin to Hall of Famer Dazzy Vance. They had no idea how impressive the kicker would be.

One final note: Marichal also is a kind of patron saint for pitchers. On August 22, 1965, bat in hand, Marichal attacked Los Angeles Dodger catcher Johnny Roseboro. The offense: Roseboro was throwing the ball back to the pitcher's mound too close to Marichal's head.

Even at the plate, Marichal (a lifetime .165 hitter, good enough for best among right-handed pitchers from Lagunda Verde) was an original.

No. 68

WILLIE McCOVEY

Of the Top 10 home run hitters at the beginning of 1999, there was a Babe, a Hammerin' Hank, a Splendid Splinter and a Mr. October. Only one was nicknamed for his fielding.

Willie "Stretch" McCovey squeaked into the Top 10 with his minor league mentor, Ted Williams, at 521 homers: both were bumped off the list in 1999 by Mark McGwire. But unlike his idol Williams, McCovey was as stellar playing the field as hitting balls into it and over it.

McCovey led the National League three times in dingers and twice in RBI. He was the MVP in 1969 and a year later drew the ultimate compliment, leading the league in intentional walks. He got 45 of them, a major league record.

Full Name: Willie Lee "Stretch" McCovey

Position: 1B, OF   Debut: July 1959, San Francisco Giants

Born: 1/10/1938, Mobile, Alabama   Bats: Left

Height: 6'4"; Weight: 210   Throws: Left

BATTING SUMMARY STATISTICS

Year	Team	AVG	G	AB	R	H	HR	RBI	BB	SO	SB
1959	San Francisco-NL	.354	52	192	32	68	13	38	22	35	2
1960	San Francisco-NL	.238	101	260	37	62	13	51	45	53	1
1961	San Francisco-NL	.271	106	328	59	89	18	50	37	60	1
1962	San Francisco-NL	.293	91	229	41	67	20	54	29	35	3
1963	San Francisco-NL	.280	152	564	103	158	44	102	50	119	1
1964	San Francisco-NL	.220	130	364	55	80	18	54	61	73	2
1965	San Francisco-NL	.276	160	540	93	149	39	92	88	118	0
1966	San Francisco-NL	.295	150	502	85	148	36	96	76	100	2
1967	San Francisco-NL	.276	135	456	73	126	31	91	71	110	3
1968	San Francisco-NL	.293	148	523	81	153	36	105	72	71	4
1969	San Francisco-NL	.320	149	491	101	157	45	126	121	66	0
1970	San Francisco-NL	.289	152	495	98	143	39	126	137	75	0
1971	San Francisco-NL	.277	105	329	45	91	18	70	64	57	0

Year	Team	AVG	G	AB	R	H	HR	RBI	BB	SO	SB
1972	San Francisco-NL	.213	81	263	30	56	14	35	38	45	0
1973	San Francisco-NL	.266	130	383	52	102	29	75	105	78	1
1974	San Diego-NL	.253	128	344	53	87	22	63	96	76	1
1975	San Diego-NL	.252	122	413	43	104	23	68	57	80	1
1976	San Diego-NL	.203	71	202	20	41	7	36	21	39	0
1976	Oakland-AL	.208	11	24	0	5	0	0	3	4	0
1977	San Francisco-NL	.280	141	478	54	134	28	86	67	106	3
1978	San Francisco-NL	.228	108	351	32	80	12	64	36	57	1
1979	San Francisco-NL	.249	117	353	34	88	15	57	36	70	0
1980	San Francisco-NL	.204	48	113	8	23	1	16	13	23	0
Career Totals:		.270	2588	8197	1229	2211	521	1555	1345	1550	26

But through most of his career spanning an amazing four decades (1959–80) he wasn't best player on the San Francisco Giants, wasn't the best slugger, wasn't even the best Willie. Although long overshadowed by Willie Mays, McCovey didn't pull a prima donna act. Instead, he hit baseballs, and scooped them up at first base.

To honor leadership and team spirit, the Giants found an easy choice for its model. It's the Willie Mac Award. And no one had to ask which Willie to engrave on it.

No. 69

BILL DICKEY

Please forgive a moment of personal reflection here. Back in the early 1970s kids didn't have the great game jerseys that proliferated in the merchandising years that followed. So some kids would take a white T-shirt and an indelible marker and write a hero's name on the back and his number. Many a "Mantle" and "B. Robinson" sweated through to tiny shoulders in that era. One day a kid came to a sandlot in Ballston Spa, NY, with the name "Dickey" on his back. Many laughed and made crude if not imaginative comments on the name, wondering who the heck "Dickey" was.

Full Name: William Malcolm Dickey

Position: Catcher   Debut: August 1928, New York Yankees

Born: 6/6/1907, Bastrop, Louisiana   Bats: Left

Height: 6'1.5"; Weight: 185   Throws: Right

BATTING SUMMARY STATISTICS

Year	Team	AVG	G	AB	R	H	HR	RBI	BB	SO	SB
1928	New York-AL	.200	10	15	1	3	0	2	0	2	0
1929	New York-AL	.324	130	447	60	145	10	65	14	16	4
1930	New York-AL	.339	109	366	55	124	5	65	21	14	7
1931	New York-AL	.327	130	477	65	156	6	78	39	20	2
1932	New York-AL	.310	108	423	66	131	15	84	34	13	2
1933	New York-AL	.318	130	478	58	152	14	97	47	14	3
1934	New York-AL	.322	104	395	56	127	12	72	38	18	0
1935	New York-AL	.279	120	448	54	125	14	81	35	11	1
1936	New York-AL	.362	112	423	99	153	22	107	46	16	0
1937	New York-AL	.332	140	530	87	176	29	133	73	22	3
1938	New York-AL	.313	132	454	84	142	27	115	75	22	3
1939	New York-AL	.302	128	480	98	145	24	105	77	37	5
1940	New York-AL	.247	106	372	45	92	9	54	48	32	0
1941	New York-AL	.284	109	348	35	99	7	71	45	17	2
1942	New York-AL	.295	82	268	28	79	2	37	26	11	2
1943	New York-AL	.351	85	242	29	85	4	33	41	12	2
1946	New York-AL	.261	54	134	10	35	2	10	19	12	0
Career Totals:		.313	1789	6300	930	1969	202	1209	678	289	36

It turns out Billy Hewitt was right, even if his mom—strongly—disagreed when she saw the shirt. So in the spirit of better late than never, let's remember just what Bill Dickey did.

For starters the Yankees retired his number, but you might not recall that either because the number was shared by Yogi Berra. In the powerhouse Yankees teams from his rookie year in 1928 to 1946, the guy behind the catcher's mask and teammate of Gehrig and DiMaggio was easily overlooked—yet essential.

Well, he was overlooked as much as a guy who hit .313 for a career, ended up eighth in World Series RBI and drove in more than 100 in four straight seasons can be overlooked. Truth is, Dickey, who once drove in five in a World Series game, was one of the best offensive catchers ever.

Of course, the day he drove in five in the World Series, against the

New York Giants in 1936, teammate Tony Lazzeri matched the feat, powered by a grand slam. Even on that day Dickey didn't get the spotlight.

No. 70

AL SIMMONS

A ballplayer can't be judged by stats alone. And almost every great hitter must take a solid, traditional stance in the batter's box.

Then there was Al Simmons.

"Bucketfoot Al" had a stance so askew it seemed like he was halfway to bailing out.

Until he hit.

Take 1925 through 1931. With the Philadelphia Athletics Simmons batted .373 during that slice of his career, averaging 200 hits and 111 RBI a season. Put just a couple of seasons together like that today and you could buy a small island republic.

Full Name: Aloysius Harry "Bucketfoot Al" Simmons
   (b: Aloys Szymanski)

Position: Outfield

Born: 5/22/1902, Milwaukee,
   Wisconsin

Height: 5'11"; Weight: 190

Debut: April 1924, Philadelphia Athletics

Bats: Right

Throws: Right

Batting Summary Statistics

Year	Team	AVG	G	AB	R	H	HR	RBI	BB	SO	SB
1924	Philadelphia-AL	.308	152	594	69	183	8	102	30	60	16
1925	Philadelphia-AL	.387	153	654	122	253	24	129	35	41	7
1926	Philadelphia-AL	.341	147	583	90	199	19	109	48	49	11
1927	Philadelphia-AL	.392	106	406	86	159	15	108	31	30	10

Year	Team	AVG	G	AB	R	H	HR	RBI	BB	SO	SB
1928	Philadelphia-AL	.351	119	464	78	163	15	107	31	30	1
1929	Philadelphia-AL	.365	143	581	114	212	34	157	31	38	4
1930	Philadelphia-AL	.381	138	554	152	211	36	165	39	34	9
1931	Philadelphia-AL	.390	128	513	105	200	22	128	47	45	3
1932	Philadelphia-AL	.322	154	670	144	216	35	151	47	76	4
1933	Chicago-AL	.331	146	605	85	200	14	119	39	49	5
1934	Chicago-AL	.344	138	558	102	192	18	104	53	58	3
1935	Chicago-AL	.267	128	525	68	140	16	79	33	43	4
1936	Detroit-AL	.327	143	568	96	186	13	112	49	35	6
1937	Washington-AL	.279	103	419	60	117	8	84	27	35	3
1938	Washington-AL	.302	125	470	79	142	21	95	38	40	2
1939	Boston-NL	.282	93	330	39	93	7	43	22	40	0
1939	Cincinnati-NL	.143	9	21	0	3	0	1	2	3	0
1939	NL Totals	.274	102	351	39	96	7	44	24	43	0
1940	Philadelphia-AL	.309	37	81	7	25	1	19	4	8	0
1941	Philadelphia-AL	.125	9	24	1	3	0	1	1	2	0
1943	Boston-AL	.203	40	133	9	27	1	12	8	21	0
1944	Philadelphia-AL	.500	4	6	1	3	0	2	0	0	0
Career Totals:		.334	2215	8759	1507	2927	307	1827	615	737	88

But Simmons had a flaw. He couldn't figure out whether to hit for power or for average. So he did it the old fashioned way: he did both. It was an amazing and lucrative career, but you have to feel sorry for the guy in 1927. He batted .392—and was second in the league. Still, Simmons finished his 20 seasons as one of the best ever, with a .334 average, 73 hits short of 3,000, and 307 home runs.

The outfielder born Aloys Szymanski to Polish immigrants was also a key to the Philadelphia A's led by Jimmie Foxx and a cast of some of the game's best ever. They won the 1929 and 1930 World Series then lost the following year. Simmons hit .300, .364 and .333, with two homers in each series. He played in the postseason again, losing with Cincinnati in the 1939 series, but ended his career fourth in World Series slugging percentage at .658.

His motivation to do all this was simple as his numbers are staggering: "You gotta hate those pitchers," he said, according to *Baseball: An Illustrated History* by Geoffrey C. Ward and Ken Burns. "They're trying to take the bread and butter right out of your mouth."

Bucketfoot couldn't have missed many meals.

No. 71

DENNIS ECKERSLEY

What do you call a pitcher with 361 games started, 100 complete games, a no-hitter, a 20-win season, nine seasons with double-digit wins and nearly 200 victories overall?

Easy: the best reliever of all time.

Dennis Eckersley, with the long black hair and thick mustache, may have looked more in place in the '70s rock band the Eagles than in the majors, but he belonged on the mound, in the late innings when the game was on the line.

Eckersley got his no-hitter with the Cleveland Indians on May 30, 1977, a 1–0 win over the California Angels. He won 20 games the next season for the Boston Red Sox. In nine of his first 12 seasons, beginning in 1975, he registered double-digit wins, with no less than 25 starts in a full season.

In 1987 the Oakland A's converted the 32-year-old Eckersley to a reliever. During the A's three-pennant run from 1988 to 1990, which included the 1989 World Series title, Eckersley registered 45, 33, and 48 saves. In 1992 he clocked out with 51 saves and a 7–1 record.

Despite his dominance, Eckersley may be best remembered for giving up gimpy Kirk Gibson's inspirational home run that won Game One of the 1988 World Series for the Los Angeles Dodgers. But more of note should be his 353 career saves that put him ahead of Rollie Fingers (and behind Lee Smith and Jeff Reardon). And just consider how many more he would have had if he hadn't "wasted" all those years as a starter.

No. 72

PAUL WANER

One look at an old black-and-white photo of Paul Waner and you'd think he was huge. Feet solidly planted, slightly wider than his broad

Full Name: Paul Glee "Big Poison" Waner

Position: OF, 1B   Debut: April 1926, Pittsburgh Pirates

Born: 4/16/1903,   Bats: Left
Harrah, Oklahoma

Height: 5'8.5"; Weight: 153   Throws: Left

BATTING SUMMARY STATISTICS

Year	Team	AVG	G	AB	R	H	HR	RBI	BB	SO	SB
1926	Pittsburgh-NL	.336	144	536	101	180	8	79	66	19	11
1927	Pittsburgh-NL	.380	155	623	114	237	9	131	60	14	5
1928	Pittsburgh-NL	.370	152	602	142	223	6	86	77	16	6
1929	Pittsburgh-NL	.336	151	596	131	200	15	100	89	24	15
1930	Pittsburgh-NL	.368	145	589	117	217	8	77	57	18	18
1931	Pittsburgh-NL	.322	150	559	88	180	6	70	73	21	6
1932	Pittsburgh-NL	.341	154	630	107	215	8	82	56	24	13
1933	Pittsburgh-NL	.309	154	618	101	191	7	70	60	20	3
1934	Pittsburgh-NL	.362	146	599	122	217	14	90	68	24	8
1935	Pittsburgh-NL	.321	139	549	98	176	11	78	61	22	2
1936	Pittsburgh-NL	.373	148	585	107	218	5	94	74	29	7
1937	Pittsburgh-NL	.354	154	619	94	219	2	74	63	34	4
1938	Pittsburgh-NL	.280	148	625	77	175	6	69	47	28	2
1939	Pittsburgh-NL	.328	125	461	62	151	3	45	35	18	0
1940	Pittsburgh-NL	.290	89	238	32	69	1	32	23	14	0
1941	Brooklyn-NL	.171	11	35	5	6	0	4	8	0	0
1941	Boston-NL	.279	95	294	40	82	2	46	47	14	1
1941	NL Totals	.267	106	329	45	88	2	50	55	14	1
1942	Boston-NL	.258	114	333	43	86	1	39	62	20	2
1943	Brooklyn-NL	.311	82	225	29	70	1	26	35	9	0
1944	Brooklyn-NL	.287	83	136	16	39	0	16	27	7	0
1944	New York-AL	.143	9	7	1	1	0	1	2	1	1
1945	New York-AL	-	1	0	0	0	0	0	1	0	0
Career Totals:		.333	2549	9459	1627	3152	113	1309	1091	376	104

shoulders. Narrow, steely eyes. Set jaw. It's the way comic book artists are taught to draw superheroes.

But "Big Poison" was just 5-foot, 8-inches tall, about 150 pounds—until he had a bat in his hand. Then he was bigger than life.

He hit over .350 six years, nailing .380 in 1927 and .370 the next. He had 200 or more hits in eight amazing seasons, a National League record.

He was also smart. While that Ruth guy in the American League was getting all that attention for hitting a lot of home runs while striking out and popping out a lot more, Waner looked deeper into the game.

As a top outfielder, he knew the kind of hit that gave fielders the most trouble. The foul lines, he figured, shouldn't be seen as boundaries, but paths. If you pulled the ball too hard or waited on the pitch too long, it would simply go foul. If you hit it right, you had extra bases.

Brilliant, yet simple. Rule the rules. The result included 603 doubles and 190 triples among his 3,152 hits from 1926 to 1945. He mustered a .333 lifetime average despite hanging on for too many years and hanging out in too many bars.

Big Poison knew his poison. Many say he lost some great years, and some batting titles, because he was too hung over.

Could be. His benders were the stuff of legend, the stories that add the slap-on-the-back laughs that add to baseball's rich tradition. Big Poison is remembered as a player who had too many too often.

But he's also remembered as a guy who could have been among the handful of the game's greatest. Only he knew which memory was comforting and which one was haunting.

No. 73

DUKE SNIDER

Duke Snider wasn't the best center fielder ever. He wasn't even the third-best center fielder among the legends who starred there in New York City during the 1940s and '50s. But while Willie Mays, Joe DiMaggio and Mickey Mantle are all among the handful of all-time greats and belong to immortality, the Silver Fox belonged to something much more tangible, much more real. Edwin Donald Snider belonged to Brooklyn. He was the Duke of Flatbush.

A left-handed power hitter and extremely polished fielder, Snider was the muscle of a Brooklyn Dodger team that won five National League

Full Name: Edwin Donald "The Silver Fox" Snider

Position: Outfield   Debut: April 1947, Brooklyn Dodgers

Born: 9/19/1926, Los Angeles,   Bats: Left
California

Height: 6'; Weight: 190   Throws: Right

BATTING SUMMARY STATISTICS

Year	Team	AVG	G	AB	R	H	HR	RBI	BB	SO	SB
1947	Brooklyn-NL	.241	40	83	6	20	0	5	3	24	2
1948	Brooklyn-NL	.244	53	160	22	39	5	21	12	27	4
1949	Brooklyn-NL	.292	146	552	100	161	23	92	56	92	12
1950	Brooklyn-NL	.321	152	620	109	199	31	107	58	79	16
1951	Brooklyn-NL	.277	150	606	96	168	29	101	62	97	14
1952	Brooklyn-NL	.303	144	534	80	162	21	92	55	77	7
1953	Brooklyn-NL	.336	153	590	132	198	42	126	82	90	16
1954	Brooklyn-NL	.341	149	584	120	199	40	130	84	96	6
1955	Brooklyn-NL	.309	148	538	126	166	42	136	104	87	9
1956	Brooklyn-NL	.292	151	542	112	158	43	101	99	101	3
1957	Brooklyn-NL	.274	139	508	91	139	40	92	77	104	3
1958	Los Angeles-NL	.312	106	327	45	102	15	58	32	49	2
1959	Los Angeles-NL	.308	126	370	59	114	23	88	58	71	1
1960	Los Angeles-NL	.243	101	235	38	57	14	36	46	54	1
1961	Los Angeles-NL	.296	85	233	35	69	16	56	29	43	1
1962	Los Angeles-NL	.278	80	158	28	44	5	30	36	32	2
1963	New York-NL	.243	129	354	44	86	14	45	56	74	0
1964	San Francisco-NL	.210	91	167	16	35	4	17	22	40	0
Career Totals:		.295	2143	7161	1259	2116	407	1333	971	1237	99

pennants between 1949 and 1956, including the glorious 1955 season that saw the Bums finally dethrone the New York Yankees in the World Series. Even after the heart was ripped out of Brooklyn when the Dodgers headed west, Snider remained the core of the team for several years, leading Los Angeles to the 1959 World Series crown.

From 1949 to 1957 Snider hit no fewer than 21 home runs in a season, and in his last five years in Ebbets Field he hit at least 40 in each campaign. He is among the all-time leaders in World Series home runs and RBI.

"Brooklyn was a lovely place to hit," Snider said in a *New York Times* story. "When they tore down Ebbets Field, they tore down a little piece of me."

Snider, a lifetime .295 hitter, hit 407 home runs in his career; appropriately, his milestone 400th came as a member of the Brooklyn Dodgers' stepchild, the New York Mets. Inappropriately, he ended his career in San Francisco, in the uniform of the hated Giants. Like the Dodgers leaving Brooklyn, it just wasn't right.

No. 74
Cool Papa Bell

How fast was Cool Papa Bell? Let's go to the expert, Satchel Paige.

"One day I was pitchin' to Cool, he drilled one right through my legs and was hit in the back by his own ground ball when he slid into second."

What, not good enough? Try this one:

"That man was so fast," Satchel said, "he could turn out the light and jump in bed before the room got dark."

There are more stories, dozens of 'em, of the outfielder's superhuman speed. They are probably just as bogus as Satchel's are and probably just as close to truth as they are as far from fact. So, OK, you are in no mood for hyperbole. Try this:

James Thomas "Cool Papa" Bell was timed circling the bases in 12 seconds. The man was fast, give him that.

The switch-hitter who threw left played a shallow center field, in part to mask a so-so arm, in part because he could run down anything in the park. He had no power but sported, according to one estimate, a .341 lifetime average in a career that spanned from 1922 to 1946 for the St. Louis Stars, Detroit Wolves, Kansas City Monarchs, Chicago American Giants, Pittsburgh Crawfords, Homestead Grays and a stint in the Mexican League.

But as we stressed, the Negro League stats are spotty at best and don't represent total accomplishments. "I remember one game I got five hits and stole five bases, but none of it was written down because they forgot to bring the scorebook to the game that day," Bell once said.

Do you believe that story? If not, there are plenty more about Cool Papa Bell.

No. 75

HARMON KILLEBREW

Quick: Who hit the most home runs in the 1960s?
Hank Aaron, of course. Wrong.
Willie Mays? Nope.
Orlando Cepeda? Willie McCovey? Mickey Mantle? Willie Stargell?
C'mon, will you look at the title of the chapter? Geez.

That's right. It was Harmon Killebrew, who pounded 393 round-trippers in the 1960s, predominantly for the Minnesota Twins. Over his 22-year career with the Washington Senators and their later incarnation as the Twins (he ended his career with a season with the Kansas City Royals), "Killer" hit 573 home runs—without ever bunting for a base hit or to sacrifice. It was just not his way.

The Washington Senator was first discovered by an Idaho senator who tipped off Nats owner Clark Griffith. Washington made him a bonus baby—a whopping (and it was) $30,000.

Full Name: Harmon Clayton "Killer" Killebrew
Position: 3B, 1B, OF   Debut: June 1954, Washington Senators
Born: 6/29/1936, Payette, Idaho   Bats: Right
Height: 5'11"; Weight: 213   Throws: Right

BATTING SUMMARY STATISTICS

Year	Team	AVG	G	AB	R	H	HR	RBI	BB	SO	SB
1954	Washington-AL	.308	9	13	1	4	0	3	2	3	0
1955	Washington-AL	.200	38	80	12	16	4	7	9	31	0
1956	Washington-AL	.222	44	99	10	22	5	13	10	39	0
1957	Washington-AL	.290	9	31	4	9	2	5	2	8	0
1958	Washington-AL	.194	13	31	2	6	0	2	0	12	0
1959	Washington-AL	.242	153	546	98	132	42	105	90	116	3
1960	Washington-AL	.276	124	442	84	122	31	80	71	106	1
1961	Minnesota-AL	.288	150	541	94	156	46	122	107	109	1
1962	Minnesota-AL	.243	155	552	85	134	48	126	106	142	1
1963	Minnesota-AL	.258	142	515	88	133	45	96	72	105	0

Year	Team	AVG	G	AB	R	H	HR	RBI	BB	SO	SB
1964	Minnesota-AL	.270	158	577	95	156	49	111	93	135	0
1965	Minnesota-AL	.269	113	401	78	108	25	75	72	69	0
1966	Minnesota-AL	.281	162	569	89	160	39	110	103	98	0
1967	Minnesota-AL	.269	163	547	105	147	44	113	131	111	1
1968	Minnesota-AL	.210	100	295	40	62	17	40	70	70	0
1969	Minnesota-AL	.276	162	555	106	153	49	140	145	84	8
1970	Minnesota-AL	.271	157	527	96	143	41	113	128	84	0
1971	Minnesota-AL	.254	147	500	61	127	28	119	114	96	3
1972	Minnesota-AL	.231	139	433	53	100	26	74	94	91	0
1973	Minnesota-AL	.242	69	248	29	60	5	32	41	59	0
1974	Minnesota-AL	.222	122	333	28	74	13	54	45	61	0
1975	Kansas City-AL	.199	106	312	25	62	14	44	54	70	1
Career Totals:		.256	2435	8147	1283	2086	573	1584	1559	1699	19

Baseball has had some dumb rules over the years, like best of nine World Series, all night World Series games (sorry kids on the East Coast), no pepper games signs, artificial turf and, we can't emphasize this enough, the designated hitter. Then there was the bonus baby clause.

Under the guidelines in the 1950s, a player given a bonus was required to stay with the parent club two seasons rather than go down to the minors for some experience. So—surprise—a lot of these guys tanked early and never recovered. Harmon Killebrew could have been one of them, but he was sent down to the minors in his third season, not to emerge as a regular major leaguer until four years later.

Then the second-third-first baseman and outfielder started hitting home runs, including 42 as a "rookie" to lead the American League in 1959. In the 1960s Killebrew led the league in homers another five times, six times smacking 40 or more home runs in a season. So, ready: Who hit the most home runs in the 1960s?

Killer question, ain't it?

No.76

MARTIN DIHIGO

Martin Dihigo wasn't really a hitter, but he was a feared batter. Dihigo wasn't what you call a pitcher, either, but he was among the most stingy on the mound. And he wasn't considered a glove man, but you could put him anywhere on the diamond.

What Martin Dihigo was was a baseball player, maybe the most versatile man ever to play the game.

"The greatest player I ever saw was a black man," Johnny Mize once said. "He's in the Hall of Fame, although not a lot of people have heard of him. His name is Martin Dihigo."

Baseball was not always the hyperspecialized game it often resembles today. One example: shortstop Bert Campaneris played all nine positions in a September 1965 game for the Kansas City Athletics. And once in a while position players like Ted Williams have been called on to pitch an inning or two.

Then there's the truly multidimensional. Pete Rose played five positions, all adequately, over the course of his Hall of…, er, illustrious career. Three major leaguers won MVP awards at two different positions. And, of course, Babe Ruth was a dominating pitcher before the Yankees made the perilous decision to move him full-time to right field and created a legend.

That said, no one matched the virtuosity of Martin Dihigo, who not only starred at every position save catcher, but in three different leagues— Negro, Mexican and Cuban—over three different decades.

Dihigo played across the diamond in both the infield and outfield in a career that spanned from 1923 to 1945 and for teams that included the Cuban Stars (East), Homestead Grays, Hilldale, Darby Daisies and New York Cubans (he also managed in his career). A lanky Cuban (he was possibly 6-foot-4, although some sources list him at 6-foot-3 and even 6-foot-1, with a weight varying from 190 to 225 pounds), the right-hander was the rarest of talents, a "six-tool" player who could run, field, throw, hit, hit for power—and pitch.

Some resources list Dihigo's position as "utility," but the term has no resemblance to contemporary definition for a .220 infielder hanging onto a job by scraping by at a few positions. He led the Eastern Colored

League in home runs in 1926 and 1927 (tying the second year). He finished second in homers in the American Negro League in 1929 (19), while compiling a .386 average. But his most startling season would not come until 1938, while playing in the Mexican League.

That year he led the league with an 18–2 mound record and a microscopic 0.90 ERA.

Dihigo also led the league in hitting with a .387 average.

Pitching record, ERA and batting average: talk about an unorthodox Triple Crown.

Dihigo is a member of baseball halls of fame in three countries—Mexico, Cuba and the United States. He was inducted into Cooperstown in 1977, six years after he died.

For a man who could play any position, for any team, in any country, one Hall of Fame simply would have not been enough.

No. 77

LOU BROCK

Sometimes you can be absolutely certain something awful is going to happen and be just as absolutely certain you can do nothing about it: a coffee cup falls in your lap, a TV show is produced by Aaron Spelling, the doctor says his next move may give you some "discomfort." For pitchers, it was Lou Brock standing on first base.

It's enough to make a fan question the IQ of pitchers and catchers: "Hey! It's Lou Brock! You think he might try to steal?" But of course knowing he was going to steal just made it worse when he did. And he did it at a level unmatched in his day.

"If you aim to steal 30 to 40 bases a year, you do it by surprising the other side," Brock told reporters. "But if your goal is 50 to 100 bases, the element of surprise doesn't matter. You go even though they know you're going to go. Then each steal becomes a contest, matching your skills against theirs."

Full Name: Louis Clark Brock

Position: Outfield   Debut: September 1961, Chicago Cubs

Born: 6/18/1939, El Dorado, Arkansas Bats: Left

Height: 5'11.5"; Weight: 170   Throws: Left

BATTING SUMMARY STATISTICS

Year	Team	AVG	G	AB	R	H	HR	RBI	BB	SO	SB
1961	Chicago-NL	.091	4	11	1	1	0	0	1	3	0
1962	Chicago-NL	.263	123	434	73	114	9	35	35	96	16
1963	Chicago-NL	.258	148	547	79	141	9	37	31	122	24
1964	Chicago-NL	.251	52	215	30	54	2	14	13	40	10
1964	St. Louis-NL	.348	103	419	81	146	12	44	27	87	33
1964	NL Totals	.315	155	634	111	200	14	58	40	127	43
1965	St. Louis-NL	.288	155	631	107	182	16	69	45	116	63
1966	St. Louis-NL	.285	156	643	94	183	15	46	31	134	74
1967	St. Louis-NL	.299	159	689	113	206	21	76	24	109	52
1968	St. Louis-NL	.279	159	660	92	184	6	51	46	124	62
1969	St. Louis-NL	.298	157	655	97	195	12	47	50	115	53
1970	St. Louis-NL	.304	155	664	114	202	13	57	60	99	51
1971	St. Louis-NL	.313	157	640	126	200	7	61	76	107	64
1972	St. Louis-NL	.311	153	621	81	193	3	42	47	93	63
1973	St. Louis-NL	.297	160	650	110	193	7	63	71	112	70
1974	St. Louis-NL	.306	153	635	105	194	3	48	61	88	118
1975	St. Louis-NL	.309	136	528	78	163	3	47	38	64	56
1976	St. Louis-NL	.301	133	498	73	150	4	67	35	75	56
1977	St. Louis-NL	.272	141	489	69	133	2	46	30	74	35
1978	St. Louis-NL	.221	92	298	31	66	0	12	17	29	17
1979	St. Louis-NL	.304	120	405	56	123	5	38	23	43	21
Career Totals:		.293	2616	10332	1610	3023	149	900	761	1730	938

Most pitchers and catchers were clearly overmatched. Brock led the National League in steals eight times. His rap sheet included 118 in 1974, and he finished with 938. But in his last of 19 seasons, 1979, his totals really fell off. He only stole 21 bases. He was also 40 years old.

But to steal you have to get on base. And Brock did that often, perhaps surprisingly so. He's in the 3,000-hit club and he hit over .300 in eight seasons (including his last, at .304). In 1968 he led the NL in doubles, triples and steals—the first in the senior circuit to do that since Honus Wagner. And speaking of smashing records of the all-time greats, Brock's career-steals mark eclipsed the one held tightly by Ty Cobb.

Brock's seven stolen bases in a World Series was a record in 1967. So he did it again in 1968 to capture the career World Series mark.

And all this for a guy who was once figured no better than Doug Clemens. Who? Clemens is one of three Cardinals traded in 1964 for Brock, Jack Spring and Paul Toth of the Chicago Cubs. Clemens went on to play a season and a half in Chicago, then finished his .229 career in Philadelphia. The others in the trade? Pitcher Ernie Broglio, who had a 77–74 career with a 3.94 ERA; and Bobby Shantz, who went 119–99 in a solid career with a 3.38 ERA, but not in 1964. He went 2–5 and then went home for good.

Wouldn't you love to have been in the school cafeteria at lunch trading time, holding a bag of carrot sticks, and have one of these front-office boys from Chicago sit next to you?

Brock, shall we say, turned out to be a bargain—as well as a pitcher's cold-sweat nightmare.

So next time that hot coffee is free-falling toward your lap as your mind flashes glimpses of painful burns and bandages where you don't want them, think of those pitchers watching Brock on first. And consider yourself lucky.

No. 78

MORDECAI "THREE FINGER" BROWN

There's this tremendous temptation by some of us whose thoughts often stray far from reality to think of somehow going up to Mordecai Centennial "Three Finger" Brown and saying he never really needed one of the most colorful nicknames in baseball. To paraphrase the weepy line in the Tom Cruise movie *Jerry Maguire*, "You had me at Mordecai."

But it's true that the index-finger-challenged pitcher from 1904 to 1916 was and is first remembered for the coolest of nicknames.

Full Name: Mordecai Peter Centennial "Three Finger" Brown

Position: Pitcher   Debut: April 1903, St. Louis Cardinals

Born: 10/19/1876, Nyesville,   Bats: Both
Indiana

Height: 5'10"; Weight: 175   Throws: Right

PITCHING SUMMARY STATISTICS

Year	Team	W	L	PCT	ERA	G	SV	IP	BB	SO
1903	St. Louis-NL	9	13	.409	2.60	26	0	201.0	59	83
1904	Chicago-NL	15	10	.600	1.86	26	1	212.1	50	81
1905	Chicago-NL	18	12	.600	2.17	30	0	249.0	44	89
1906	Chicago-NL	26	6	.813	1.04	36	3	277.1	61	144
1907	Chicago-NL	20	6	.769	1.39	34	3	233.0	40	107
1908	Chicago-NL	29	9	.763	1.47	44	5	312.1	49	123
1909	Chicago-NL	27	9	.750	1.31	50	7	342.2	53	172
1910	Chicago-NL	25	14	.641	1.86	46	7	295.1	64	143
1911	Chicago-NL	21	11	.656	2.80	53	13	270.0	55	129
1912	Chicago-NL	5	6	.455	2.64	15	0	88.2	20	34
1913	Cincinnati-NL	11	12	.478	2.91	39	6	173.1	44	41
1914	St. Louis-FL	12	6	.667	3.29	26	0	175.0	43	81
1914	Brooklyn-FL	2	5	.286	4.21	9	0	57.2	18	32
1914	FL Totals	14	11	.560	3.52	35	0	232.2	61	113
1915	Chicago-FL	17	8	.680	2.09	35	4	236.1	64	95
1916	Chicago-NL	2	3	.400	3.91	12	0	48.1	9	21
Career Totals:		239	130	.648	2.06	481	49	3172.1	673	1375

As an Indiana farm boy, Brown lost the index finger on his throwing hand to a corn-mulcher. Soon after, he mangled two more fingers chasing a runaway hog. They were the best breaks Brown ever had.

His delivery from that hand that almost made him a lefty confounded physics and batters. He remains one of the best of all time, the top starter on a Chicago Cubs team in 1906 in which the relative weakness was called batting. It was kind of a Bizarro BoSox, where the worst starter had an ERA of 2.21.

But with an infield of Tinkers, Evers and Chance and a pitching staff whose ERAs added together were lower than some stars today, the Cubs managed to beat just about everybody in the National League.

The team ERA was 1.75, No. 2 in history after the staff's 1907 mark. In that pennant-winning '06 season, the Cubs pitched 32 shutouts and won 55 of their last 65 games to win the flag by 20 games over New York. The World Series, however, went to the crosstown White Sox.

Brown's contribution was monumental, putting him on the Cubs' all-time team. In his career he was 239–131 (with 57 shutouts), posted the third-best lifetime ERA of all time at 2.06 (1.04 in 1906), won five World Series games with a 2.81 ERA, and won 20 or more games a season from 1906 to 1911 (56–18 in 1908–9).

Ty Cobb once praised Christy Mathewson's famous fadeaway pitch but then added that it was nothing like Three Finger's curve.

No. 79

DIZZY DEAN

Dizzy Dean was better than he was.

If that sounds like a Dizzy Dean-ism, one of a library full of malaprops and language butchering attributed to the man as a broadcaster, it isn't. It's the truth.

Dean the broadcaster spent decades delivering a folksy stand-up and shrewdly made $100,000 a year making America laugh at how dumb he was. He mixed the play-by-play with down-home philosophy in often intentionally busted English, without apology: "Let the teachers teach English, and I will teach baseball. There is a lot of people in the United States who say 'isn't,' and they ain't eating."

He'll go down as one of the most colorful, most remembered and most popular sports broadcasters of all time. But he was better than that.

Consider October 9, 1934, the seventh game of the World Series. Dizzy had already pitched two games, winning the first game against the Detroit Tigers. For the seventh game, the St. Louis Cardinal got the call, as he did so often, a workhorse with the image of a jackass.

The week before he had pitched the Cardinals to three wins in the thick of a pennant race. His last World Series appearance had been 48 hours before, a series in which he'd already hurled two complete games and

Full Name: Jay Hanna "Dizzy" Dean

Position: Pitcher

Debut: September 1930,
St. Louis Cardinals

Born: 1/16/1910, Lucas, Arkansas

Bats: Right

Height: 6'2"; Weight: 182

Throws: Right

PITCHING SUMMARY STATISTICS

Year	Team	W	L	PCT	ERA	G	SV	IP	BB	SO
1930	St. Louis-NL	1	0	1.000	1.00	1	0	9.0	3	5
1932	St. Louis-NL	18	15	.545	3.30	46	2	286.0	102	191
1933	St. Louis-NL	20	18	.526	3.04	48	4	293.0	64	199
1934	St. Louis-NL	30	7	.811	2.66	50	7	311.2	75	195
1935	St. Louis-NL	28	12	.700	3.04	50	5	325.1	77	190
1936	St. Louis-NL	24	13	.649	3.17	51	11	315.0	53	195
1937	St. Louis-NL	13	10	.565	2.69	27	1	197.1	33	120
1938	Chicago-NL	7	1	.875	1.81	13	0	74.2	8	22
1939	Chicago-NL	6	4	.600	3.36	19	0	96.1	17	27
1940	Chicago-NL	3	3	.500	5.17	10	0	54.0	20	18
1941	Chicago-NL	0	0	-	18.00	1	0	1.0	0	1
1947	St. Louis-AL	0	0	-	0.00	1	0	4.0	1	0
Career Totals:		150	83	.644	3.02	317	30	1967.1	453	1163

pinch-run in another (he'd been hit in the head while running and joked at the hospital that the X-rays of his head found nothing).

"Apparently Dizzy was bent on making this a shutout," the *New York Times* reported. "Whenever the Tigers threatened, Dizzy merely turned on the heat and poured his blazing fastball and sharp-breaking curve right down the middle.... It was superhuman."

He'd finish that series with a championship, two wins and a loss, 17 strikeouts, an ERA of 1.73 and a batting average of .250 with two doubles, three runs and an RBI.

For a man who always seemed to be just as good as he had to be— "Heck, if anybody told me I was settin' a record I'd of got me some more strikeouts," he said after fanning 17 in a 1933 game—he seemed tested that October. He came through.

It's hard to believe that even Dizzy Dean, the broadcaster, could describe the pitcher, who bore down while having fun, who was fiercely competitive while disarming, who was smart enough to sometimes play dumb.

From 1933 to 1936 he had 102 wins. He'd finish his 12-year career

150–83, with a 3.03 ERA. He led National League pitching categories 20 times in everything from wins (30–7 in 1934) to shutouts, strikeouts, complete games, even saves once.

The man born in 1911 in Lucas, Ark., was a man ahead of his times in so many ways. But braver than his boasts was the praise he showered on talent, regardless of color, something that undoubtedly made official baseball see red. He called Satchel Paige the best he'd seen. "If Satch and I were pitching on the same team we'd cinch the pennant by July 4 and go fishing until World Series time," he said.

Check the record books. Dizzy Dean was very, very good. But he was better than he was.

No. 80

ROD CAREW

"Just try to make contact with the ball."

That's the basic tenant of hitting, one drilled into players from backyards to Camden Yard. But it's not as easy as that. Ask Michael Jordan.

Rod Carew was the best man to make contact with the ball in his time, 1967–85. Even Ted Williams thought so. The Panama-born infielder for the Minnesota Twins and California Angels hit over .300 in 10 seasons, totaled more than 3,000 hits and left the game with a .328 career batting average and 18 All-Star Game appearances. In addition, in 1969 he tied Pete Reiser's major league record by stealing home seven times.

He led the American League in batting average seven times, but 1977 was his show stopper. He hit .388, had the league's second-best slugging average at .577 (behind AL leader Jim Rice in Boston and ahead of Reggie Jackson in New York), had 239 hits (14th best in history when he retired), and led the league in runs and triples.

All this while playing on a team that put few runners on base ahead of him that season. The Twins finished fourth in the AL West.

Over 19 years Carew just made contact—extremely often. At age 40 he knew it was time to retire. He'd only hit .280.

Full Name: Rodney Cline Carew

Position: 2B, 1B, DH

Born: 10/1/1945, Gatun, C.Z.

Height: 6'; Weight: 182

Debut: April 1967, Minnesota Twins

Bats: Left

Throws: Right

BATTING SUMMARY STATISTICS

Year	Team	AVG	G	AB	R	H	HR	RBI	BB	SO	SB
1967	Minnesota-AL	.292	137	514	66	150	8	51	37	91	5
1968	Minnesota-AL	.273	127	461	46	126	1	42	26	71	12
1969	Minnesota-AL	.332	123	458	79	152	8	56	37	72	19
1970	Minnesota-AL	.366	51	191	27	70	4	28	11	28	4
1971	Minnesota-AL	.307	147	577	88	177	2	48	45	81	6
1972	Minnesota-AL	.318	142	535	61	170	0	51	43	60	12
1973	Minnesota-AL	.350	149	580	98	203	6	62	62	55	41
1974	Minnesota-AL	.364	153	599	86	218	3	55	74	49	38
1975	Minnesota-AL	.359	143	535	89	192	14	80	64	40	35
1976	Minnesota-AL	.331	156	605	97	200	9	90	67	52	49
1977	Minnesota-AL	.388	155	616	128	239	14	100	69	55	23
1978	Minnesota-AL	.333	152	564	85	188	5	70	78	62	27
1979	California-AL	.318	110	409	78	130	3	44	73	46	18
1980	California-AL	.331	144	540	74	179	3	59	59	38	23
1981	California-AL	.305	93	364	57	111	2	21	45	45	16
1982	California-AL	.319	138	523	88	167	3	44	67	49	10
1983	California-AL	.339	129	472	66	160	2	44	57	48	6
1984	California-AL	.295	93	329	42	97	3	31	40	39	4
1985	California-AL	.280	127	443	69	124	2	39	64	47	5
Career Totals:		.328	2469	9315	1424	3053	92	1015	1018	1028	353

No. 81

BUCK LEONARD

Buck Leonard was Lou Gehrig to Josh Gibson's Babe Ruth. Together they led the Homestead Grays to nine consecutive Negro National League titles, from 1937 to 1945. Catcher Gibson provided the monstrous home runs, while first baseman Leonard hit line drives off and over the wall from the left side of the plate.

"We went to their games," Leonard said of Ruth and Gehrig in a 1994 interview quoted by the Associated Press. "We watched those boys. We imitated them. We wanted to be just like them."

But Leonard and Gibson weren't. They were stars to be sure, among the best in the game, but Lou and the Babe did not play more than 200 games in a season (exhibitions included) for $80 a month. And the Yankees certainly didn't spend the off-season working on the railroad, shining shoes, or scrambling elsewhere for a few bucks like Leonard did.

Walter Fenner Leonard—who was talked to by the Washington Senators about breaking the color barrier several years before Jackie Robinson, but was too old to break into the majors by the time black players were let in—still left his mark on big leaguers.

"Buck Leonard hit a home run so far off Bob Feller that it cleared the fence, the bleachers, a row of houses, and hit a big old water tower out there," Negro Leaguer Ted "Double Duty" Radcliffe said in an Associated Press story in 1997, after Leonard died at age 90. "It rained in that town for five weeks."

Leonard played in the Negro Leagues through the 1950 season. He then played five more years in Mexico, retiring at the age of 48. Counting semipro ball, he spent more than three decades playing the game.

According to one source, Leonard hit .341 over a 17-year Negro National League career; another source has it at .346, while the Hall of Fame and *The Baseball Encyclopedia* list Leonard as hitting .324.

We have had to put disclaimers on Negro League players' stats throughout this book, and every time the authors get angrier and angrier. The social injustice, of course, is readily apparent. But the ban was also a grand larceny against the game and its fans.

The Negro Leaguers in here need not be "defended" for their inclusion, just as their exclusion was indefensible. Remember that next time you see a big old dented water tower.

No. 82

ROLLIE FINGERS

He looked like a silent-film villain dressed by a color-blind wardrobe man, his handlebar mustache waxed and perfect, his yellow/green/white Oakland A's uniform the antithesis to the brush-cut conservatism that was much of baseball in the early 1970s. Rollie Fingers was a failed starter— he said nerves got to him—but he was perfect for the role he glamorized, the closer.

Full Name: Roland Glen Fingers

Position: Pitcher

Born: 8/25/1946, Steubenville, Ohio

Height: 6'4"; Weight: 195

Debut: September 1968, Oakland Athletics

Bats: Right

Throws: Right

PITCHING SUMMARY STATISTICS

Year	Team	W	L	PCT	ERA	G	SV	IP	BB	SO
1968	Oakland-AL	0	0	-	27.00	1	0	1.1	1	0
1969	Oakland-AL	6	7	.462	3.71	60	12	119.0	41	61
1970	Oakland-AL	7	9	.438	3.65	45	2	148.0	48	79
1971	Oakland-AL	4	6	.400	2.99	48	17	129.1	30	98
1972	Oakland-AL	11	9	.550	2.51	65	21	111.1	32	113
1973	Oakland-AL	7	8	.467	1.92	62	22	126.2	39	110
1974	Oakland-AL	9	5	.643	2.65	76	18	119.0	29	95
1975	Oakland-AL	10	6	.625	2.98	75	24	126.2	33	115
1976	Oakland-AL	13	11	.542	2.47	70	20	134.2	40	113
1977	San Diego-NL	8	9	.471	2.99	78	35	132.1	36	113
1978	San Diego-NL	6	13	.316	2.52	67	37	107.1	29	72
1979	San Diego-NL	9	9	.500	4.52	54	13	83.2	37	65
1980	San Diego-NL	11	9	.550	2.80	66	23	103.0	32	69
1981	Milwaukee-AL	6	3	.667	1.04	47	28	78.0	13	61
1982	Milwaukee-AL	5	6	.455	2.60	50	29	79.2	20	71
1984	Milwaukee-AL	1	2	.333	1.96	33	23	46.0	13	40
1985	Milwaukee-AL	1	6	.143	5.04	47	17	55.1	19	24
Career Totals:		114	118	.491	2.90	944	341	1701.1	492	1299

There were other high-profile relievers before Fingers—it was said when Whitey Ford even gave a speech in 1961, Luis Arroyo would have to come on to finish—but it was Rollie more than anyone who made the job once reserved for secondary pitchers of primary prominence. In the 1972 World Series, the first of three straight won by the A's, Fingers saved games Two and Seven and won Game Four, appearing in six of the seven games. In 1974 he won Game One, saved by Jim "Catfish" Hunter, and saved Game Three—won by Hunter—and Game Four, nabbing the MVP award.

In the strike-shortened 1981 season, Fingers, pitching for the Milwaukee Brewers, won the Cy Young Award and MVP, posting 28 saves and a 1.04 ERA. His 341 career saves set the standard that has since been broken. But it is tough to come up with a supposed "bad guy" who was as good as Rollie Fingers.

No. 83

BILL TERRY

Everything you need to know about Bill Terry is in some staggering statistic. The last National Leaguer to hit .400 had a career batting average of .341, hit .372 in 1929, .401 in 1930, and over .320 seven more years. He also had more than 200 hits and more than 100 RBI in each of six seasons.

But all you need to love Bill Terry is one story.

Like most anyone other than Moses, Terry hated his boss. Manager John McGraw of the New York Giants was many things, but the description "great manager" is about all that can be printed in most books. Left to the imagination are the other, more colorful phrases for the man who could be cruel to players, using quick and repeated references to ethnic backgrounds, physical shortcomings, and mothers.

Bill Terry had enough. So for two years this superstar refused to talk to the manager who frequently referred to the great Frankie Frisch as "Krauthead" during the rise of Hitler's Germany. Terry didn't take a swing at McGraw, he didn't whine to the owner or press, he didn't demand to be traded.

Instead, Terry stayed, and never responded to the manager's taunts.

For McGraw, who loved to get a rise out of players he berated, the silent treatment must have been slow torture.

No. 84

ROBIN YOUNT

Even as he was winning the 1989 American League Most Valuable Player Award, Robin Yount seemed out of place.

"I always thought of myself as a shortstop," Yount told a Wisconsin radio station in 1999. "I always felt like I was misplaced in the outfield. I learned to enjoy playing center field. But I still always felt like a shortstop."

Yount must have felt out of place in Cooperstown in the summer of

Full Name: Robin R. Yount

Position: SS, OF, DH

Born: 9/16/1955, Danville, Illinois

Height: 6'; Weight: 170

Debut: April 1974, Milwaukee Brewers

Bats: Right

Throws: Right

BATTING SUMMARY STATISTICS

Year	Team	AVG	G	AB	R	H	HR	RBI	BB	SO	SB
1974	Milwaukee-AL	.250	107	344	48	86	3	26	12	46	7
1975	Milwaukee-AL	.267	147	558	67	149	8	52	33	69	12
1976	Milwaukee-AL	.252	161	638	59	161	2	54	38	69	16
1977	Milwaukee-AL	.288	154	605	66	174	4	49	41	80	16
1978	Milwaukee-AL	.293	127	502	66	147	9	71	24	43	16
1979	Milwaukee-AL	.267	149	577	72	154	8	51	35	52	11

Year	Team	AVG	G	AB	R	H	HR	RBI	BB	SO	SB
1980	Milwaukee-AL	.293	143	611	121	179	23	87	26	67	20
1981	Milwaukee-AL	.273	96	377	50	103	10	49	22	37	4
1982	Milwaukee-AL	.331	156	635	129	210	29	114	54	63	14
1983	Milwaukee-AL	.308	149	578	102	178	17	80	72	58	12
1984	Milwaukee-AL	.298	160	624	105	186	16	80	67	67	14
1985	Milwaukee-AL	.277	122	466	76	129	15	68	49	56	10
1986	Milwaukee-AL	.312	140	522	82	163	9	46	62	73	14
1987	Milwaukee-AL	.312	158	635	99	198	21	103	76	94	19
1988	Milwaukee-AL	.306	162	621	92	190	13	91	63	63	22
1989	Milwaukee-AL	.318	160	614	101	195	21	103	63	71	19
1990	Milwaukee-AL	.247	158	587	98	145	17	77	78	89	15
1991	Milwaukee-AL	.260	130	503	66	131	10	77	54	79	6
1992	Milwaukee-AL	.264	150	557	71	147	8	77	53	81	15
1993	Milwaukee-AL	.258	127	454	62	117	8	51	44	93	9
Career Totals:		.285	2856	11008	1632	3142	251	1406	966	1350	271

1999, as he was only 43 years old yet an inductee to the Hall of Fame (by comparison, fellow 1999 inductee Nolan Ryan was still playing at that age). Then again Yount was always the kid, and always a Milwaukee Brewer, from the time he came up in 1974 as an 18-year-old shortstop.

Yount was one of the most dependable players in the game, leading the American League in doubles, triples and fielding average twice each. The versatile athlete who left the Brewers for a short spell during spring training in 1978 to become a pro golfer had a monster year in 1982 in leading the Brewers to the pennant, earning the shortstop the MVP.

Most veterans, when they get on in years, move to first base. Yount instead was shifted to the outfield in 1985. As he did in the infield he led the league in fielding and in 1989 was again named MVP. He joined Stan Musial and Hank Greenberg (both of whom played the outfield and first base) as the only players to win Most Valuable Player Awards at two different positions.

Yount retired 1993 at age 38 with 3,142 hits, 251 home runs, 126 triples, 1,406 RBI and 271 stolen bases. Cooperstown is where he should feel comfortable. It is where he belongs.

No. 85

WADE BOGGS

Wade Boggs was the master of repetition. He always woke up at the same time before a game, always ate the same food (chicken), and always took batting and fielding practice at the same times. Call it routine, call it superstition. He also had one more: doubling off the Green Monster at Fenway Park. If there were ever a hitter and a ballpark made for each other, it was Boggs and Fenway, his home for 11 seasons with the Boston Red Sox.

Weight back, holding the swing until the last possible moment before taking an inside-out cut, the left-handed Boggs was a master at hitting the other way, where the near but tall wall in Boston looms. Boggs hit at least 40 doubles in nine of his 11 years in Boston, leading the league in 1988 and 1989.

A five-time batting champion in the 1980s, including four in a row from 1985 to 1988, Boggs led the Red Sox to within one win of the World Series in 1986, where Boston inevitably lost in seven to the New York Mets. Boggs would get a championship ring in 1996 as a member of the once-hated New York Yankees.

In 1999 41-year-old Boggs got his 3,000th hit—and a sure ticket to Cooperstown—as a member of his hometown Tampa Bay Devil Rays (he retired after the season). Boggs became the 23rd player to reach the milestone—but the first to do it with a home run (off Cleveland Indian Chris Haney). Odder still, it was just the 118th home run of his career and second of that season. If history were to have been served, it would have been a double to left.

No. 86

PIE TRAYNOR

Some guys quietly go about making marks for themselves and their teams that, in retrospect, are as astounding as they are forgotten. Take Harold "Pie" Traynor. From 1920 to 1937 he made extraordinary play at third base seem routine, while methodically banging away toward a lifetime batting average of .320, one of the Top 50 of all time.

Look at strikeouts, for example. Traynor would strike out like anyone, but he did it at a rate of one every couple weeks. Not every couple innings or games. Weeks. In 7,559 at bats over 17 seasons, he whiffed 278 times. That includes a total of seven strikeouts in 1929.

Mike Schmidt struck out 180 times in 1975 alone.

Full Name: Harold Joseph Traynor

Position: 3B, SS   Debut: September 1920, Pittsburgh Pirates

Born: 11/11/1899, Framingham,   Bats: Right
    Massachusetts

Height: 6'; Weight: 170   Throws: Right

BATTING SUMMARY STATISTICS

Year	Team	AVG	G	AB	R	H	HR	RBI	BB	SO	SB
1920	Pittsburgh-NL	.212	17	52	6	11	0	2	3	6	1
1921	Pittsburgh-NL	.263	7	19	0	5	0	2	1	2	0
1922	Pittsburgh-NL	.282	142	571	89	161	4	81	27	28	17
1923	Pittsburgh-NL	.338	153	616	108	208	12	101	34	19	28
1924	Pittsburgh-NL	.294	142	545	86	160	5	82	37	26	24
1925	Pittsburgh-NL	.320	150	591	114	189	6	106	52	19	15
1926	Pittsburgh-NL	.317	152	574	83	182	3	92	38	14	8
1927	Pittsburgh-NL	.342	149	573	93	196	5	106	22	11	11
1928	Pittsburgh-NL	.337	144	569	91	192	3	124	28	10	12
1929	Pittsburgh-NL	.356	130	540	94	192	4	108	30	7	13
1930	Pittsburgh-NL	.366	130	497	90	182	9	119	48	19	7
1931	Pittsburgh-NL	.298	155	615	81	183	2	103	54	28	6
1932	Pittsburgh-NL	.329	135	513	74	169	2	68	32	20	6

Year	Team	AVG	G	AB	R	H	HR	RBI	BB	SO	SB
1933	Pittsburgh-NL	.304	154	624	85	190	1	82	35	24	5
1934	Pittsburgh-NL	.309	119	444	62	137	1	61	21	27	3
1935	Pittsburgh-NL	.279	57	204	24	57	1	36	10	17	2
1937	Pittsburgh-NL	.167	5	12	3	2	0	0	0	1	0
Career Totals:		.320	1941	7559	1183	2416	58	1273	472	278	158

But it's guys like Schmidt and other slugging third basemen who make our collective memory of Pie more than a bit fuzzy. Brooks Robinson and several others push Traynor further out of focus.

But Traynor's numbers, if not remembered, are memorable, especially in the context of his era.

His 2,291 putouts are the fifth-best mark for third basemen, and he led the National League seven times in the department. *The Sporting News* pegged him as the best third baseman in both leagues seven times. And while not a slugger (58 career home runs), he got on base while not losing more than 28 at bats in any year to strikeouts. In 1930, when he hit .366, he had 182 hits.

In 130 games.

When Bill Mazeroski was chosen to the Pittsburgh Pirates' Team of the Century, he told *Pittsburgh Post-Gazette* columnist Bob Smizik that he was honored to be named to the team chosen not through some data-crunching computer but by the hearts of Pirates fans. But the living legend found one thing hard to believe. He couldn't believe he got more votes than Roberto Clemente, Ralph Kiner, Honus Wagner—and Pie Traynor.

No. 87
PAUL MOLITOR

In the long, arrogant history of humanity, you come to realize most of us are just big, dumb goofballs. Cases in point: We should have known Van Gogh was a genius before he died, that the League of Nations was

destined to fail, that Prohibition could never work, and that those med-
dling kids would always unmask the bad guy in *Scooby-Doo*. We also
should have known Paul Molitor was great well before he became one of
the greatest to play in the postseason.

But for most people outside the Midwest, Molitor was that guy who
spent most of his career playing on one of those M-teams in the AL—
pretty good hitter, though.... No. He was amazing.

The Minnesota native who mostly played for the Milwaukee Brewers and the Twins (with an amazing short stint in Toronto) was very Midwest—workmanlike, quiet, making no waves.

Just hits. Lots of them. He ended his 21 seasons hitting .306 with
3,319 hits—eighth best all-time—and had a 39-game hitting streak in 1987.
Effective to the end of his career as a designated hitter at 41 years old, he
hit his 3,000th hit in 1996. It was a triple.

He also ended his days 10th in at bats and tied for 10th in doubles,
while racking up the 15th-highest total of runs. That's no doubt partly
attributable to the guy's speed and savvy on the base paths. He once stole
three bases in one inning (1987) and holds the American League mark
for most steals in a season without being caught, 20 (in 1994).

Those of us who overlooked Paul Molitor for so long despite all this
and five All-Star Game appearances better watch our backs. There's probably a "kick me" sign there.

No. 88

ALBERT BELLE

Albert Belle is probably the only player in this book who the authors
would never want to have on their team. Or the team they root for. Then
again, or on the opposing team.

The man is an end-stage cancer in the clubhouse and a headcase on
and off the field. But as Babe Ruth said of Ty Cobb, he sure can hit. God
Almighty, that man can hit.

Belle became a regular in the outfield in 1991, hitting .282 with 28 home runs and 95 RBI for the Cleveland Indians. Since then Belle has hit at least 30 homers and driven in 101 or more runs every year, leading the American League in RBI three times and home runs once. He has hit as many as 50 homers in a season (1995, before the number became a fad), driven in as many as 152 runs (1998, with the Chicago White Sox), and hit as high as .357 (1994, with Cleveland).

Yes, he is a weapon, but he is also a bomb waiting to go off in the clubhouse. Belle left Cleveland for Chicago, then signed with the Baltimore Orioles in 1999. He is at times surly and sullen (OK, most times), the anti–Ernie Banks of baseball. But there is no denying the man can hit. Even the Babe would have said so.

No. 89

ROBIN ROBERTS

George Will, the conservative columnist who proves baseball makes strange bench fellows, was asked to pick his All-Stars from among men who played a significant part of their careers in one of baseball's most historic decades, the 1950s. His pitching staff was Whitey Ford, Warren Spahn, Bob Lemon, Early Winn and Robin Roberts.

Will, who has a side line of writing some of the best baseball pieces ever, including the bestseller *Men at Work*, is among those to make the case that this era—after World War II and before America's cultural wars turned red hot—was baseball's golden age.

Rarely have so many great pitchers taken the mound in the same span. And, appropriately, Roberts starred in a game in that decade's first year that even Hollywood would figure was over the top.

October 1, 1950. Roberts's Philadelphia Phillies were taking on the Brooklyn Dodgers at the season's end, with the National League pennant at stake. Roberts had 19 wins and he'd never had 20. In his last six starts, he pitched well but missed the W. In the last critical week of the Whiz Kids' effort to avoid becoming the Fizz Kids, Roberts started three games.

A scoreless battle against Don Newcombe ensued until the ninth inning, when both teams forced a run. Top of the 10th, Roberts, who had pitched a near perfect game, also had six assists and a putout. Now he had the bat in his hand. The "big bonus boy," as the *New York Times* called him, singled up the middle to start the inning, and jump-start Philadelphia's offense.

Eddie Waitkus, after trying to bunt, popped a fly ball into short center with no one around. Roberts hustled to second.

Richie Ashburn bunted. Roberts slid hard to try to break up the play at third and was called out, but the momentum he started couldn't be. Ashburn was safe. Waitkus was safe. The Dodgers were not.

Dick Sisler followed with a pop over the left field fence. After Newcombe recovered and struck out Del Ennis and forced Puddin' Head Jones into a ground out, Roberts had to write the Whiz Kids' storybook ending.

He did. Roy Campanella's line drive was caught in deep left field by Jack Mayo, who had just been put into the game as Sisler's defensive replacement. Then Roberts struck out pinch hitter Jim Russell and forced Tommy Brown to pop out to Waitkus at first base.

"I felt strong all the way," said Roberts of the five-hitter, with red, swollen eyes from stinking flecks of lime off the foul line he got when he slid into third.

Teammate Jocko Thompson said Roberts wasn't bothered by the problem with his eyes while pitching in the bottom of the 10th. "That didn't bother Robby," he told the *New York Times* during the locker room celebration. "He'd keep pitching if he were blind."

In the World Series the Phillies would be swept by DiMaggio's Yankees. Roberts pitched 11 hard innings, gave up 11 hits, had five strikeouts and posted a 1.64 ERA in his loss.

It was his only World Series game but not for lack of personal success. He won 20 or more games six years in a row on his way to a 286–245 career mark. In those years, 1950–55, he led the league in wins four times (28–7 in '52), starts six times, innings pitched five times, complete games four times and strikeouts twice.

In a decade that included hurlers like Newcombe, Warren Spahn, Sal Maglie, Whitey Ford, Carl Erskine and a young Don Drysdale, Roberts shone like the fins on a new Cadillac.

No. 90

JOE CRONIN

No one in baseball history has done what Joe Cronin has done.

In 20 seasons as a shortstop, second baseman, third baseman, first baseman and pinch hitter he averaged .301, led the American League in doubles twice (1933, 1938) and triples (1932), hit better than .300 in 11 seasons and had more than 100 RBI eight years.

But he did more. He was named manager of the Washington Senators at 26 years old, replacing Walter Johnson, while continuing to be a shortstop who could hit. Later he moved himself out of the lineup to make way for a better shortstop, then took the bench, but didn't sit down much. He led the American League with 18 pinch hits in 1943 (hitting .429 in the clutch). He also once hit homers in both ends of a doubleheader. By the time "The Boy Manager" was done managing, he had a .540 winning percentage, two AL pennants, and had guided a green kid from California named Ted Williams to greatness.

Full Name: Joseph Edward Cronin

Position: SS, PM, 3B

Debut: April 1926, Pittsburgh Pirates

Born: 10/12/1906, San Francisco, California

Bats: Right

Height: 5'11.5"; Weight: 180

Throws: Right

BATTING SUMMARY STATISTICS

Year	Team	AVG	G	AB	R	H	HR	RBI	BB	SO	SB
1926	Pittsburgh-NL	.265	38	83	9	22	0	11	6	15	0
1927	Pittsburgh-NL	.227	12	22	2	5	0	3	2	3	0
1928	Washington-AL	.242	63	227	23	55	0	25	22	27	4
1929	Washington-AL	.281	145	494	72	139	8	61	85	37	5
1930	Washington-AL	.346	154	587	127	203	13	126	72	36	17
1931	Washington-AL	.306	156	611	103	187	12	126	81	52	10
1932	Washington-AL	.318	143	557	95	177	6	116	66	45	7
1933	Washington-AL	.309	152	602	89	186	5	118	87	49	5
1934	Washington-AL	.284	127	504	68	143	7	101	53	28	8

Year	Team	AVG	G	AB	R	H	HR	RBI	BB	SO	SB
1935	Boston-AL	.295	144	556	70	164	9	95	63	40	3
1936	Boston-AL	.281	81	295	36	83	2	43	32	21	1
1937	Boston-AL	.307	148	570	102	175	18	110	84	73	5
1938	Boston-AL	.325	143	530	98	172	17	94	91	60	7
1939	Boston-AL	.308	143	520	97	160	19	107	87	48	6
1940	Boston-AL	.285	149	548	104	156	24	111	83	65	7
1941	Boston-AL	.311	143	518	98	161	16	95	82	55	1
1942	Boston-AL	.304	45	79	7	24	4	24	15	21	0
1943	Boston-AL	.312	59	77	8	24	5	29	11	4	0
1944	Boston-AL	.241	76	191	24	46	5	28	34	19	1
1945	Boston-AL	.375	3	8	1	3	0	1	3	2	0
Career Totals:		.301	2124	7579	1233	2285	170	1424	1059	700	87

But he did more. He was the Boston Red Sox general manager for 10 years until 1959, when he became the president of the American League.

Oh, one other thing. Cronin is the subject of baseball's best family story. In 1934, while Cronin was on his honeymoon, his father-in-law and boss, Senators owner Clark Griffith, sold the manager/shortstop/son-in-law to the Red Sox.

It must have been an expensive wedding.

No. 91

JOHNNY MIZE

Pressure made Johnny Miller go from being bigger than almost anything professional golf had ever seen to the broadcast booth, talking about poorer golfers doing what he no longer could. Even in the movies, pressure was the central plot point of the World War II epic *Twelve O'Clock High*, in which the war-weary squadron leader eventually became comatose when faced with one more bombing mission.

Johnny Mize knew pressure. But he thrived on it.

Full Name: John Robert "The Big Cat" Mize

Position: First Base   Debut: April 1936, St. Louis Cardinals

Born: 1/7/1913, Demorest, Georgia   Bats: Left

Height: 6'2"; Weight: 215   Throws: Right

BATTING SUMMARY STATISTICS

Year	Team	AVG	G	AB	R	H	HR	RBI	BB	SO	SB
1936	St. Louis-NL	.329	126	414	76	136	19	93	50	32	1
1937	St. Louis-NL	.364	145	560	103	204	25	113	56	57	2
1938	St. Louis-NL	.337	149	531	85	179	27	102	74	47	0
1939	St. Louis-NL	.349	153	564	104	197	28	108	92	49	0
1940	St. Louis-NL	.314	155	579	111	182	43	137	82	49	7
1941	St. Louis-NL	.317	126	473	67	150	16	100	70	45	4
1942	New York-NL	.305	142	541	97	165	26	110	60	39	3
1946	New York-NL	.337	101	377	70	127	22	70	62	26	3
1947	New York-NL	.302	154	586	137	177	51	138	74	42	2
1948	New York-NL	.289	152	560	110	162	40	125	94	37	4
1949	New York-NL	.263	106	388	59	102	18	62	50	19	1
1949	New York-AL	.261	13	23	4	6	1	2	4	2	0
1950	New York-AL	.277	90	274	43	76	25	72	29	24	0
1951	New York-AL	.259	113	332	37	86	10	49	36	24	1
1952	New York-AL	.263	78	137	9	36	4	29	11	15	0
1953	New York-AL	.250	81	104	6	26	4	27	12	17	0
Career Totals:		.312	1884	6443	1118	2011	359	1337	856	524	28

October 7, 1949. The Yankees have their hands full against the Brooklyn Dodgers in the third game of the World Series. The Yankees had eked out a 1–0 win on a ninth-inning homer in the first game and lost the second game, 1–0.

Now in Brooklyn a day later, the Yankees are in a 1–1 tie going into the ninth inning. Enter Johnny Mize, with the winning run and insurance run on the bases. With all of Brooklyn shouting, Mize strokes a single, scoring two runs.

In the World Series decided by seven runs over five games, in which the DiMaggio-Rizzuto-Berra Yankees batted just .226 and the Dodgers with Duke Snider, Pee Wee Reese, Gil Hodges, Jackie Robinson and Roy Campanella hit just .210, Mize batted 1.000. His two clutch hits turned the tide for the Yankees, who won by their biggest margins after the third game.

In his 15-year career, the Big Cat hit .312 while belting 359 homers and amassing the eighth-best slugging percentage of all time at .562. He led the National League in dingers four times (including 51 in 1947 and 43 in 1940), three times in RBI, once in runs, and once in average (.349 in 1939, although he also hit .364 in 1937). In addition, he led the league in slugging average four times (over .600 three times) and hit over .300 his first nine seasons.

But the Yankees, who seemed to have everything in the late 1940s and early 1950s, wanted Mize's power when DiMaggio was briefly ailing. In 1949 they got him. But the Bronx Bombers wouldn't need Mize every day, just when it counted. In four years spent mostly as a pinch hitter, he hit .295 for the Yankees. Under pressure. As a starter during the same period he had hit .264.

More pressure: in five World Series, all with the Yankees, he hit .375 as a pinch hitter and recorded the most World Series pinch hits even though others had more at bats.

Johnny Mize, almost exclusively a first baseman, wouldn't be in everyone's starting nine. But he'd be in the lineup of everyone who knows baseball—and pressure.

No. 92

FRANKIE FRISCH

He was a three-sport star in college, a star basketball forward and second-team All-America halfback. Frankie Frisch was the Fordham Flash (How fun is that to say? C'mon, you know you want to: *Fordham Flash Frankie Frisch/Fordham Flash Frankie Frisch...*), but the open-field runner was to make his mark bringing his football mentality to his third sport.

Back in the 1920s, when Frisch broke in with John McGraw's New York Giants, most baseball players just didn't go to college (although McGraw did). But the switch-hitting second baseman brought an intelligence and belligerence to the field that helped lead the Giants and later

Full Name: Frank Francis "The Fordham Flash" Frisch

Position: 2B, 3B, SS   Debut: June 1919, New York Giants
Born: 9/9/1898, Bronx, New York   Bats: Both
Height: 5'11"; Weight: 165   Throws: Right

BATTING SUMMARY STATISTICS

Year	Team	AVG	G	AB	R	H	HR	RBI	BB	SO	SB
1919	New York-NL	.226	54	190	21	43	2	24	4	14	15
1920	New York-NL	.280	110	440	57	123	4	77	20	18	34
1921	New York-NL	.341	153	618	121	211	8	100	42	28	49
1922	New York-NL	.327	132	514	101	168	5	51	47	13	31
1923	New York-NL	.348	151	641	116	223	12	111	46	12	29
1924	New York-NL	.328	145	603	121	198	7	69	56	24	22
1925	New York-NL	.331	120	502	89	166	11	48	32	14	21
1926	New York-NL	.314	135	545	75	171	5	44	33	16	23
1927	St. Louis-NL	.337	153	617	112	208	10	78	43	10	48
1928	St. Louis-NL	.300	141	547	107	164	10	86	64	17	29
1929	St. Louis-NL	.334	138	527	93	176	5	74	53	12	24
1930	St. Louis-NL	.346	133	540	121	187	10	114	55	16	15
1931	St. Louis-NL	.311	131	518	96	161	4	82	45	13	28
1932	St. Louis-NL	.292	115	486	59	142	3	60	25	13	18
1933	St. Louis-NL	.303	147	585	74	177	4	66	48	16	18
1934	St. Louis-NL	.305	140	550	74	168	3	75	45	10	11
1935	St. Louis-NL	.294	103	354	52	104	1	55	33	16	2
1936	St. Louis-NL	.274	93	303	40	83	1	26	36	10	2
1937	St. Louis-NL	.219	17	32	3	7	0	4	1	0	0
Career Totals:		.316	2311	9112	1532	2880	105	1244	728	272	419

the St. Louis Cardinals "Gashouse Gang" to eight pennants, six second-place finishes and three world championships in his 19-year career.

The college man was smart enough to serve as player-manager the last five years of his playing career and later skippered the Pittsburgh Pirates and Chicago Cubs before becoming an announcer.

The consummate practitioner of the head-first slide more than four decades before Pete Rose, Frisch hit .300 or better 11 straight seasons (13 overall, to retire with a .316 average) and three times led the National League in steals. He was also one of the best in the field at second; in 1927 he handled more than 1,000 chances, with only 22 errors.

There is an old story about a reporter wanting to do a story about the perfect composite player, one that would combine the hitting of Cobb, the fielding of Wagner, the determination of Dean. A veteran manager said why go to the bother of making up such a fictitious player: "What couldn't Frankie Frisch do?"

No. 93

Luis Aparacio

Donie Bush was one of the best fielding shortstops of his era, a regular for the Detroit Tigers during the 1910s. Over the years he saw all the fielding greats at short, from Joe Cronin to Lou Boudreau, Phil Rizzuto and Pee Wee Reese.

But the best? Luis Aparacio. "I wouldn't except anybody, from Honus Wagner on up," Bush said in the early 1960s. "There weren't any of them as good defensively as this kid."

Before there was the "Wizard of Oz" there was "Little Looie," a 5-foot-9 Venezuelan. A starter for 18 seasons of his 20-season career, Aparacio retired holding the records for most games (2,581), assists (8,016), double plays (1,553) and chances (12,564) for his position. The 1956 Rookie of the Year led the Chicago White Sox—the "Go-Go Sox"—to the pennant in 1959, and after being traded to the Baltimore Orioles in 1963 led the O's to the World Series title in 1966 (he was later traded back to the White Sox, and finished his career with the Boston Red Sox).

And eight years before Maury Wills, Aparacio reintroduced the steal to the offensive arsenal, leading the American League in steals his first nine years in the majors (1956–64). He was successful almost four out of five times for his career that totaled 506 steals. Yes, Ozzie Smith, the Wizard, may be the best glove man ever, and Rey Ordonez could someday give him a run. But never forget Aparacio. He used a heavier glove during warm-ups to make his own feel lighter during the game. Aparacio probably could have won the nine Gold Gloves he snared using an oven mitt.

Full Name: Luis Ernesto Aparacio (b: Aparicio y Montiel)

Position: Shortstop

Born: 4/29/1934, Maracaibo, Venezuela

Height: 5'9"; Weight: 160

Debut: April 1956, Chicago White Sox

Bats: Right

Throws: Right

BATTING SUMMARY STATISTICS

Year	Team	AVG	G	AB	R	H	HR	RBI	BB	SO	SB
1956	Chicago-AL	.266	152	533	69	142	3	56	34	63	21
1957	Chicago-AL	.257	143	575	82	148	3	41	52	55	28
1958	Chicago-AL	.266	145	557	76	148	2	40	35	38	29
1959	Chicago-AL	.257	152	612	98	157	6	51	53	40	56
1960	Chicago-AL	.277	153	600	86	166	2	61	43	39	51
1961	Chicago-AL	.272	156	625	90	170	6	45	38	33	53
1962	Chicago-AL	.241	153	581	72	140	7	40	32	36	31
1963	Baltimore-AL	.250	146	601	73	150	5	45	36	35	40
1964	Baltimore-AL	.266	146	578	93	154	10	37	49	51	57
1965	Baltimore-AL	.225	144	564	67	127	8	40	46	56	26
1966	Baltimore-AL	.276	151	659	97	182	6	41	33	42	25
1967	Baltimore-AL	.233	134	546	55	127	4	31	29	44	18
1968	Chicago-AL	.264	155	622	55	164	4	36	33	43	17
1969	Chicago-AL	.280	156	599	77	168	5	51	66	29	24
1970	Chicago-AL	.313	146	552	86	173	5	43	53	34	8
1971	Boston-AL	.232	125	491	56	114	4	45	35	43	6
1972	Boston-AL	.257	110	436	47	112	3	39	26	28	3
1973	Boston-AL	.271	132	499	56	135	0	49	43	33	13
Career Totals:		.262	2599	10230	1335	2677	83	791	736	742	506

No. 94

IVAN RODRIGUEZ

There was another catcher with the nickname Pudge before Ivan Rodriguez: the great Carlton Fisk of arm-waving, home-run fame with the Boston Red Sox and later the Chicago White Sox. But there may have never been a better catcher behind the plate than the 1990s Pudge of the Texas Rangers.

It took several seasons for Rodriguez to become a force at the plate, a multiple Silver Slugger Award winner who worked to evolve into a solid .300 hitter. Then in 1999 Pudge exploded, hitting .332 with 35 home runs—an American League record for catchers—and 113 RBI for the Western Division champions. He even stole 24 bases, which along with his homers made him the first catcher to join the 20/20 club.

The scary part is Rodriguez, just 27 during his 1999 MVP season, would still be a perennial all-star if he hit .220. He is one of the few catchers who radically alter opponents' strategy because of his skill behind the plate. A good defensive catcher will throw out 35 percent of steal attempts. In 1999 Rodriguez nailed 53 percent, while allowing only one passed ball the entire season. He may save as many runs as he knocks in.

And still he might get better. There may have been another Pudge, but someday we might say there never was another catcher quite like Ivan Rodriguez.

No. 95

Chuck Klein

Sometimes a guy like Adlai E. Stevenson comes along (stick with us here, we'll make a baseball point in a moment). The Democrat was widely regarded even by Republicans as one of the great intellects of the 1950s, an honorable and capable statesman. But he ran for president against a guy named Dwight D. Eisenhower. The first time was just seven years after Ike had done nothing less than win World War II. Ike got seven million more votes than Stevenson did in 1952, and 10 million more in the 1956 rematch.

It's not that Ike wasn't great; we like Ike. But so was Stevenson. Most people will just never know it. Such is the plight of Chuck Klein (See? The baseball point).

Full Name: Charles Herbert Klein

Position: Outfield

Born: 10/7/1904, Indianapolis, Indiana

Height: 6'; Weight: 185

Debut: July 1928, Philadelphia Phillies

Bats: Left

Throws: Right

BATTING SUMMARY STATISTICS

Year	Team	AVG	G	AB	R	H	HR	RBI	BB	SO	SB
1928	Philadelphia-NL	.360	64	253	41	91	11	34	14	22	0
1929	Philadelphia-NL	.356	149	616	126	219	43	145	54	61	5
1930	Philadelphia-NL	.386	156	648	158	250	40	170	54	50	4
1931	Philadelphia-NL	.337	148	594	121	200	31	121	59	49	7
1932	Philadelphia-NL	.348	154	650	152	226	38	137	60	49	20
1933	Philadelphia-NL	.368	152	606	101	223	28	120	56	36	15
1934	Chicago-NL	.301	115	435	78	131	20	80	47	38	3
1935	Chicago-NL	.293	119	434	71	127	21	73	41	42	4
1936	Chicago-NL	.294	29	109	19	32	5	18	16	14	0
1936	Philadelphia-NL	.309	117	492	83	152	20	86	33	45	6
1936	NL Totals	.306	146	601	102	184	25	104	49	59	6
1937	Philadelphia-NL	.325	115	406	74	132	15	57	39	21	3
1938	Philadelphia-NL	.247	129	458	53	113	8	61	38	30	7
1939	Philadelphia-NL	.191	25	47	8	9	1	9	10	4	1
1939	Pittsburgh-NL	.300	85	270	37	81	11	47	26	17	1
1939	NL Totals	.284	110	317	45	90	12	56	36	21	2
1940	Philadelphia-NL	.218	116	354	39	77	7	37	44	30	2
1941	Philadelphia-NL	.123	50	73	6	9	1	3	10	6	0
1942	Philadelphia-NL	.071	14	14	0	1	0	0	0	2	0
1943	Philadelphia-NL	.100	12	20	0	2	0	3	0	3	1
1944	Philadelphia-NL	.143	4	7	1	1	0	0	0	2	0
Career Totals:		.320	1753	6486	1168	2076	300	1201	601	521	79

Klein, who played primarily with the Philadelphia Phillies and Chicago Cubs, hit 300 career home runs from 1928 to 1944, with 2,076 hits, 1,201 RBI and a .320 average for his career. He's fourth all-time in single-season total bases, having collected 445 in 1930, more than guys like Jimmie Foxx and Stan Musial (Klein's 420 bases in 1932 also put him at No. 8). In the Top 10 only Lou Gehrig and Klein appear twice, not Ruth, nor Foxx, nor Musial.

Klein, the National League MVP in 1932, won the Triple Crown in 1933. Now just consider the Triple Crown. Since 1900 only 14 players have been tops in batting, home runs and RBI.

Nineteen thirty-three. Rarely has a player dominated a league like Klein. He hit .368, had 28 homers, 120 RBI. But he also led the league in hits (223), slugging (.602), total bases (365—66 more than the next best), was second in runs (101), second in home run percentage (4.6) and fourth in stolen bases (15).

In his only World Series, in 1935, Klein hit a single in the ninth inning of Game Three that nearly pulled off a comeback for the Cubs against the Tigers. In Game Five he hit a homer with a man on to give the Cubs a 3–1 win. The Cubs, of course, would lose the series, four games to two. Klein hit .333.

For a career Klein ended up sixth in single-season hits at 250 in 1930 and 43rd all-time in batting average.

So why isn't there a Chuck Klein youth baseball league? Or even a deli sandwich? There are several reasons: Gehrig, Foxx, Ruth and Simmons. It was a tough era to be great.

OK, here's a what-if. What if Rogers Hornsby, Mel Ott and Hack Wilson had retired a few years earlier? If not for three men, Klein would have ruled the senior circuit without peer.

Figure this guy's luck: of the very, very few Triple Crown winners since the gasoline engine was invented, only once was it shared in the same year by two players: in 1933 arguably the greatest achievement in baseball went to the already famous Jimmie Foxx, and Chuck Klein.

No. 96

RALPH KINER

Many baseball fans today know Ralph Kiner best as the voice of the New York Mets, a colorful commentator who has been with the team since its birth in 1962. His malaprops—wishing all fathers happy birthday on Father's Day and repeatedly calling Gary Carter "Gary Cooper" are just two examples—are as much a part of his announcing legend as his colorful and insightful anecdotes from the game's past.

Full Name: Ralph McPherran Kiner

Position: Outfield

Born: 10/27/1922, Santa Rita,
New Mexico

Height: 6'2"; Weight: 195

Debut: April 1946, Pittsburgh Pirates

Bats: Right

Throws: Right

BATTING SUMMARY STATISTICS

Year	Team	AVG	G	AB	R	H	HR	RBI	BB	SO	SB
1946	Pittsburgh-NL	.247	144	502	63	124	23	81	74	109	3
1947	Pittsburgh-NL	.313	152	565	118	177	51	127	98	81	1
1948	Pittsburgh-NL	.265	156	555	104	147	40	123	112	61	1
1949	Pittsburgh-NL	.310	152	549	116	170	54	127	117	61	6
1950	Pittsburgh-NL	.272	150	547	112	149	47	118	122	79	2
1951	Pittsburgh-NL	.309	151	531	124	164	42	109	137	57	2
1952	Pittsburgh-NL	.244	149	516	90	126	37	87	110	77	3
1953	Pittsburgh-NL	.270	41	148	27	40	7	29	25	21	1
1953	Chicago-NL	.283	117	414	73	117	28	87	75	67	1
1953	NL Totals	.279	158	562	100	157	35	116	100	88	2
1954	Chicago-NL	.285	147	557	88	159	22	73	76	90	2
1955	Cleveland-AL	.243	113	321	56	78	18	54	65	46	0
Career Totals:		.279	1472	5205	971	1451	369	1015	1011	749	22

But Kiner is also one of the greatest sluggers the game has known. It is Kiner—not Ruth or Aaron or McGwire—who led his league in home runs the first seven years of his career, a record. A pure slugger who is the only player to homer in three consecutive All-Star Games, the right-handed left fielder averaged nearly 37 home runs a season in his 10-year career with the Pittsburgh Pirates (seven seasons) Chicago Cubs (two) and Cleveland Indians. Twice he hit more than 50 home runs in a season. He also led the league three times in RBI.

A back sprain ended Kiner's career after 1955 at age 33. He then went on to become a minor league executive before be turned to broadcasting. But long before he started telling stories in the booth, he was the story on the field.

No. 97
ROBERTO ALOMAR

So author McGuire's daughter Zoe went as Robbie Alomar for Halloween in 1996. She was three months old, drooling was her primary talent, and well, it just seemed right.

It was a month before that Alomar vapor-locked, spitting in the face of umpire John Hirschbeck after being called out on strikes (PS: That Halloween mom went as the ump). Alomar, a second baseman then with the Baltimore Orioles, did not have a reputation of being a jerk. He quickly apologized and kept out of trouble since the incident that painted him the personification of all that was wrong with sport. Eventually, the focus returned to Alomar the player—a career .300 hitter and perennial Gold Glove winner.

A 10-time All-Star, including nine straight selections, Roberto Alomar came up with the San Diego Padres in 1988. His trade to the Blue Jays prior to the 1991 season paved the way for his becoming the cornerstone of the Toronto team that won back-to-back World Series titles in 1992 and 1993. He has hit .347 in 12 World Series games and .316 in 28 League Championship Series contests.

Alomar and Omar Vizquel on the Cleveland Indians are among the better double-play combinations ever paired, rally killers up the middle. To go along with his solid bat that shows occasional pop (151 career home runs, including 24 in 1999), Alomar is an established threat on the field—and not just to umpires.

No. 98
SADAHARU OH

Let's get right to it, and try to win you some money:

The Question: What player hit in the same batting order as the two greatest career home-run hitters of all time?

Let the guy with you at the bar scratch his head and suffer for a while, trying to figure out who played on the same teams as Babe Ruth and Henry Aaron. Then deliver the knockout blow:

The Answer: Davey Johnson. He played with Aaron ... and Sadaharu Oh.

Oh, by verifiable numbers anyway, is the greatest home run hitter ever, with 868 round-trippers in Japan's Central League in the 1960s and 70s (Negro Leaguer Josh Gibson is credited by some with hitting more, but not in official league games).

At the plate the Yomiuri Giant legend looked like an approximation of Mel Ott: a left-handed hitter with his front right leg poised high (Oh started his stance that way, initially to rid himself of a hitch in his swing). The two men's uniforms were even the same.

Granted, Oh played in some bandboxes: the park where he hit most of his home runs, the Giants' Korakuen Stadium, measured only 298 feet down the lines and 388 feet to center, comparable to other Japanese parks (American parks are usually a minimum of 310 down the lines and 400 to center, although the dimensions vary from city to city).

But Oh played in a Central League that would only play 130 games a year, and was often among the leaders in walks. And from 1962 to 1976, Oh hit between 44 and 55 homers a season. That's consistency you can bet on.

No. 99

ED WALSH

Here's a dream: you're a starting pitcher in Chicago. Here's a nightmare: the team's nickname is the Hitless Wonders.

Such was the lot drawn by Big Ed Walsh in 1904. But he was a spitter, not a quitter, and instead of whining, he won. At the end of 14 years, all but the last with the White Sox, the spit-balling Walsh won 195 games against 126 losses. Fifty-seven were by shutout. But here's the only stat

Full Name: Edward Augustine "Big Ed" Walsh
Position: Pitcher   Debut: May 1904, Chicago White Sox
Born: 5/14/1881, Plains, Pennsylvania   Bats: Right
Height: 6'1"; Weight: 193   Throws: Right

PITCHING SUMMARY STATISTICS

Year	Team	W	L	PCT	ERA	G	SV	IP	BB	SO
1904	Chicago-AL	6	3	.667	2.60	18	1	110.2	32	57
1905	Chicago-AL	8	3	.727	2.17	22	0	136.2	29	71
1906	Chicago-AL	17	13	.567	1.88	41	1	278.1	58	171
1907	Chicago-AL	24	18	.571	1.60	56	4	422.1	87	206
1908	Chicago-AL	40	15	.727	1.42	66	6	464.0	56	269
1909	Chicago-AL	15	11	.577	1.41	31	2	230.1	50	127
1910	Chicago-AL	18	20	.474	1.27	45	5	369.2	61	258
1911	Chicago-AL	27	18	.600	2.22	56	4	368.2	72	255
1912	Chicago-AL	27	17	.614	2.15	62	10	393.0	94	254
1913	Chicago-AL	8	3	.727	2.58	16	1	97.2	39	34
1914	Chicago-AL	2	3	.400	2.82	8	0	44.2	20	15
1915	Chicago-AL	3	0	1.000	1.33	3	0	27.0	7	12
1916	Chicago-AL	0	1	.000	2.70	2	0	3.1	3	3
1917	Boston-NL	0	1	.000	3.50	4	0	18.0	9	4
Career Totals:		195	126	.607	1.82	430	34	2964.1	617	1736

you need to see how good he was, and how he could help make the Hit-less Wonders win games:

Career ERA: 1.82.

Yes, it was a different game then. Hitters didn't smack 40—or even 20 home runs—a season. But neither did a starter routinely leave a game when he was tired or getting blown away.

Walsh weighed in at a then-huge 6-foot-1 and 193 pounds. He wore the short-billed caps of the day and the stern look of a man with the—let's say audacity—to throw something as dangerous as a spitball at human beings.

In 14 years Walsh started 315 games and completed 250. By comparison, in 16 years Whitey Ford started 438 games and completed 156.

But Walsh had more than good work habits. He led the American League in wins in 1908 with a ridiculous 40–15 record and 1.42 ERA, completing 42 of 49 starts. Oh, included in those stats is a 5–1 record as a reliever, to go along with six saves. That year he led the league in wins, winning percentage, games, starts, complete games, innings pitched, strikeouts (269), shutouts (11) and saves.

In the 1906 World Series the Hitless Wonders faced the crosstown Cubs, a powerful sure bet to win. Then Walsh took the mound. In the third game Walsh threw a record 12 strikeouts, shutting the Cubs out. Two days later Walsh shutout the Cubs again, giving up just two hits. He ended the series with 17 strikeouts and a championship.

And a 1.80 ERA. Which, for Ed Walsh, was average.

No. 100

RYNE SANDBERG

Ryne Sandberg was a throw-in by the Philadelphia Phillies in a January 1982 trade in which Larry Bowa also went to the Chicago Cubs for Ivan DeJesus. Sandberg, who played only 13 games with six at bats the season before, had been groomed as a utility guy, a nice bench player.

In his first year with the Cubs, Sandberg played third base, putting up respectable if not stellar numbers. When Chicago acquired Ron "The Penguin" Cey prior to the 1983 season, Sandberg was shifted again.

And arguably the best defensive second baseman ever came of age.

Sandberg qualified as one of those "they-find-a-way-to-beat-you" guys, whether it was with the long ball, a double off the ivy or with his unparalleled glove. This was never more true than in Sandberg's MVP season of 1984, the year the Cubs won an unexpected Eastern Division title. Sandberg hit .314 with 19 home runs and 84 RBI. While he did not post overwhelming numbers (although he did lead the National League in triples and runs), there was little doubt he was the most *valuable* player to his team.

Ryno changed his swing and developed into a deep threat, leading the National League in home runs with 40 in 1990. But the constant was his glove. From June 21, 1989, to May 17, 1990, Sandberg did not make an error at second, a streak of 123 consecutive games and 582 chances.

Fifteen times the nine-time Gold Glover had streaks of 30 or more games without an error.

Ryne Sandberg's raw statistics don't hold up to some other legendary players, and he barely squeaks into our Top 100. But he was more than a throw-in.

INDEX